T2-CSE-396

*Reform, Crisis, and
Confusion, 1900–1929*

Random House Readings in American History
VOLUME 5

Series Editors:

ALLEN WEINSTEIN

Smith College

FRANK OTTO GATELL

University of California, Los Angeles

Reform, Crisis, and Confusion, 1900–1929

Edited by

R. JACKSON WILSON

UNIVERSITY OF WISCONSIN

 RANDOM HOUSE, New York

FIRST PRINTING

Copyright © 1970 by Random House, Inc. All rights reserved under
International and Pan-American Copyright Conventions. Published in
the United States by Random House, Inc., New York, and simultaneously
in Canada by Random House of Canada Limited, Toronto.

Library of Congress Catalog Card Number: 76–96275

Manufactured in the United States of America.

Preface

The following volume is one of six in the *Random House Readings in American History* series. In each volume, the editor develops a coherent view of his own scholarly period, presenting a cross section of provocative new research that has influenced recent interpretations of American history. Each editor introduces his own period, discusses the literature bearing on its central themes, and offers the reader a sampling of current scholarship. The six volumes, arranged chronologically, contain major recent articles or portions of recent books on the evolving structure of American political, economic, social, and cultural life. They offer the student, when read either as single volumes or as a series, an exploration of the American past through the eyes of a half-dozen historical specialists. Each volume contains its own angle of vision, its own particular style of argument, and its own distinct flavor.

The choice of selections and the introductory material are the work of the volume editor. Scholars may disagree over aspects of the periodization employed. None of the volume editors, however, found difficulty in treating within this framework the central themes of each succeeding era in American life. Although the most significant problems faced by previous generations of Americans are explored in each volume, the editors have not aimed at a "problems" approach. Similarly, although they discuss the flow of historical argument within their periods, they do not march "conflicting interpretations" quickstep across the pages simply to give each what Herodotus called its "due meed of glory." Instead, the participating scholars have tried to sift the present state of knowledge on their period in order to determine the major themes and characteristics. In the present volume, Professor R. Jackson Wilson of the University of Wisconsin analyzes the distinct nature of the changes and troubles in the United States in the years 1900–1929.

Students can assess for themselves the quality of Professor Wilson's judgments by careful examination of the readings, discussion with their own instructors, and reference to other historians mentioned in the text. The results may prove tentative and uncertain, a familiar state of affairs for the working historian. Yet, hopefully, the selections that follow will provoke in some a passion for continued reading in the national past, while providing for others an entry into that normally contentious world, the historians' America.

Allen Weinstein

Frank Otto Gatell

CONTENTS

Reform, Crisis, and Confusion, 1900–1929

Introduction

At the end of World War II, most educated Americans inherited a con-
ventionalized picture of the years of their fathers—the progressive period
of the first two decades of the century and the "roaring twenties" that
followed. According to this picture, during the administrations of Theodore Roosevelt and Woodrow Wilson, the people (most of them, at
least) rose against the abuses committed by corporate and political leaders.
Through new political spokesmen, Americans achieved reform on every
front: legislation governing wages and hours, child-labor laws, food and
drug controls, action against trusts and monopolies. Then, just as reform
was about to reach a height of achievement, it was cut off. A reluctant
nation, which would have been more content to seek its domestic promise,
was drawn into war in 1917 and was confronted with the demands of
world power. After the war, a tired people, finally sick of the power
politics of old Europe, withdrew from both domestic reform and world
leadership. Wilson, who had combined reform vigor and high idealism,
was replaced by Harding, who brought to Washington only cronies and
"normalcy." Calvin Coolidge and Herbert Hoover continued a regime
of inactive, pro-corporate government. In foreign policy, the outcome
was a period of isolationism whose price had to be paid between 1941
and 1945. During the twenties, American social life was a matter of jazz,
ballyhoo, flagpole sitters, flappers, speak-easies, and the Ku Klux Klan.
The only relief in sight was a literary and artistic renaissance wrought
in Paris and New York by expatriates and bohemians. But the reform
impulse, always latent in American life, had to lie dormant for a decade,
awaiting the crash of 1929, the depression, and the election of Franklin Roosevelt.

This was the picture of the first three decades of the century that
most literate Americans held in 1945. The picture might vary from
class to class and from one section of the country to another. A young

Negro in the South or an aged Polish immigrant in Milwaukee might not respond to the picture at all. But for those Americans to whom formal history had any relevance, the story seemed plain. As it was drawn by professional historians, of course, the picture was considerably more subtle and varied. Still, most practicing historians worked within some variant of the popular view of modern American history.

This conventional version of the recent American past, which influenced the work of almost every historian throughout the 1940s, rested on several underlying assumptions. First, and probably most important, most historians were sympathetic with the progressive reformers. One historian or another might find fault with Roosevelt's inconsistency or Wilson's stubbornness, but as a group, American historians were themselves of a liberal, progressive cast of mind. They accepted, on the whole, the idea that American history was a series of periodic confrontations between vested interests and reform leaders who represented an aroused people. This view led directly to the second main assumption of the conventional history of progressivism: a confidence that the reformers had been motivated by a fairly straightforward desire to change conditions that were objectively bad. The primary cause of progressivism, then, was actually existing evil conditions in industry and government. Third, historians tended to agree that World War I had spelled a "farewell to reform." This opinion, in turn, committed them to a sharp periodization of twentieth-century history in which the progressive period, the twenties, and the New Deal were seen as three sharply separate entities marked off by two climactic events, the Great War and the Great Depression.

Soon after World War II, the conventional account of American history in the twentieth century began to be challenged. The pace of the challenge accelerated sharply after about 1955. By the end of the 1960s, almost no part of the older version of things remained unquestioned. Historians had begun to discover a new past. The events, to be sure, remained substantially the same: progressivism, World War I, and the Republican "ascendancy" of Harding, Coolidge, and Hoover. What had changed were historians' perceptions of the *meaning* of the United States' emergence into modernity.

The essays collected in this volume are a sampling of the newer interpretations. They do not, in any useful sense, represent the work of a particular "school" of historians, and they do not always fit together in obvious ways. Deep changes in interpretation seldom emerge suddenly and cleanly. As a result, some of the historians whose work is included in this collection still retain parts of the inherited framework. But collectively, the essays do represent a considerable challenge to the inherited conventions of national history, a challenge that will probably determine the way American history is written and thought of in the 1970s.

It is possible to make several generalizations about the directions in which the reinterpretation of the period 1900–1929 is moving. Historians are much more likely today than they were twenty years ago to be suspicious of the progressive reformers; at the same time, they are less likely to be resentful toward men like Coolidge and Hoover. A related preoccupation of contemporary historians is with the causes of the progressive movement. More and more, historians are concerned with the *subjective* motivations of the reformers, with their private ambitions, fears, and even neuroses, rather than with the objective evils that they confronted. Also, many historians are no longer content to think of progressivism as a conflict between liberal reformers and businessmen, entrepreneurs, or capitalists. Instead, the current fashion is to view political progressivism as something of a businessmen's movement and even to argue that on crucial issues, progressive policy was actually controlled by wealthy industrialists. This view, in turn, implies another major change in interpretation. Formerly, intellectuals were given considerable credit for the directions that reform took. The tendency of historians now is to question the importance of intellectuals' contribution to progressivism and, at the same time, to question whether intellectuals were devoted to "democracy" or, instead, to a subtle and sinister form of élitism. Also, historians are no longer certain that war spelled the end of reform. If businessmen-reformers were interested in achieving a controlled economy through reform, then the wartime controls of labor, transportation, prices, and agriculture could be viewed as the consummation of their program and not as a defeat. And if intellectuals-as-reformers were more interested in social planning by a trained élite than in popular democracy, then the war could have represented to them a new opportunity for planning rather than a farewell to visions of progress.

These emergent questions about the nature of progressivism entail corresponding questions about the 1920s. Generally, the present drift is toward making less sharp the divisions between the two "periods." In matters of foreign policy, for example, it seems that many progressives were militant imperialists or expansionists and that the war was a logical outcome of their foreign policy of involvement. Correspondingly, the policy of the 1920s was by no means isolationist but was rather a consistent extension of the expansionist humor of the preceding decade. Similarly, historians who treat progressivism as essentially a businessmen's movement can see the pro-corporate policies of the 1920s as an *outcome* of progressivism, rather than a reversal. Other historians, working in social and intellectual history, have discovered that characteristics which used to be associated with the 1920s really had their beginnings before 1917. The alienation and rebellion of intellectuals, for example, now seems to be a product of the prewar years and not a phenomenon of the Lost Generation. These historians have also made clear that the movement for prohibition was as much a part of the progressive experience as of the 1920s and that such indications of social instability as a rising divorce rate belonged to the years before the war just as much as to the decade of the flapper and the gin mill. Political historians have raised doubts whether progressivism "died" in the 1920s or was merely redefined and redirected. The outcome of these new questions is a tendency to view the years 1900-1929 as something of a unity, punctuated at some points by reform, at others by war, and at others by a heightened instability of social conventions, but still an integral, reasonably continuous whole.

PART I
Progressivism: The Politics of Reform

The Status Revolution and Progressive Leaders

RICHARD HOFSTADTER

Professor Richard Hofstadter's *The Age of Reform* has proved to be one of the most influential books on American history that has been written since World War II. In this book, he deals with various reform movements from the Populism of the 1890s to the New Deal of the 1930s, but his most important chapters are on the progressive movement. The most innovative chapter concerns the reasons why a broad section of the middle classes "went Progressive" and why, more particularly, the "intellectuals"—ministers, professors, and lawyers—provided a "large and strategic section of Progressive leadership."

According to Professor Hofstadter, anyone who wants to understand the motivation of the progressive leadership must do more than merely point to the objective evils that the reformers attacked. Indeed, the objective situation probably had been worse in the "crisis of the 1890s" than in the years after 1900. The upper middle classes, and the professional groups in them especially, became progressive because of their anxieties about their own social status in a nation increasingly dominated by new business wealth and corporate power. The movement, then, could be best understood as the attempt of such men to regain control of their own experience by political means.

Richard Hofstadter is, by any useful measure, one of the two or three best American historians of the postwar decades. Much of his work has been derivative, resting finally on the research of other scholars, but he has always brought to his subjects a critical imagination that lifts them from the level of the scholarly monograph to cultural commentary of a high order. He is the DeWitt Clinton Professor of History at Columbia University and is the author of The American Political Tradition *(1948),* The Age of Reform *(1963),* Social Darwinism in American Thought *(1955),* Anti-Intellectualism in American Life *(1963), and* The Progressive Historians *(1968), among others. Of particular interest is the closing chapter of* The Progressive Historians, *in which he attempts to define the intellectual dilemmas of postwar historians in America.*

I. The Plutocracy and the Mugwump Type

Populism had been overwhelmingly rural and provincial. The ferment of the Progressive era was urban, middle-class, and nationwide. Above all, Progressivism differed from Populism in the fact that the middle classes of the cities not only joined the trend toward protest but took over its leadership. While Bryan's old followers still kept their interest in certain reforms, they now found themselves in the company of large numbers who had hitherto violently opposed them. As the demand for reform spread from the farmers to the middle class and from the Populist Party into the major parties, it became more powerful and more highly regarded. It had been possible for their enemies to brand the Populists as wild anarchists, especially since there were millions of Americans who had never laid eyes on either a Populist or an anarchist. But it was impossible to popularize such a distorted image of the Progressives, who flourished in every section of the country, everywhere visibly, palpably, almost pathetically respectable. . . .

Clearly, the need for political and economic reform was now felt more widely in the country at large. Another, more obscure process, traceable to the flexibility and opportunism of the American party system, was also at work: successful resistance to reform demands required a partial incorporation of the reform program. As Bryan Democracy had taken over much of the spirit and some of the program of Populism, Theodore Roosevelt, in turn, persistently blunted Bryan's appeal by appropriating Bryan's issues in modified form. In this way Progressivism became nationwide and bipartisan, encompassing Democrats and Republicans, country and city, East, West, and South. A working coalition was forged between the old Bryan country and the new reform movement in the cities, with-

CONDENSED FROM *The Age of Reform*, BY RICHARD HOFSTADTER. © COPYRIGHT 1955 BY RICHARD HOFSTADTER. REPRINTED BY PERMISSION OF ALFRED A. KNOPF, INC. AND JONATHAN CAPE, LTD.

out which the broad diffusion and strength of Progressivism would have
been impossible. Its spirit spread so widely that by the time of the three-
cornered Presidential contest of 1912 President Taft, who was put in the
position of the "conservative" candidate, got less than half the combined
popular vote of the "Progressives," Wilson and Roosevelt.

After 1900 Populism and Progressivism merged, though a close student
may find in the Progressive era two broad strains of thought, one influenced chiefly by the Populist inheritance, the other mainly a product
of urban life. Certainly Progressivism was characterized by a fresh, more
intimate and sympathetic concern with urban problems—labor and social
welfare, municipal reform, the interest of the consumer. However, those
achievements of the age that had a nationwide import and required
Congressional action, such as tariff and financial legislation, railroad and
trust regulation, and the like, were dependent upon the votes of the Senators from the agrarian regions and were shaped in such a way as would
meet their demands.

While too sharp a distinction between Populist and Progressive thinking
would distort reality, the growth of middle-class reform sentiment, the
contributions of professionals and educated men, made Progressive
thought more informed, more moderate, more complex than Populist
thought had been. Progressivism, moreover, as the product of a more
prosperous era, was less rancorous. With the exception of a few internally controversial issues of a highly pragmatic sort, the Populists had
tended to be of one mind on most broad social issues, and that mind was
rather narrow and predictable. The Progressives were more likely to be
aware of the complexities of social issues and more divided among themselves. Indeed, the characteristic Progressive was often of two minds on
many issues. Concerning the great corporations, the Progressives felt that
they were a menace to society and that they were all too often manipu-
lated by unscrupulous men; on the other hand, many Progressives were
quite aware that the newer organization of industry and finance was a
product of social evolution which had its beneficent side and that it was
here to stay. Concerning immigrants, they frequently shared Populist
prejudices and the Populist horror of ethnic mixture, but they were somewhat more disposed to discipline their feelings with a sense of some obli-
gation to the immigrant and the recognition that his Americanization was
a practical problem that must be met with a humane and constructive
program. As for labor, while they felt, perhaps more acutely than most
Populists of the nineties, that the growth of union power posed a distinct
problem, even a threat, to them, they also saw that labor organization
had arisen in response to a real need among the urban masses that must
in some way be satisfied. As for the bosses, the machines, the corruptions
of city life, they too found in these things grave evils; but they were
ready, perhaps all too ready, to admit that the existence of such evils was
in large measure their own fault. Like the Populists the Progressives

were full of indignation, but their indignation was more qualified by a sense of responsibility, often even of guilt, and it was supported by a greater capacity to organize, legislate, and administer. But lest all this seem unfair to the Populists, it should be added that the Progressives did not, as a rule, have the daring or the originative force of the Populists of the 1890's, and that a great deal of Progressive political effort was spent enacting proposals that the Populists had outlined fifteen or even twenty years earlier.

Curiously, the Progressive revolt—even when we have made allowance for the brief panic of 1907 and the downward turn in business in 1913— took place almost entirely during a period of sustained and general prosperity. The middle class, most of which had been content to accept the conservative leadership of Hanna and McKinley during the period of crisis in the mid-nineties, rallied to the support of Progressive leaders in both parties during the period of well-being that followed. This fact is a challenge to the historian. Why did the middle classes undergo this remarkable awakening at all, and why during this period of general prosperity in which most of them seem to have shared? What was the place of economic discontents in the Progressive movement? To what extent did reform originate in other considerations?

Of course Progressivism had the adherence of a heterogeneous public whose various segments responded to various needs. But I am concerned here with a large and strategic section of Progressive leadership, upon whose contributions the movement was politically and intellectually as well as financially dependent, and whose members did much to formulate its ideals. It is my thesis that men of this sort, who might be designated broadly as the Mugwump type, were Progressives not because of economic deprivations but primarily because they were victims of an upheaval in status that took place in the United States during the closing decades of the nineteenth and the early years of the twentieth century. Progressivism, in short, was to a very considerable extent led by men who suffered from the events of their time not through a shrinkage in their means but through the changed pattern in the distribution of deference and power.

Up to about 1870 the United States was a nation with a rather broad diffusion of wealth, status, and power, in which the man of moderate means, especially in the many small communities, could command much deference and exert much influence. The small merchant or manufacturer, the distinguished lawyer, editor, or preacher, was a person of local eminence in an age in which local eminence mattered a great deal. In the absence of very many nationwide sources of power and prestige, the pillars of the local communities were men of great importance in their own right. What Henry Adams remembered about his own bailiwick was, on the whole, true of the country at large: "Down to 1850, and even later, New England society was still directed by the professions. Lawyers, physicians, professors, merchants were classes, and acted not as individuals, but as though they were clergymen and each profession were a church."[1]

In the post-Civil War period all this was changed. The rapid development of the big cities, the building of a great industrial plant, the construction of the railroads, the emergence of the corporation as the dominant form of enterprise, transformed the old society and revolutionized the distribution of power and prestige. During the 1840's there were not twenty millionaires in the entire country; by 1910 there were probably more than twenty millionaires sitting in the United States Senate.[2] By the late 1880's this process had gone far enough to become the subject of frequent, anxious comment in the press. In 1891 the *Forum* published a much-discussed article on "The Coming Billionaire," by Thomas G. Shearman, who estimated that there were 120 men in the United States each of whom was worth over ten million dollars.[3] In 1892 the *New York Tribune*, inspired by growing popular criticism of the wealthy, published a list of 4,047 reputed millionaires, and in the following year a statistician of the Census Bureau published a study of the concentration of wealth in which he estimated that 9 per cent of the families of the nation owned 71 per cent of the wealth.[4]

The newly rich, the grandiosely or corruptly rich, the masters of great corporations, were bypassing the men of the Mugwump type—the old gentry, the merchants of long standing, the small manufacturers, the established professional men, the civic leaders of an earlier era. . . . In a strictly economic sense these men were not growing poorer as a class, but their wealth and power were being dwarfed by comparison with the new eminences of wealth and power. They were less important, and they knew it.

Against the tide of new wealth the less affluent and aristocratic local gentry had almost no protection at all. . . . To face the insolence of the local boss or traction magnate in a town where one's family had long been prominent was galling enough; it was still harder to bear at a time when every fortune, every career, every reputation, seemed smaller and less significant because it was measured against the Vanderbilts, Harrimans, Goulds, Carnegies, Rockefellers, and Morgans.[5]

While men of the Mugwump type flourished during those decades most conspicuously about Boston, a center of seasoned wealth and seasoned conscience, where some of the most noteworthy names in Massachusetts were among them,[6] they were also prominent in a metropolis like New York and could be found in some strength in such Midwestern cities as Indianapolis and Chicago. Nonetheless, one senses among them the prominence of the cultural ideals and traditions of New England, and beyond these of old England. Protestant and Anglo-Saxon for the most part, they were very frequently of New England ancestry; and even when they were not, they tended to look to New England's history for literary, cultural, and political models and for examples of moral idealism.

Their conception of statecraft was set by the high example of the Found-ing Fathers, or by the great debating statesmen of the silver age, Webster, Sumner, Everett, Clay, and Calhoun. Their ideal leader was a well-to-do, well-educated, high-minded citizen, rich enough to be free from motives of what they often called "crass materialism," whose family roots were deep not only in American history but in his local community. Such a person, they thought, would be just the sort to put the national interest, as well as the interests of civic improvement, above personal motives or political opportunism. And such a person was just the sort, as Henry Adams never grew tired of complaining, for whom American political life was least likely to find a place. To be sure, men of the Mugwump type could and did find places in big industry, in the great corporations, and they were sought out to add respectability to many forms of enter-prise. But they tended to have positions in which the initiative was not their own, or in which they could not feel themselves acting in harmony with their highest ideals. They no longer called the tune, no longer com-manded their old deference. They were expropriated, not so much economically as morally. . . .

The typical Mugwump was a conservative in his economic and political views. He disdained, to be sure, the most unscrupulous of the new men of wealth, as he did the opportunistic, boodling, tariff-mongering politi-cians who served them. But the most serious abuses of the unfolding economic order of the Gilded Age he either resolutely ignored or ac-cepted complacently as an inevitable result of the struggle for existence or the improvidence and laziness of the masses.[7] As a rule, he was dog-matically committed to the prevailing theoretical economics of *laissez faire*. His economic program did not go much beyond tariff reform and sound money—both principles more easily acceptable to a group whose wealth was based more upon mercantile activities and the professions than upon manufacturing and new enterprises—and his political program rested upon the foundations of honest and efficient government and civil-service reform. He was a "liberal" in the classic sense. Tariff reform, he thought, would be the sovereign remedy for the huge business combina-tions that were arising. . . . He imagined that most of the economic ills that were remediable at all could be remedied by free trade, just as he believed that the essence of government lay in honest dealing by honest and competent men. . . . It was in fact intellect and social position, among other things, that insulated the Mugwump from the sources of voting power. If he was critical of the predatory capitalists and their political allies, he was even more contemptuously opposed to the "radical" agrarian movements and the "demagogues" who led them, to the city workers when, led by "walking delegates," they rebelled against their employers, and to the urban immigrants and the "unscrupulous bosses" who intro-duced them to the mysteries of American civic life. He was an impeccable constitutionalist, but the fortunes of American politics had made him an equally firm aristocrat. He had his doubts, now that the returns were in, about the beneficence of universal suffrage.[8] The last thing he would have dreamed of was to appeal to the masses against the plutocracy, and to appeal to them against the local bosses was usually fruitless. The Mugwump was shut off from the people as much by his social reserve and his amateurism as by his candidly conservative views. In so far as he sought popular support, he sought it on aristocratic terms.

One of the changes that made Progressivism possible around the turn of the century was the end of this insulation of the Mugwump type from mass support. For reasons that it is in good part the task of these pages to explore, the old barriers melted away. How the Mugwump found a following is a complex story, but it must be said at once that this was impossible until the Mugwump type itself had been somewhat transformed. The sons and successors of the Mugwumps had to challenge their fathers' ideas, modify their doctrinaire commitment to *laissez faire*, replace their aristocratic preferences with a startling revival of enthusiasm for popular government, and develop greater flexibility in dealing with the demands of the discontented before they could launch the movement that came to dominate the political life of the Progressive era.

But if the philosophy and the spirit were new, the social type and the social grievance were much the same. The Mugwump had broadened his base. One need not be surprised, for instance, to find among the Progressive leaders in both major parties a large number of well-to-do men whose personal situation is reminiscent of the Mugwumps of an earlier generation. As Professor George Mowry has remarked, "few reform movements in American history have had the support of more wealthy men."[9] . . . As yet no study has been made of reform leaders in both major parties, but the systematic information available on leaders of the Progressive Party of 1912 is suggestive. Alfred D. Chandler, Jr., surveying the backgrounds and careers of 260 Progressive Party leaders throughout the country, has noted how overwhelmingly urban and middle-class they were. Almost entirely native-born Protestants, they had an extraordinarily high representation of professional men and college graduates. The rest were businessmen, proprietors of fairly large enterprises. None was a farmer, only one was a labor-union leader, and the white-collar classes and salaried managers of large industrial or transportation enterprises were completely unrepresented. Not surprisingly, the chief previous political experience of most of them was in local politics. But on the whole, as Chandler observes, they "had had little experience with any kind of institutional discipline. In this sense, though they lived in the city, they were in no way typical men of the city. With very rare exceptions, all these men had been and continued to be their own bosses. As lawyers, businessmen, and professional men, they worked for themselves and had done so for most of their lives. As individualists, unacquainted with institutional discipline or control, the Progressive leaders represented, in spite of their thoroughly urban backgrounds, the ideas of the older, more rural America."[10] From the only other comparable study, George Mowry's survey of the California Progressives, substantially the same conclusions emerge. The average California Progressive was "in the jargon of his day, 'well fixed.' He was more often than not a Mason, and almost invariably a member of his town's chamber of commerce. . . . He apparently had been, at least until 1900, a conservative Republican, satisfied with McKinley and his Republican predecessors."[11]

While some of the wealthier reformers were self-made men, like John P. Altgeld, Hazen Pingree, the Mayor of Detroit and Governor of Michigan, and Samuel ("Golden Rule") Jones, the crusading Mayor of Toledo, more were men of the second and third generation of wealth or (notably Tom Johnson and Joseph Fels) men who had been declassed for a time and had recouped their fortunes. Progressive ideology, at any rate, distinguished consistently between "responsible" and "irresponsible" wealth—a distinction that seems intimately related to the antagonism of those who had had money long enough to make temperate and judicious use of it for those who were rioting with new-found means.

· · ·

II. The Alienation of the Professionals

Whenever an important change takes place in modern society, large sections of the intellectuals, the professional and opinion-making classes, see the drift of events and throw their weight on the side of what they feel is progress and reform. In few historical movements have these classes played a more striking role than in Progressivism. While those intellectuals and professional men who supported Progressive causes no doubt did so in part for reasons that they shared with other members of the middle classes, their view of things was also influenced by marked changes within the professions themselves and by changes in their social position brought about by the growing complexity of society and by the status revolution.

In the previous era, during the industrial and political conflicts of the 1870's and 1880's, the respectable opinion-making classes had given almost unqualified support to the extreme conservative position on most issues. The Protestant ministry, for instance, was "a massive, almost unbroken front in its defense of the status quo."[12] Most college professors preached the great truths of *laissez faire* and the conservative apologetics of social Darwinism, and thundered away at labor unions and social reformers. Lawyers, except for a rare small-town spokesman of agrarian unrest or little business, were complacent. And while an occasional newspaper editor launched an occasional crusade, usually on a local issue, the press was almost as unruffled.

Beginning slowly in the 1890's and increasingly in the next two decades, members of these professions deserted the standpat conservatism of the post-Civil War era to join the main stream of liberal dissent and to give it both moral and intellectual leadership. The reasons for this reversal are complex. But if the professional groups changed their ideas and took on new loyalties, it was not in simple response to changes in the nature of the country's problems—indeed, in many ways the problems of American life were actually less acute after 1897—but rather because they had become disposed to see things they had previously ignored and to agitate themselves about things that had previously left them unconcerned. What interests me here is not the changed external condition of American society, but the inward social and psychological position of the professionals themselves that made so many of them become the advisers and the gadflies of reform movements. The alienation of the professionals was in fact a product of many developments, but among these the effects of the status revolution must be given an important place. Conditions varied from profession to profession, but all groups with claims to learning and skill shared a common sense of humiliation and common grievances against the plutocracy.

The contrast between the attitude of the clergy in the 1870's and that of the 1890's measures the change. When the hard times following the panic of 1873 resulted in widespread labor unrest, culminating in the railway strikes of 1877, the Protestant religious press was bloodthirsty in its reaction. The laborers were described as "wild beasts" and "reckless desperadoes," and some of the religious papers suggested that if they could not be clubbed into submission they should be mowed down with cannon and Gatling guns. During the social conflicts of the 1880's, ministers expressed an attitude only slightly less hysterical. By the 1890's a liberal minority was beginning to express a far milder view of strikes, though the chief religious papers were still completely hostile, for instance, to the American Railway Union in the Pullman strike of 1894. By this time, however, a substantial reversal of opinion was under way, and the ideas of social Christianity and the social gospel had profoundly modified the outlook of many ministers in the major denominations. From 1895 through the Progressive era "the doctrines developed by the [early social-gospel] generation . . . increasingly dominated the most articulate sections of American Protestantism."[13]

The clergy were probably the most conspicuous losers from the status revolution. They not only lost ground in all the outward ways, as most middle-class elements did, but were also hard hit in their capacity as moral and intellectual leaders by the considerable secularization that took place in American society and intellectual life in the last three decades of the nineteenth century. On one hand, they were offended and at times antagonized by the attitudes of some of the rich men in their congregations.[14] On the other, they saw the churches losing the support of the working class on a large and ominous scale. Everywhere their judgments seemed to carry less weight. Religion itself seemed less

important year by year, and even in their capacity as moral and intellectual leaders of the community the ministers now had to share a place
with the scientists and social scientists. . . .

The general decline in deference to the ministerial role was shown
nowhere more clearly than in the failure of the lay governors of Protestant congregations to maintain the standard of living of their pastors
under the complex conditions of urban life and the rising price level of
the period after 1897. Not only were the clergy less regarded as molders
of opinion, but they were expected to carry on the arduous work of
their pastorates with means that were increasingly inadequate and to
defer meekly to far more affluent vestrymen.[15]

In the light of this situation, it may not be unfair to attribute the
turning of the clergy toward reform and social criticism not solely to
their disinterested perception of social problems and their earnest desire
to improve the world, but also to the fact that as men who were in
their own way suffering from the incidence of the status revolution they
were able to understand and sympathize with the problems of other
disinherited groups. The increasingly vigorous interest in the social
gospel, so clearly manifested by the clergy after 1890, was in many
respects an attempt to restore through secular leadership some of the
spiritual influence and authority and social prestige that clergymen had
lost through the upheaval in the system of status and the secularization
of society. . . .

The situation of the professors is in striking contrast to that of
the clergy—and yet the academic man arrived by a different path
at the same end as the cleric. While the clergy were being in a considerable measure dispossessed, the professors were rising. The challenge
they made to the *status quo* around the turn of the century, especially
in the social sciences, was a challenge offered by an advancing group,
growing year by year in numbers, confidence, and professional standing.
Modern students of social psychology have suggested that certain social-
psychological tensions are heightened both in social groups that are
rising in the social scale and in those that are falling;[16] and this may
explain why two groups with fortunes as varied as the professoriat and
the clergy gave so much common and similar support to reform ideologies.

Unlike the clergy, academic men in America before 1870 had had
no broad public influence, no professional traditions or self-awareness,
hardly even any very serious professional standards.[17] The sudden emergence of the modern university, however, transformed American scholar-
ship during the last three decades of the century. Where there had been
only a number of denominational colleges, there were now large univer-
sities with adequate libraries, laboratories, huge endowments, graduate
schools, professional schools, and advancing salaries. The professoriat
was growing immensely in numbers, improving in professional standards,
gaining in compensation and security, and acquiring a measure of influence and prestige in and out of the classroom that their predecessors

of the old college era would never have dreamed of. And yet there was a pervasive discontent. . . . The professors had their intimate experience with and resentments of the plutocracy. . . . Professors in America had always had the status of hired men, but they had never had enough professional pride to express anything more than a rare momentary protest against this condition. Now, even though their professional situation was improving, they found in themselves the resources to complain against their position;[18] not the least of their grievances was the fact that their professional affairs were under the control of the plutocracy, since boards of trustees were often composed of those very businessmen who in other areas of life were becoming suspect for their predatory and immoral lives. Further, academic men in the social sciences found themselves under pressure to trim their sails ideologically; and caste self-consciousness was heightened by a series of academic-freedom cases involving in some instances the more eminent members of the emerging social sciences—Richard T. Ely, Edward A. Ross, J. Allen Smith, and others. In 1915 this rising self-consciousness found expression in the formation of the American Association of University Professors. . . .

The legal profession, which stands in a more regular and intimate relation with American politics than any other profession or occupation, affords a good example of the changing position of the middle-class professional in the development of corporate society. The ambiguous situation of many lawyers, which often involved both profitable subservience to and personal alienation from corporate business, contributed significantly to the cast of Progressive thought and the recruitment of Progressive leaders. While many lawyers could participate in Progressive politics in the spirit of good counselors caring for their constituents, many also felt the impact of the common demand for reform as a response to changes in their own profession.

In the opening decades of the century the American legal profession was troubled by an internal crisis, a crisis in self-respect precipitated by the conflict between the image of legal practice inherited from an earlier age of more independent professionalism and the realities of modern commercial practice. . . .

At the turn of the century lawyers as a group were far less homogeneous than they had been fifty years before. The large, successful firms, which were beginning even then to be called "legal factories," were headed by the wealthy, influential, and normally very conservative minority of the profession that tended to be most conspicuous in the Bar Associations. In their firms were many talented young lawyers, serving their time as cheap labor. There was a second echelon of lawyers in small but well-established offices of the kind that flourished in smaller cities; lawyers of this sort, who were commonly attached to and often shared the outlook of new enterprisers or small businessmen, frequently staffed and conducted local politics. A third echelon, consisting for the most part of small partnerships or individual practitioners, usually carried on a catch-as-catch-can practice and eked out modest livings. As the situation of the independent practitioners deteriorated, they often drifted into ambulance-chasing and taking contingent fees. Much of the talk in Bar Associations about improving legal ethics represented the unsympathetic efforts of the richer lawyers with corporate connections to improve the reputation of the profession as a whole at the expense of their weaker colleagues. . . .

With the rise of corporate industrialism and finance capitalism, the law, particularly in the urban centers where the most enviable prizes were to be had, was becoming a captive profession. Lawyers kept saying that the law had lost much of its distinctly professional character and had become a business. Exactly how much truth lay in their laments cannot be ascertained until we know more about the history of the profession; but whether or not their conclusions were founded upon a false sentimentalization of an earlier era, many lawyers were convinced that their profession had declined in its intellectual standards and in its moral and social position. Around the turn of the century, the professional talents of courtroom advocacy and briefmaking were referred to again and again as "lost arts," as the occupation of the successful lawyer centered more and more upon counseling clients and offering business advice. General and versatile talent, less needed than in the old days, was replaced by specialized practice and the division of labor within law firms. The firms themselves grew larger; the process of concentration and combination in business, which limited profitable counseling to fewer and larger firms, engendered a like concentration in the law. Metropolitan law firms, as they grew larger and more profitable, moved into closer relationships with and became "house counsel" of the large investment houses, banks, or industrial firms that provided them with most of their business. But the relation that was the source of profit brought with it a loss of independence to the great practitioners. The smaller independent practitioner was affected in another, still more serious way: much of his work was taken from him by real estate, trust, and insurance companies, collection agencies, and banks, which took upon themselves larger and larger amounts of what had once been entirely legal business.[19] A speaker at the meeting of the Baltimore Bar Association in 1911 estimated that 70 per cent of the members of the profession were not making a suitable living. "Corporations doing our business are working . . . to our detriment," he said. "Slowly, but with persistence, the corporations are pushing the lawyer to the wall. They advertise, solicit, and by their corporate influence and wealth monopolize the legal field."[20] . . .

Thus internal conditions, as well as those outward events which any lawyer, as a citizen, could see, disposed a large portion of this politically decisive profession to understand the impulse toward change. That impecunious young or small-town lawyers or practitioners associated with small business, and academic teachers of law, should often have approached the problems of law and society from a standpoint critical of the great corporations is not too astonishing—though among these elements only one, the teacher, was consistently articulate. Somewhat more noteworthy is the occasional evidence of a mixed state of mind even among some of the outstanding corporation lawyers, for whom allegiance to the essentials of the *status quo* was qualified by a concern with its unremedied abuses and a feeling of irritation with its coarsest representatives. The top leaders of the law, in their strategic place as the source of indispensable policy advice to the captains of industry, probably enjoyed more wealth and as much power as lawyers had ever had. But their influence was of course no longer *independently* exercised; it was exerted through the corporation, the bank, the business leader. . . . The corporation lawyer lived in frequent association with business-men who were oppressively richer, considerably less educated, and sometimes less scrupulous than himself. By professional tradition and training he saw things with much more disinterested eyes than they did; and although it was his business to serve and advise them, he some-times recoiled. . . . Such men turned to public service with a sense of release. . . .

It may be objected that the progressivism espoused by corpora-tion lawyers on a moral holiday would be a rather conservative sort of thing. In fact it was, but this was not out of harmony with the general tone of the Progressive movement, especially in the Eastern states, where this kind of leadership played an important role. There Progressivism was a mild and judicious movement, whose goal was not a sharp change in the social structure, but rather the formation of a responsible élite, which was to take charge of the popular impulse toward change and direct it into moderate and, as they would have said, "con-structive" channels—a leadership occupying, as Brandeis so aptly put it, "a position of independence between the wealthy and the people, prepared to curb the excesses of either."

III. From the Mugwump to the Progressive

What I have said thus far about the impact of the status revolution may help to explain the occurrence of the Progressive movement, but will not account for its location in time. A pertinent question remains to be answered: as the status revolution had been going on at least since the Civil War and was certainly well advanced by the 1890's, why did the really powerful outburst of protest and reform come only with the first fifteen years of the twentieth century? Why did our middle classes, after six years of civic anxieties and three years of acute and ominous depression, give Hanna and McKinley a strong vote of confidence in 1896? And then after this confidence seemed in fact to have been justi-fied by the return of prosperity, when the nation's sense of security and power had been heightened by a quick victory in what John Hay called "our splendid little war," and when a mood of buoyant optimism had again become dominant, why should they have turned about and given ardent support to the forces that were raking American life with criticism?

First, it must be said that in some areas of American life those phenomena that we associate with the Progressive era were already much in evidence before 1900. In a limited and local way the Progressive movement had in fact begun around 1890. On the part of some business interests the movement for cheap transportation and against monopoly had already waxed strong enough to impel a reluctant Congress to pass the Interstate Commerce Act in 1887 and the Sherman Act in 1890.[21] Likewise the crusade for municipal reform was well under way in the 1890's. A very large number of local organizations dedicated to good government and a variety of reforms had sprung into existence, and in some cities they had already achieved more than negligible changes.[22] Finally, the state legislatures had already begun to pass the sort of social legislation—regulation of hours and conditions of labor, for instance— that was later fostered more effectually by the Progressives.[23]

These were the timid beginnings of a movement that did not become nationwide until the years after 1901. One important thing that kept them from going further during the nineties was that the events of that decade frightened the middle classes so thoroughly that they did not dare dream of taking seriously ideas that seemed to involve a more fundamental challenge to established ways of doing things. The Progressive appeal was always directed very largely to people who felt that they did have something to lose. Populism, which was widely portrayed as "menacing socialism in the Western states," the Homestead and Pullman strikes with their violence and class bitterness, the march of Coxey's army, the disastrous slump in business activity, and the lengthening breadlines seemed like the beginnings of social revolution; and in the imagination of the timid bourgeois, Bryan, Altgeld, and Debs seemed like the Dantons, Robespierres, and Marats of the coming upheaval. Hence there was a disposition among the middle classes to put aside their own discontents and grievances until the time should come when it seemed safe to air them.[24]

More pertinent, perhaps, is the fact that the Progressive ferment was the work of the first generation that had been born and raised in the midst of the status revolution. In 1890 the governing generation still consisted of men born in the 1830's and 1840's, who through force of habit still looked upon events with the happier vision of the mid-nineteenth century. During the next twenty years the dominant new influence came from those who were still young enough in the nineties to have their thinking affected by the hard problems just emerging, problems for which the older generation, reared in the age of the great transcontinental settlement, had no precedents and no convincing answers. The crisis of the nineties was a searing experience. During the depression of 1893–7 it was clear that the country was being profoundly shaken, that

men everywhere were beginning to envisage a turning-point in national
development, after which one could no longer live within the framework of the aspirations and expectations that had governed American
life for the century past. Americans had grown up with the placid
assumption that the development of their country was so much unlike
what had happened elsewhere that the social conflicts troubling other
countries could never become a major problem here. By the close of
the century, however, younger Americans began to feel that it would
be their fate to live in a world subject to all the familiar hazards of
European industrialism. "A generation ago," said one of the characters
in Henry Blake Fuller's *With the Procession* (1895), "we thought . . .
that our pacific processes showed social science in its fullest development. But today we have all the elements possessed by the old world
itself, and we must take whatever they develop, as the old world does.
We have the full working apparatus finally, with all its resultant noise,
waste, stenches, stains, dangers, explosions."[25]

The generation that went Progressive was the generation that came
of age in the nineties. Contemporaries had often noticed how large a
portion of the leaders at any Populist convention were the silver-haired
veterans of old monetary reform crusades; Progressivism, however,
passed into the hands of youth—William Allen White remembered them
in his autobiography as the "hundreds of thousands of young men in
their twenties, thirties, and early forties" whose "quickening sense of
the inequities, injustices, and fundamental wrongs" of American society
provided the motive power of reform.[26] The ascension of Theodore
Roosevelt to the presidency, the youngest man ever to occupy the
White House, was no more than symbolic of the coming-of-age of a
generation whose perspectives were sharply demarcated from those of
their fathers and who felt the need of a new philosophy and a new
politics.[27] T. R. himself had been thirty-two in 1890, Bryan only thirty,
La Follette thirty-five, Wilson thirty-four. Most of the Progressive leaders, as well as the muckraking journalists who did so much to form
Progressive opinion, were, at the opening of that crucial *fin de siècle*
decade, in their early thirties, or perhaps younger, and hence only
around forty when the Progressive era got under way.[28]

The Progressive leaders were the spiritual sons of the Mugwumps,
but they were sons who dropped much of the ideological baggage of
their parents. Where the Mugwumps had been committed to aristocracy,
in spirit if not in their formal theories of government, the Progressives
spoke of returning government to the people; and where the Mugwumps
had clung desperately to liberal economics and the clichés of *laissez faire*,
the Progressives were prepared to make use of state intervention wherever
it suited their purposes. The Mugwumps had lacked a consistent and
substantial support among the public at large. The Progressives had an
almost rabidly enthusiastic following. The Mugwumps, except on spora-
dic occasions, were without allies among other sectors of the country.

The Progressives had, on a substantial number of national issues, reliable allies in the very agrarian rebels for whom the Mugwumps had had nothing but contempt. In many ways the Mugwump type was refashioned into the Progressive by the needs and demands of its own followers. . . . I may anticipate here at least one constellation of events that had vital importance, which centered on the reversal in the price trend. The unorganized middle class now found itself in the midst of a steady upward trend in the price cycle that was linked with the growing organization of American industry and labor. Prices, which began to go up after 1897, continued to go up steadily throughout the Progressive era, and indeed even more steeply during the war that followed. In the years between 1897 and 1913 the cost of living rose about 35 per cent. Those of us who have endured the inflation of the past fifteen years may smile at such a modest rise in prices; but the price movement of 1897–1913 was not accepted complacently by the generation that experienced it—particularly not by those who lacked the means to defend themselves against it by augmenting their incomes or by those who found the growth in their incomes largely eaten up by the higher cost of living. Just as the falling prices of the period 1865–96 had spurred agrarian discontents, so the rising prices of this era added to the strength of the Progressive discontents.

Rising prices in themselves were trouble enough; but the high cost of living took on added significance because it was associated in the public mind with two other unwelcome tendencies: the sudden development of a vigorous, if small, labor movement, and an extraordinary acceleration in the trustification of American industry. Both of these took place with alarming suddenness in the years from 1898 to 1904. John Moody singles out 1898 as "the year in which the modern trust-forming period really dates its beginning."[29] General business prosperity, rising prices, and an active securities market spurred on this burst of trust formation. Of the 318 trusts listed by Moody in 1904, 82, with a total capitalization of $1,196,700,000, had been organized before 1898. But 234, with a capitalization of over $6,000,000,000, had been organized in the years between January 1, 1898 and January 1, 1904.[30] Thus in this short period almost three quarters of the trusts and almost six sevenths of the capital in trusts had come into existence. It was during the last years of McKinley's administration and the early years of Roosevelt's that such frighteningly large organizations as the United States Steel Corporation, Standard Oil, Consolidated Tobacco, Amalgamated Copper, International Mercantile Marine Company, and the American Smelting and Refining Company were incorporated. Major local consolidations simultaneously took place in the fields of the telephone, telegraph, gas, traction, and electric power and light.

Far less spectacular, but nonetheless nettlesome to the middle-class mentality, were the developments in labor organization. During the long price decline of 1865–96 the real wages of labor had been advancing steadily at the average rate of 4 per cent a year.[31] But beginning with the upward trend of prices in 1897, these automatic gains not only ceased but were turned into losses, as unorganized workers found themselves unable to keep abreast of the steady advance in commodity prices. While real annual wages rose slightly during the period 1900–14, real hourly wages remained almost stationary.[32] Under the spur of rising prices and the favorable auspices of good business conditions, the young A.F. of L. seized its opportunity to organize skilled workers. By 1911 the membership of all American trade unions was five times what it had been in 1897; that of the A.F. of L. was almost seven times as large. Total union membership had grown from 447,000 to 2,382,000,[33] and, as in the case of industry, most of this new organization was concentrated in a sharp organizing drive between 1897 and 1904, a drive marked by a large increase in the number of strikes.

The price rise after 1897 was a part of a world-wide trend, connected with the discovery of new gold supplies and new refining processes. How much of it can properly be laid to the growing organization of industry is a moot point. What is most relevant here, however, is that the restive consuming public was not content to attribute the high cost of living to such impersonal causes. The average middle-class citizen felt the pinch in his pocketbook.[34] On one side he saw the trusts mushrooming almost every day and assumed that they had something to do with it. On the other he saw an important segment of the working class organizing to protect itself, and in so doing also contributing, presumably, a bit more to higher prices. He saw himself as a member of a vast but unorganized and therefore helpless consuming public. He felt that he understood very well what Woodrow Wilson meant when he declared that "The high cost of living is arranged by private understanding,"[35] and he became indignant. The movement against the trusts took on new meaning and new power. To be sure, there had always been antitrust sentiment, and the argument that the trusts would squeeze the consumers after they had eliminated their competitors had been familiar for more than a generation. So long, however, as prices were declining, this fear had lacked urgency. Now that prices were rising, it became a dominant motif in American life.[36]

·   ·   ·

Notes

1. *The Education of Henry Adams* (New York, Modern Library ed., 1931), p. 32; cf. Tocqueville: *Democracy in America* (New York, 1912), Vol. I, pp. 40–1.

2. Sidney Ratner: *American Taxation* (New York, 1942), pp. 136, 275.

3. Thomas G. Shearman: "The Coming Billionaire," *Forum*, Vol. X (January 1891), pp. 546–57; cf. the same author's "The Owners of the United States," *ibid.*, Vol. VIII (November 1889), pp. 262–73.

4. Ratner, *op. cit.*, p. 220 . . . Out of the alarm of the period over the concentration of wealth arose the first American studies of national wealth and income. For a

review of these studies, see C. L. Merwin: "American Studies of the Distribution of Wealth and Income by Size," in *Studies in Income and Wealth,* Vol. III (New York, 1939), pp. 3–84.

5. It may be significant that the era of the status revolution was also one in which great numbers of patriotic societies were founded. Of 105 patriotic orders founded between 1783 and 1900, 34 originated before 1870 and 71 between 1870 and 1900. A high proportion of American patriotic societies is based upon descent and length of family residence in the United States, often specifically requiring family participation in some such national event as the American Revolution. The increase of patriotic and genealogical societies during the status revolution suggests that many old-family Americans, who were losing status in the present, may have found satisfying compensation in turning to family glories of the past. Of course, a large proportion of these orders were founded during the nationalistic outbursts of the nineties; but these too may have had their subtle psychological relation to status changes. Note the disdain of men like Theodore Roosevelt for the lack of patriotism and aggressive nationalism among men of great wealth. On the founding of patriotic societies, see Wallace E. Davies: *A History of American Veterans' and Hereditary Patriotic Societies, 1783–1900,* unpublished doctoral dissertation, Harvard University, 1944, Vol. II, pp. 441 ff.

6. Notably Charles Francis Adams, Jr., Edward Atkinson, Moorfield Storey, Leverett Saltonstall, William Everett, Josiah Quincy, Thomas Wentworth Higginson.

7. For a cross-section of the views of this school, see Alan P. Grimes: *The Political Liberation of the New York Nation, 1865–1932* (Chapel Hill, 1953), chapter ii.

8. Grimes, *op. cit.,* chapter iii.

9. George Mowry: *Theodore Roosevelt and the Progressive Movement* (Madison, 1946), p. 10.

10. Alfred D. Chandler, Jr.: "The Origins of Progressive Leadership," in Elting Morison, ed.: *The Letters of Theodore Roosevelt,* Vol. VIII (Cambridge, 1954), pp. 1462–5. Chandler found the 260 leaders distributed as follows: business, 95; lawyers, 75; editors, 36; other professional (college professors, authors, social workers, and a scattering of others), 55. Chandler also found significant regional variations. In the cities of the Northeast and the old Northwest, the role of the intellectuals and professionals was large, while the businessmen were chiefly those who managed old, established enterprises. In the South, however, a rising social élite of aggressive new businessmen took part. In the West and the rural areas, editors and lawyers dominated party leadership, while the businessmen tended to be from businesses of modest size, like cattle, real estate, lumber, publishing, small manufacturing.

11. George Mowry: *The California Progressives* (Berkeley, 1951), pp. 88–9; see generally chapter iv, which contains an illuminating brief account of 47 Progressive leaders. Three fourths of these were college educated. There were 17 lawyers, 14 journalists, 11 independent businessmen and real-estate operators, 3 doctors, 3 bankers. Of the ideology of this group Mowry observed that they were opposed chiefly to "the impersonal, concentrated, and supposedly privileged property represented by the behemoth corporation. Looking backward to an older America [they] sought to recapture and reaffirm the older individualistic values in all the strata of political, economic, and social life." *Ibid.,* p. 89.

12. Henry F. May: *Protestant Churches and Industrial America* (New York, 1949), p. 91.

13. *Ibid.,* pp. 202–3.

14. An interesting but by no means representative case was the controversy between W. S. Rainsford, rector of St. George's (Episcopal) Church in New York City, and one of his vestrymen, J. Pierpont Morgan. See Rainsford: *Story of a Varied Life* (Garden City, 1924), p. 281.

15. In 1918 a *Literary Digest* survey showed that only 1,671 of the 170,000 ministers in the United States paid taxes on incomes over $3,000. In 1920 a survey by the Interchurch World Movement found that the average annual pastoral income was $937. *Christian Advocate,* Vol. XCV (July 22, 1920), p. 985. Preachers were well aware that they had reached a point at which their wages were lower than those of many skilled workers, especially masons, plumbers, plasterers, and bricklayers. On preachers' salaries, see *Homiletic Review,* Vol. LXXXVI (December 1923), p. 437; Vol. LXXXVII (January 1924), p. 9.

16. Cf. Joseph Greenbaum and Leonard I. Pearlin: "Vertical Mobility and Preju-dice," in Reinhard Bendix and Seymour M. Lipset, eds.: *Class, Status and Power* (Glencoe, Illinois, 1953), pp. 480–91; Bruno Bettelheim and Morris Janowitz: "Ethnic Tolerance: a Function of Personal and Social Control," *American Journal of Sociology*, Vol. IV (1949), pp. 137–45. . . .

17. Richard Hofstadter and Walter P. Metzger: *The Development of Academic Freedom in the United States* (New York, 1955), esp. chapters v, vi, ix.

18. Cf. the lament of John Dewey in 1902: "The old-fashioned college faculty was pretty sure to be a thoro-going democracy in its way. Its teachers were selected more often because of their marked individual traits than because of pure scholar-ship. Each stood his own and for his own." "Academic Freedom," *Education Review*, Vol. XXIII (January 1902), p. 13. This very idealization of the professional past was a product of the rise of the profession. For the falseness of this idealization, see Hofstadter and Metzger, *op. cit.*, chapters v and vi, and *passim*.

19. See Joseph Katz: *The American Legal Profession, 1890–1915*, unpublished M.A. thesis, Columbia University, 1953, for an illuminating discussion of trends in the profession during this period.

20. "Corporate Monopoly in the Field of Law," 15 *Law Notes* (1911), p. 22.

21. The traditional emphasis on agrarian discontent has diverted attention from the pressure from business for such measures. See Lee Benson: *New York Merchants and Farmers in the Communications Revolution*, unpublished Ph.D. dissertation, Cornell University, 1952.

22. Clifford W. Patton: *The Battle for Municipal Reform* (Washington, 1940), chapter iv. William Howe Tolman: *Municipal Reform Movements in the United States* (New York, 1895) has a suggestive summary of over seventy such organizations.

23. Legislation in this field before and after 1900 may be compared in Elizabeth Brandeis's treatment of the subject, John R. Commons, ed.: *History of Labor in the United States*, Vol. III (New York, 1935), pp. 399 ff. The chief fields that had been entered by state legislatures before 1900 were child labor, hours of women's labor, and employers' liability.

24. There were, for instance, Eastern urban election districts, normally heavily Democratic, in which Bryan's support fell drastically in 1896 from its normal level both before and after.

25. Henry Blake Fuller: *With the Procession* (New York, 1895), p. 245.

26. White: *Autobiography* (New York, 1946), p. 367.

27. As a consequence of the sharp difference in the viewpoint of the generations, family conflicts around the turn of the century tended to take on an ideological coloring. For the treatment of this theme in the works of the most popular Progressive novelist, see Richard and Beatrice Hofstadter: "Winston Churchill: a Study in the Popular Novel," *American Quarterly*, Vol. II (Spring 1950), pp. 12–28.

28. Cf. Mowry: "Compositely, the California progressive leader was a young man, often less than forty years old. . . . In 1910 the average age of ten of the most promi-nent Progressives was thirty-eight." *The California Progressives*, pp. 87, 313.

29. John Moody: *The Truth about the Trusts* (New York, 1904), p. 486.

30. Henry R. Seager and Charles A. Gulick, Jr.: *Trust and Corporation Problems* (New York, 1929), pp. 60–7.

31. Black: *Parity, Parity, Parity*, p. 74.

32. Paul H. Douglas: *Real Wages in the United States, 1890–1926* (Boston, 1930), p. 111.

33. Leo Wolman: *The Growth of Trade Unionism* (New York, 1924), p. 33. Figures for all unions are estimates; they exclude the membership of company unions.

34. Those portions of the middle classes that were on fixed salaries lost ground; notable among them were postal employees, many clerical workers, government employees, and ministers. Harold U. Faulkner: *The Decline of Laissez Faire* (New York, 1951), p. 252.

35. *The Public Papers of Woodrow Wilson*, Vol. II (New York, 1925), p. 462. For a discussion of the cost-of-living issue by a contemporary, see Frederic C. Howe: *The High Cost of Living* (New York, 1917).

36. Cf. Walter Weyl, *op. cit.*, p. 251: "The universality of the rise of prices has begun to affect the consumer as though he were attacked by a million gnats. The chief offense of the trust becomes its capacity to injure the consumer."

Introduction to *The New Radicalism in America*

CHRISTOPHER LASCH

Professor Christopher Lasch's *The New Radicalism in America* takes up where Professor Hofstadter's *The Age of Reform* leaves off. The latter attempts to explain why a broad section of the middle classes, and with it a large group of working clerics, professors, and lawyers, became Progressives. Professor Lasch looks within this group to a smaller, more élite body that he terms "intellectuals" and attempts to explain why so many intellectuals—as distinguished from Professor Hofstadter's professionals—became radicals during the progressive period.

Professor Lasch has taken many of his cues from Professor Hofstadter. He looks to the subjective conditions created by a crisis in middle-class culture, but he extends Professor Hofstadter's interpretation to include such nearly psychoanalytic facts as anxiety about the collapse of parental authority and fear of powerlessness. Also, he is more critical of the reformer-intellectuals. They responded, according to him, primarily to their own class interests, and they persistently confused those interests with the good of the society as a whole. Consequently, they also confused culture and politics and left this legacy to later twentieth-century intellectuals—a legacy of confusion that intellectuals in America have not yet been able to escape.

Christopher Lasch, once Professor Richard Hofstadter's student at Columbia University, is one of the most vocal historians of what is sometimes called "The New Left." He is one of several young historians in the 1960s who have called themselves "radicals" and yet have been able to exert a considerable influence on the academic "establishment." He is Professor of History at Northwestern University, and the author of American Liberals and the Russian Revolution *(1962),* The New Radicalism in America *(1965), and* The Agony of the American Left *(1969).*

The main argument of this book is that modern radicalism or liberalism can best be understood as a phase of the social history of the intellectuals. In the United States, to which this study is confined, the connection is particularly clear. There, the rise of the new radicalism coincided with the emergence of the intellectual as a distinctive social type.

The intellectual may be defined, broadly, as a person for whom thinking fulfills at once the function of work and play; more specifically, as a person whose relationship to society is defined, both in his eyes and in the eyes of the society, principally by his presumed capacity to comment upon it with greater detachment than those more directly caught up in the practical business of production and power. Because his vocation is to be a critic of society, in the most general sense, and because the value of his criticism is presumed to rest on a measure of detachment from the current scene, the intellectual's relation to the rest of society is never entirely comfortable; but it has not always been as uncomfortable as it is today in the United States. "Anti-intellectualism" offers only a partial explanation of the present tension between intellectuals and American society. The rest of the explanation lies in the increased sensitivity of intellectuals to attacks on themselves as a group. It lies in the intellectuals' own sense of themselves, not simply as individuals involved in a common undertaking, the somewhat hazardous business of criticism, but as members of a beleaguered minority. The tension is a function, in other words, of the class consciousness of the intellectuals themselves.

Intellectuals have existed in all literate societies, but they have only recently come to constitute a kind of subculture. In fact, the word

FROM THE INTRODUCTION TO *The New Radicalism in America, 1889–1963*, BY CHRISTOPHER LASCH. © COPYRIGHT BY CHRISTOPHER LASCH. REPRINTED BY PERMISSION OF ALFRED A. KNOPF, INC.

"intellectual" does not seem to have found its way into American usage much before the turn of the century. Before that, most intellectuals belonged to the middle class, and though they may sometimes have felt themselves at odds with the rest of the community, they did not yet conceive of themselves as a class apart. The modern intellectual, even when he chooses to throw himself into the service of his country or attempts to embrace the common life about him, gives himself away by the very self-consciousness of his gestures, He agonizes endlessly over the "role of the intellectuals." A hundred years ago these discussions, and the passion with which they are conducted, would have been incomprehensible.

The growth of a class (or more accurately, a "status group") of intellectuals[1] is part of a much more general development: the decline of the sense of community, the tendency of the mass society to break down into its component parts, each having its own autonomous culture and maintaining only the most tenuous connections with the general life of the society—which as a consequence has almost ceased to exist. The most obvious victims of this process in our own time are adolescents, who live increasingly in a world all their own. The emergence of the intellectual class in the first couple of decades of the present century reveals the workings of the same process at a somewhat earlier period in time.

The intellectual class, then, is a distinctively modern phenomenon, the product of the cultural fragmentation that seems to characterize industrial and postindustrial societies. It is true that in the United States the agencies of social cohesion (church, state, family, class) were never very strong in the first place. Nevertheless, there existed during the first two and a half centuries of American history a sort of cultural consensus at the heart of which was a common stake in capitalism and a common tradition of patriarchal authority. There were social classes but, compared to Europe or even to American society during the colonial period, remarkably little class-consciousness; and whatever the real opportunities for social advancement, the myth of equal opportunity was sufficiently strong to minimize the tensions and resentments which later came to characterize American society. "The whole society," wrote Tocqueville in 1831, "seems to have melted into a middle class. . . . All the Americans whom we have encountered up to now, even to the simplest *shop salesman*, seem to have received, or wish to appear to have received, a good education. Their manners are grave, deliberate, reserved, and they all wear the same clothes. All the customs of life show this mingling of the two classes which in Europe take so much trouble to keep apart."[2] Divisive influences tended to be local and regional rather than social; and the very intensity of local and regional rivalries enhanced the social solidarity of each particular part of the country, so that Southerners, for instance, found what seemed to be a common interest in resisting the encroachments of the Yankee. Under these conditions men of intellectual inclination had very little sense of themselves as a class. The South—the preindustrial

society par excellence—offers a particularly striking example of the degree
to which such men shared the general aspirations of the *bourgeoisie*, the
highest form of which, as is customary in bourgeois societies, was to set up
as country gentlemen on lordly estates.[3]

It was only in the North that writers and thinkers began to acquire a
sense of being at odds with the rest of society. The transcendentalists and
reformers of the 1830's and 1840's, in their protest against the materialism
of a society dominated by the Cotton Whigs, in some respects anticipated
the attacks of modern intellectuals on the middle class. But the truth of the
matter is suggested by the ease with which the reforming impulse after the
Civil War was reabsorbed into the stream of genteel culture. The war itself had a unifying effect on New England, as on the South.[4] Abolitionism
petered out in mugwumpery, a form of extreme sectional particularism.
Indeed, the whole New England tradition—with which American reform
until the twentieth century was so completely bound up—precisely embodied everything against which later intellectuals were in rebellion,
everything associated with the cultural ascendancy of the middle class.

The term "middle-class" seems nowadays to encounter as much resistance, among historians at least, as the term "intellectual." I have been
told by historians that the term means nothing, that indeed the "middle
class" is a myth. It is true that the term has often been loosely used.
But I do not understand why that should prevent its being used
quite precisely. I have used it here simply as a synonym for *bourgeoisie*,
to describe a class of people which derives its income from the ownership
of property and in particular from trade and commerce—a definition,
when applied to American society in the nineteenth century, which in-
cludes most of the farming population as well as the bulk of those who
lived in towns. It does not include the salaried employees (clerks, sales-
men, managers, professionals), whom C. Wright Mills has called the
"new" middle class—itself a creation of the twentieth century. The cultural style of the old as distinguished from the new middle class was
characterized by that combination of patriarchal authority and the sen-
timental veneration of women which is the essence of the genteel tradition. Everything I mean to catch up in the phrase "middle-class culture"
seems to me ultimately to derive from these characteristic familial arrangements. It is no wonder that the revolt of the intellectuals so often
took the form of a rebellion against the conventional family. The family
was the agency which transmitted from generation to generation—and
not only transmitted but embodied down to the last detail of domestic
architecture—the enormous weight of respectable culture; as its defenders
would have said, of civilization itself.

Everyone who has studied the history of American reform agrees
that the reform tradition underwent a fundamental change around 1900.
Some people identify the change with a changing attitude toward government, a new readiness to use government (particularly the federal

government) as an instrument of popular control. Others associate it with an abandonment of the old populistic distrust of large-scale institutions, like corporations, and an acceptance of the inevitability of the concentration of wealth and power. Still others define the change as a movement away from the dogma of natural rights toward a relativistic, environmentalist, and pragmatic view of the world.[5] All of these developments, in truth, were going on at the same time, and all of them contributed to the emergence of the new radicalism. Equally important was a tendency to see cultural issues as inseparable from political ones; so that "education," conceived very broadly, came to be seen not merely as a means of raising up an enlightened electorate but as an instrument of social change in its own right. Conversely, the new radicals understood the end of social and political reform to be the improvement of the quality of American culture as a whole, rather than simply a way of equalizing the opportunities for economic self-advancement. It is precisely this confusion of politics and culture, so essential to the new radicalism, that seems to me to betray its origins in the rise of the intellectual class; for such a program, with its suggestion that men of learning occupy or ought to occupy the strategic loci of social control, has an obvious appeal to intellectuals, and particularly to intellectuals newly conscious of their own common ties and common interests.

What I have called the new radicalism was not the same thing as the so-called progressive movement, though it took shape during the "progressive era." Progressivism was influenced by the new radicalism, but it was more deeply indebted to the populism of the nineteenth century. It was for the most part a purely political movement, whereas the new radicals were more interested in the reform of education, culture, and sexual relations than they were in political issues in the strict sense. Many of them, in fact, rejected progressivism; they saw in "uplift" only another manifestation of middle-class morality. Even those like Jane Addams who did not embrace socialism, and whose political position therefore has to be described, for lack of a better word, as "progressive" (or "liberal"), had more in common with socialists than with the kind of progressives one associates with the initiative and referendum, the campaign against the trusts, and the crusade for "good government." What distinguished her from them was not only her insistence on the preeminence of "education" but her sense of kinship with the "other half" of humanity. The intellectual in his estrangement from the middle class identified himself with other outcasts and tried to look at the world from their point of view. This radical reversal of perspective was still another distinguishing feature of the new radicalism, socialist or progressive. The particular political labels are of little importance. What matters is the point of view such people deliberately cultivated.

That point of view—the effort to see society from the bottom up, or at least from the outside in—seems to me to account for much of what was valuable and creative in the new radicalism. On the other hand, the very circumstance which made this feat possible—the estrangement of intellectuals, as a class, from the dominant values of American culture—also accounted for what seems to me the chief weakness of the new radicalism, its distrust not only of middle-class culture but of intellect itself. Detachment carried with it a certain defensiveness about the position of intellect (and intellectuals) in American life; and it was this defensiveness, I think, which sometimes prompted intellectuals to forsake the role of criticism and to identify themselves with what they imagined to be the laws of historical necessity and the working out of the popular will. At certain points in the history of the twentieth century, notably during the First World War, American intellectuals seemed too eager to participate in national crusades, too little inclined to wonder precisely how such crusades would serve the values they professed to cherish; and such episodes, together with the more recent appearance of a cold-war liberalism determined not to be outdone in its devotion to the "national purpose," have left me somewhat skeptical of "pragmatic liberalism" in its more militant and affirmative moods. I have not attempted to disguise my skepticism, or for that matter my admiration for whatever was negative and critical in the new radicalism; but I have not wished to write a tract, another *Trahison des Clercs*,[6] and I state my own prejudices here only in order to make it clear what they are, not because this book is intended to document them.

I am much less interested, in short, in praising or condemning the new radicalism than in understanding where it came from. Even the effort to understand where it came from, unfortunately, will strike some readers as an insidious attempt to discredit the ideas of radicals and reformers by "psychologizing" them away. For some people, it is enough to say that the reformers were moved by the spectacle of human injustice; to say anything more is to deny the fact of injustice. I am unable to understand this argument, nor do I know quite how to meet it (since I cannot understand it), except to say that the reformers themselves did not share this reluctance of their admirers to examine their own motives. They wrote about their motives with all the enthusiasm, and all the honesty, with which they wrote about social injustice, and I have relied very heavily on what they wrote. Of course it would be possible to ignore what they wrote about themselves, and to write instead about the evils of capitalism. But that is not the book I have chosen to write. I have written instead about some of the critics of capitalism, in the hope that their history would tell something, if not specifically about capitalism, about the peculiarly fragmented character of modern society, and beyond that, about what it means to pursue the life of reason in a world in which the irrational has come to appear not the exception but the rule.

•   •   •

Notes

1. For the distinction between classes and status groups (subcultures?), see Max Weber: "Class, Status, Party," in H. H. Gerth and C. Wright Mills, eds.: *From Max Weber: Essays in Sociology* (New York: Oxford University Press; 1958), pp. 180–94.

2. George W. Pierson: *Tocqueville and Beaumont in America* (New York: Oxford University Press; 1938), pp. 69–70.

3. See William R. Taylor: *Cavalier and Yankee* (New York: George Braziller; 1961), especially the chapter on William Wirt, pp. 67–94.

4. Antislavery politics, wrote Henry Adams (*The Education of Henry Adams* [New York: Modern Library; 1931], p. 26), represented a "violent reaction" which swept New England "back into Puritanism with a violence as great as that of a religious war."

5. See, for instance, Daniel Aaron: *Men of Good Hope* (New York: Oxford University Press; 1951); Charles Forcey: *The Crossroads of Liberalism* (New York: Oxford University Press; 1961); Eric Goldman: *Rendezvous with Destiny* (New York: Alfred A. Knopf; 1952); Morton G. White: *Social Thought in America: The Revolt against Formalism* (New York: Viking Press; 1949); John Braeman: "Seven Progressives," *Business History Review*, XXXV (Winter, 1961), pp. 581–92.

6. Julien Benda: *The Betrayal of the Intellectuals* (Boston: Beacon Press; 1959 [Paris, 1927]).

The Rebellion of the Intellectuals, 1912–1917

HENRY F. MAY

Professors Lasch's and Hofstadter's discussion of "alienation" among intellectuals suggests that the Lost Generation may have gone astray not in the twenties but before World War I. Professor Henry F. May took up this possibility the year after the publication of *The Age of Reform*. In "The Rebellion of the Intellectuals, 1912–1917," he suggests that most of the philosophical and literary characteristics that once were associated with the twenties had a firm start before American entry into the war. It was not the war that "disillusioned" men, as had traditionally been supposed. Professor May does not deny (as no historian would) that something that might be called a cultural revolution occurred in the 1920s. But his analysis of the young intellectuals of the progressive period makes it clear that this cultural transformation was not the product of events of 1919 or 1920, but was rather a part of the same long-gathering revolution that was shaking European society in the first decades of the century.

Henry Farnham May is the Margaret Byrne Professor of History at the University of California at Berkeley. His special field of emphasis is the intellectual history of the United States since the Civil War. He is the author of Protestant Churches and Industrial America *(1949),* The End of American Innocence *(1959), and coauthor of* A Synopsis of American History *(1963). In* The End of American Innocence, *Professor May works out at length the notions advanced in this essay on "The Rebellion of the Intellectuals." Also relevant to this subject is an important article of his entitled "Shifting Perspectives on the 1920s," which appeared in the* Mississippi Valley Historical Review *(1956).*

As the nineteen-twenties move from memory into history, a standard picture of the decade emerges from reminiscence and research into the textbooks. This picture is a puzzling one. The decade is still, as it was in the thirties, the last island of normalcy and isolation between wars and crises. Yet it is also, clearly, a period of major cultural revolution. Both the "revolt of the highbrows" and the "rebellion of youth," first sketched by F. L. Allen, are a standard part of our semiofficial self-picture. In response to current historical fashions and perhaps also to their own changing worries about their country, historians are giving more attention to the revolutionary aspect of this conservative decade.

Having dealt with other revolutions, historians should be able to appreciate both the importance and complexity of this one. For instance, they should be able to avoid taking to task the rebellious intellectuals of the twenties in the manner of some critics of the forties. The spokesmen of a revolution are not, after all, its sole cause, and a healthy regime is seldom overthrown. Yet anybody, today, must recognize that revolutions are expensive. They may release, as this one certainly did, a burst of creative vigor; but they inevitably leave behind division, hatred, and shock. In the twenties, for instance, beliefs and customs that still commanded the deepest loyalties of one part of the population became to another group a dead and repressive Genteel Tradition, to be ceremonially flouted whenever possible. Suspicions dating from this cultural cleavage still poison the air. The historian must hope that analysis of the revolution and its causes can eventually help a little to clear away some of the resentment.

Starting backward, as historians must, we arrive immediately at the First World War, and there many have stopped. It is obvious that Amer-

REPRINTED BY PERMISSION, FROM *American Quarterly*, 8 (SUMMER 1956), 114–126. COPYRIGHT, 1956, TRUSTEES OF THE UNIVERSITY OF PENNSYLVANIA.

ica's first major venture into world tragedy, with its rapid cycle of
national exaltation, exhaustion, and revulsion played a very large part
in the emotional life of the postwar rebels. By contrast with 1918 or
1919 or even 1925, hundreds of autobiographies paint the prewar period
as a time of unity, moderation, progress, and sheltered childhood.

Yet we all know that postwar reminiscence, whether of the old plantation or the old literary culture, is a dubious guide for history. Those
who have looked even briefly at the social and literary criticism of the
prewar years know that the period 1912–1917[1] was itself, for some, a
time of doubt and fragmentation, of upheaval in ideas, of the disintegration of tradition—in other words it was a pre-revolutionary or early
revolutionary period. Nearly every phenomenon of the twenties from
Freudianism to expatriation or the abandonment of politics was present
before the war, on a smaller scale and with certain differences. If we can
recapture any of the meaning or content of this prewar ferment, we may be
able to understand better in what sense the revolution of the twenties was
and was not postwar. In this way we may even get a few suggestions as
to the perennially baffling problem of the relation between ideas and events.

In an essay published in 1913 George Santayana made an attempt to
catch and pin down on paper "The Intellectual Temper of the Age."
To do this for one's own time is one of the hardest tasks a writer can
undertake, yet for anybody who has been for a while immersed in the
records of that period it is astonishing how well this brilliant essay seems
to order and illuminate the times. To Santayana it seemed that "the
civilisation characteristic of Christendom has not disappeared, yet another
civilisation has begun to take its place."[2] In the resulting age of confusion and transition, men were giving up the search for lasting values
and firm intellectual conclusions. Instead of these, they were placing a
premium on sheer vitality, on movement, change, and emotion. According to Santayana, who sometimes enjoyed but did not admire this taste,
the result was that in thought and art, his generation was "in full career
toward disintegration."[3]

Whether or not one shares Santayana's cool disapproval of the tendencies of his day, the vitalist spirit he describes stares out from the sources.
One recognizes on all sides its gaiety, its irresponsibility, its love of
change, and also its contempt for reason. And it does not take much
knowledge of American intellectual history to know that this spirit
meant trouble. For a century and a half the dominant ideas in the
national faith had been a confidence in secure moral values and a belief
in progress. These two commitments had often been in conflict and
formed at best a somewhat unstable compound. Now both at once were
brought under devastating attack.

If one starts, as Santayana does, with philosophy, the tendencies he
describes emerge very clearly. The young intellectuals of America were
still most widely influenced by pragmatism, by what Morton G. White
has called the revolt against formalism. Experience and movement were

reality; potentiality more important than actuality. Dewey's program for intelligence remaking both the world and itself probably attracted the largest number of conscious disciples, some of them, like Randolph Bourne, soon to break away in a more emotionally satisfying direction. But it may well be that the influence of James, with his catholic and dangerous acceptance of the irrational, personal, and mysterious went deeper in a generation nourished on idealism. Emerson, universally read though misunderstood and underrated, and Whitman, the sole American patron of some of the rebels, as well as the German idealists casually studied in college courses, must have prepared them for a philosophy of intuition. Whatever the reason, it was the destructive elements in pragmatism that were the most influential. The avant-garde of 1912–17, the aggressive young innovators, were perfectly willing to see all of life as an experiment. But their purpose in experimenting was rather to express themselves and experience emotion than to solve problems in a disciplined manner.

Those who were sensitive to Atlantic breezes felt most keenly the swelling winds of antirationalism, which had been gathering force for a long time. Nietzsche, for long known vaguely by the American public as an Anti-christ, was becoming a major prophet. The most vigorous, though not the most accurate, of his American interpreters was H. L. Mencken, who in a widely read and widely praised book published first in 1908 and again in 1913 used the German prophet to belabor religion, women, and, most roughly of all, democracy in his already familiar manner.[4] But the most fashionable of Europeans was the still living and lecturing Henri Bergson, who pushed the current tendency to an extreme, contending that reality, being in constant flux and change, is only distorted by efforts to think about it and must be apprehended through intuition. His was not the only, but it was probably the dominant direction in which philosophy was moving in 1913, and there is plenty of evidence that he was extraordinarily attractive to up-to-date American intellectuals. Irving Babbitt, already an alarmed defender of traditional values, saw the rise of Bergsonism as the culmination of a long, deplorable irrationalist trend, and found it in 1912 "allied with all that is violent and extreme in contemporary life from syndicalism to 'futurist' painting."[5]

Psychology, as well as philosophy, was dealing heavy blows to dominant assumptions and beliefs. From the time of Freud's famous trip to Clark University in 1908, the Viennese theories cropped up in popular magazines and political treatises as well as learned journals. Whether or not, as his supporters claim, Freud is to be regarded as himself a brave and determined champion of reason, the first impact of his doctrines in the United States seemed to confirm and deepen the hedonism, emotionalism, and egocentricity that were beginning to spread so widely.[6] On the other hand, Behaviorism, a movement launched in its most dogmatic form by John B. Watson in 1912, had to wait for its vogue until after the war.[7] Its extreme practicalism, its rejection not only of reason but of consciousness, its suspicion of emotion, did not fit the tastes of the prewar rebels.

It does not need demonstrating that restless and vigorous innovation in the graphic arts got its American start before the war. Two major tendencies already dazzled the intellectuals and startled the public. One was apparently native, the harsh and sometimes violent Ash Can realism of Sloan, Bellows and the *Masses* cartoons. The other was imported from Paris and consisted of a kaleidoscopic series of schools of experiment in form and technique. Commenting on "Current Impressionism," a term already well out of date but helpful as a catch-all, Louis Weinberg extended his observations from and beyond contemporary art:

> Impressionism as a technique is a means of recording the transitory nature of phenomena and the fluidity of motion. As a principle it is based on a philosophy of change. . . . But this is not alone a description of the art of our times. It is the very essence of our lives.[8]

Wherever the impressionist or vitalist tendency arose, it was expressed most frequently and characteristically not in painting or philosophy but in politics and literature. These are the forms in which most American cultural change has been recorded, and it is to them that we must turn for a slightly closer look at prewar tendencies. Santayana's brilliant summary suggests that in politics alone the current drift toward fragmentation and chaos may have reversed itself in the constructive and integrating (though to Santayana most uncongenial) movement toward collectivism.[9] In this one opinion, regarding an area which concerned him little, I think Santayana missed the current drift and underrated the force of his own generalization. It is true that progressivism, optimistic, gradual, and in some forms mildly collectivist, was the officially dominant ideology; and that socialism was a swelling movement on the left that seemed to many sober Americans to possess the future. Yet both these political tendencies were in the early teens already under devastating attack, and from much the same irrationalist quarter.

Progressivism in all its varieties took for granted one or both of the two fundamental assumptions which had so far underlain the whole American political tradition. One of these was that we possess secure criteria by which we can judge our political achievement, the other that human beings are able consciously to remold their environment. Now both of these basic assumptions were being seriously shaken by new doctrines that had penetrated the house of progressivism itself.

Recent studies have shown that moral standards of a highly traditional sort motivated a great many of the prewar progressives. Truth and falsehood, good and evil, stand out in nearly all the speeches of Theodore Roosevelt and Wilson, and good men threw out bad in most American cities. These venerable distinctions were the first to go; the younger progressive intellectuals, nourished on Dewey and H. G. Wells, were quite willing to throw out moral categories and rely on the shaping intelligence. On a popular level Lincoln Steffens spread the picture of the good boss and the honest crook. James Harvey Robinson, speaking for the main organ of the pragmatic progressives, lumped together as obsolete the ideals of "sound doctrine, consistency, fidelity to conscience, eternal verities, immutable human nature, and the imprescriptable rights of man."[10]

With these went the state and law, the traditional locus and method of American reform. Many of the ablest political theorists of various schools, led by the brilliant Harold Laski, were redefining the state almost out of existence. To some it was a congeries of associations, to others the tool of a class, to still others the expression of the wish of those at present in authority. Its acts were no more final and deserved no greater obedience than those of other human groups, and it was less likely than many to be rationally motivated. Similarly, law, to the followers of the French positivist Leon Duguit or the American Roscoe Pound was no longer either the embodiment of a principle or the command of a sovereign, but the complex resultant of social forces, prevailing opinion, and judicial will.

There remained the conscious intelligence, remolding the goals of action together with its methods. This was a moving conception, and a sufficient loyalty for many in this generation. Yet this too was seriously menaced by ideas that were attractive to the youngest generation of progressives. From the new and flourishing disciplines of sociology, anthropology, and social psychology came an increasingly fashionable emphasis on custom and group emotion. It was sometimes hard to see what function this newest tendency left for intelligence and purpose.[11]

Walter Lippmann's two prewar studies, *A Preface to Politics* (1913) and *Drift and Mastery* (1914) bring together the pragmatist attack on tradition and the implicit Freudian attack on pragmatism. Appealing for a radically instrumental state, he denounces the "routineers" who rely on political machinery, law, and conventional morality. His fellow progressives seem to draw most of his fire for their naïve adherence to literal numerical democracy and narrow utilitarian goals. What is needed in politics is passion and creative emotion, still of course somehow constructively channeled and used by the far-seeing for purposes which will transcend woman suffrage or the eight-hour day.

> . . . the goal of action is in its final analysis aesthetic and not moral—a quality of feeling instead of conformity to rule.[12]

This formulation seems to me far closer to the view of postwar literary intellectuals than to that of the progressive standard-bearers. And the sources are explicit. Lippmann's friend Graham Wallas, the British author of *Human Nature in Politics*,[13] had opened the eyes of his Harvard seminar to political psychology. Steffens had helped to guide Lippmann and so, in a negative direction, had his brief experience with municipal socialism in Schenectady. But beyond these immediate guides one finds recurring references to James, Nietzsche and Bergson and frequent, specific acknowledgment of the work of Freud.[14]

All these new insights enriched the social sciences, and for many they doubtless furnished in practice new sources of power and freedom. Traditional progressivism, with its facile assumptions and sometimes shallow purposes, needed—and for that matter still needs—rethinking. Yet much had been accomplished under the auspices of ideas that were beginning to seem stale and boring. And the new beliefs that buzzed and swarmed through the immediate postwar years were not easy to introduce into the progressive hive. To combine Lippmann or Laski with Wilson was, and soon proved to be, as difficult as to match Bergson and Nietzsche with Lyman Abbott.

It is tempting to wonder whether the actual practical difficulties of progressivism from about 1914 to 1917 were not related in part to confusion of purposes and motives. It is true at least that the Wilsonian impetus began to bog down in these years. Already one finds in the up-to-the-minute *New Republic* troubled editorials that ask the common postwar question: what has happened to the progressives?[15]

On the far left much the same process was taking place, whether one labels it fertilization or disintegration or both. Not the Marxian dialectic, but the Bergsonian and mystical syndicalism of Sorel or the anarchism of Max Stirner or Emma Goldman seemed most exciting to the younger radical intellectuals.[16] Not the earnest socialism of Milwaukee or Schenectady, with its respectability and its reliance on the discredited machinery of the state, but the romantic activism of the I.W.W. captured the emotions of the sympathizers. One of America's waves of labor violence, running through the Northwest, Colorado, West Virginia, and other centers of direct action, reflecting the primitive brutality of employers' methods in the same areas, aroused the generous emotions and seemed to some to make political action irrelevant. The climax came in 1912 at Lawrence and in 1913 at Paterson, when the I.W.W. penetrated the East and the writers and artists went to its aid, when Bill Haywood was a Greenwich Village social lion and John Reed staged an immense pageant in Madison Square Garden with the letters I.W.W. flaming from the roof in red electric signs ten feet high. Even Lippmann, viewing radicalism from the outside, approved the I.W.W. rather than the Socialist Party as less formalist and more in possession of the kind of emotional force that needed only to be constructively channeled.[17]

Naturally, when Max Eastman, a young man of impeccable ministerial stock, joined the Socialist Party, he chose the left wing rather than the gradualists. Under Eastman's editorship the *Masses*, focus of so much later radical nostalgia, became perhaps even more clearly than the sober *New Republic* the organ of youth. Publishing the magnificent and not always political cartoons of Sloan and Bellows, an occasional Picasso drawing, stories by Sherwood Anderson, and reporting by Reed, it fought for the new literature and the new sexual morality as well as the social revolution. The *Masses* was rich in humor and human emotion —qualities often enough lacking on the far left—and practically negligible in social program. Smashing idols was, in these years as after the war, a flourishing business, while Socialism as a political movement was already losing momentum in 1914–16.[18]

More spectacularly than anywhere else, the new spirit of 1910 or 1912 to 1917 was reflected in a literary renaissance. The story of this sudden creative outburst has often been told, and only two points need making for our present purpose. One of these is that literary departures in the prewar years were closely related to contemporary movements in other fields of thought, the other that prewar writing contains in embryo nearly all the developments of the twenties.

Here too the stimulus came in large part from abroad. Young Americans, brought up on Matthew Arnold and Thackeray, were following before he gave it the advice of Yeats at the *Poetry* dinner in 1912 to forget London and look to Paris for all that was excellent.[19] In Kroch's bookstore in Chicago, in the translations issued by a series of daring new publishers, in the eager if undiscriminating reviews by the young critics, this generation of rebels was nourished on a whole series of movements extending over the last generation in Europe. All the writers that had for so long been belaboring the European bourgeoisie—French symbolists and decadents and naturalists, Scandinavian pessimists and social critics, Russian apostles of mysticism and emotion; even from England D. H. Lawrence as well as Shaw, suddenly began to penetrate the American barrier. What this series of reagents produced was a series of explosions, and what exploded was more than the genteel tradition in literature, more than conventional moral categories. With the conventions of literary form and language went the underlying assumptions about thought and communication. Randolph Bourne perhaps described this grand explosion better than he realized in June, 1917:

> What becomes more and more apparent to the readers of Dostoevsky, however, is his superb modern healthiness. He is healthy because he has no sense of any dividing line between the normal and the abnormal, or even between the sane and the insane.[20]

When Harriet Monroe, full of civic feeling as well as poetic zeal, founded *Poetry* in 1912 she seemed to tap immediately a rich underground gusher of poetic impulse. Soon the flood of experiment became too thick and varied even for *Poetry* to contain and overflowed into *Others* and the *Little Review*. As in the visual arts, a rapid series of schools succeeded each other, but perhaps the literary movement most characteristic of the period and most obviously related to its philosophic tendencies was that of the Imagists, with its manifestoes in favor of complete freedom, concentration on the fleeting and immediate image for its own sake, and refusal to assign an image any "external" meaning or reference. Already before the war the revolution in the use of language was under way toward its ultimate destinations; Joyce was being published in the London *Egoist* and Gertrude Stein, settled in Paris, had developed her opinions and her characteristic style.

It would be misleading to divide this literary outpouring into precise categories, yet one can find suggestions of two emergent ways of thinking and feeling among writers. One group demanded freedom from European forms, confidence in emotion and spontaneity, and in general preached democratic optimism in the Whitman tradition. The other, more disciplined but also more deeply rebellious against American culture, called for concentration, rejection of irrelevant moral and political purposes, and the development of conscious intellectual aristocracy.

Obviously the former, democratic and optimist group is more distant than the other from postwar directions. This is the tendency one associates particularly with the sudden and brief Chicago Renaissance, with Sandburg and Lindsay and Miss Monroe, though it is found also in other areas, for instance in the organized and vigorous character of what Francis Hackett labeled and dated forever as Miss Amy Lowell's "Votes for Poetry movement."[21] Yet even the most exuberant of the Chicago poets were, like contemporary political radicals, destroying for the sake of redemption, like Sandburg's personified city "Shovelling, wrecking, planning, building, breaking, rebuilding."

And even in Chicago pessimistic and skeptical tendencies were also, and had long been, at work. Dreiser's not exactly rosy picture of American city life was finally finding its audience; and the small town, from E. A. Robinson's New England Tilbury town to Masters' Middlewestern Spoon River, was preparing the way for Winesburg and Gopher Prairie. In the bosom of *Poetry* magazine, at the official heart of the Chicago movement, Ezra Pound, the magazine's foreign editor, was chafing at its cover slogan, the statement of Whitman that "to have great poets there must be great audiences too." Pound preferred Dante's pronouncement that the wisest in the city is "He whom the fools hate worst" and denied that poets have any need for the rabble.

> It is true that the great artist has always a great audience, even in his lifetime; but it is not the *vulgo* but the spirits of irony and of destiny and of humor, sitting with him.[22]

In that sentence lies the germ of a dozen ponderous manifestoes of the postwar Young Intellectuals. Pound stayed on *Poetry* long enough to persuade Miss Monroe to publish Eliot's "Prufrock" in 1915 and then found a refuge from uplift and Whitmanism in the *Little Review*.

In the Eastern centers of the new literary movement the mixture of optimism and nihilism, of reform and rejection was somewhat different. Harvard, which was incubating an extraordinary number of important writers, seemed to produce a strange and special mixture of ideas.[23] The dominant note in its teaching of literature was aestheticism, worship of Europe, and contempt for the native production. Irving Babbitt's vigorous attack on democratic sentimentality was already a major influence. Yet Walter Lippmann, for one, managed to combine presidency of the Harvard Socialist Club with assisting Professor Santayana. A certain survival of Emersonian and Puritan responsibility seems to have been a part of the prevalent passionate concern for literature. America might be vulgar and materialistic and nearly hopeless; if so one's duty was to search the harder for seeds of literary springtime, and literary revival would bring social regeneration as well. Like so many writers after the war, Van Wyck Brooks went to Europe to look for these seeds. He found in London in 1913–14 Ezra Pound, T. S. Eliot, John Gould Fletcher, Conrad Aiken, Elinor Wylie, Robert Frost, and Walter Lippmann.[24] Across the channel he could already have run into an equally significant group of fellow-countrymen. It was in London that Brooks began to struggle seriously with the typical problem of the expatriate of the next decade: the love of European tradition and the nostalgic turning toward American vitality. He solved this problem by writing, in London in 1914, the book that most influenced the writers of the next decade, an attack on the Genteel Tradition and an appeal for a literary renaissance that seemed then, as its title implies, to mark an arrival and not just a beginning: *America's Coming-of-Age.*

From here we can see, even more clearly than Santayana could in 1913, the unrest, the disintegration of old standards, the search for vitality and movement that already was under way at that time.[25] We know, too, that what was then unrest later became cultural revolution and angry intellectual civil war. This brings us to the compelling question, what started it all? Why did this search for novelty, this gay destruction of traditional standards, occur at just this moment in the midst of an apparently placid and contented period?

This is hardly a question that can be answered with certainty. All that we know for sure is that a movement so general and noticeable in the prewar years was not started by the war. Perhaps the most obvious forces at work in early twentieth-century civilization were technological change and urban growth, but these had been at work reshaping American culture for several generations and do not afford a direct and simple explanation for the sudden restlessness of 1912–17. Moreover, an increase of mechanistic materialism rather than a new vitalism would seem a more easily understandable product of machine civilization. It may be that the prewar rebellion was in part a protest against such a long-run tendency; in 1915 the *Nation* suggested that the rising "Bergsonian school . . . owes not a little of its popularity to its expression of revolt from the dreary materialistic determinism of the closing years of the last century."[26]

One is tempted to wonder whether the new physics was at work already, disintegrating the comparatively simple universe of nineteenth-century science. It seems, however, that although the Einstein revolution was being discussed before the war by American scientists and reported in the serious periodical press, it did not directly affect as yet the literary and political intellectuals to any great extent, and it was not, as it became after the war, a newspaper sensation.[27]

In part the American intellectual rebellion may be considered merely a belated phase of a European antirationalist tendency. Yet it remains puzzling that Nietzsche and Dostoevsky and Baudelaire waited for their most telling American impact until they competed with Freud and Joyce. Part of the violence of the American literary and intellectual battles of the next decade arises from the fact that influences that had gradually permeated European thought presented themselves to many Americans all at once and in their extreme forms.

The time and special character of the prewar rebellion were, I believe, determined in part by the very surface placidity of the Progressive Era. Traditional American beliefs in moral certainty and inevitable progress had for some time been subjected to inner strain and external attack, yet in the prewar decade, for the last time, the official custodians of culture were able to maintain and defend a common front. Yet these almost hereditary leaders—Roosevelt and Royce and Howells in their several spheres —were growing weaker. A new generation, full of confidence and provided with leisure and libraries, was fairly literally looking for trouble. What attracts us about the standard culture of America in the early years of the century is its confident consensus, its lack of passion and violence. Passion and violence were exactly the demand of the young intellectuals of 1913 and 1914, of Lippmann and Brooks and Bourne and Pound. This was what they wanted, and this was what they got.

The war, then, was not the cause of the cultural revolution of the twenties. It played, however, the immense part that the Civil War played in the economic and political revolution of the mid-nineteenth century, speeding, widening and altering in kind a movement already under way.

The experiences of 1917–19 darkened and soured the mood of the rebels. Even at its most iconoclastic and even in those spokesmen who adopted the most pessimistic doctrines, the prewar renaissance was always exuberant. Pound, amid his fierce negations, still found it possible to make his famous and somewhat rash prophecy that the coming American Risorgimento would "make the Italian Renaissance look like a tempest in a teapot!"[28] The rejection of easy rationalism, the spurning of dull politics were to make America better and brighter. In the war and its aftermath, however, the rebellious generation learned something of the price of destruction and experienced personally both tragedy and (in 1919) failure. Many who had been rebellious optimists became despairing nihilists and those who had already been preaching the futility of conscious effort preached it with different emotional corollaries.

The other effect of the war was that the disintegration of traditional ideas spread far more widely among the population. Most of the prewar rebellion was confined to a small and isolated, though articulate and potentially influential, group of intellectuals. As yet the overwhelming bulk of the people took for granted the truth of the old political and moral slogans. As long as this was so, rebels could be ignored or patronized; they did not have to be feared and fought. Without the political events of 1917-19, traditional beliefs might perhaps have been slowly adapted to new realities instead of, for the moment, either smashed or blindly defended. And without the currents of doubt and disintegration already abroad, these political events themselves might have lacked their willing and ready Cassandras.

In 1913 *Sons and Lovers, A Preface to Politics,* and *Winds of Doctrine* were published, but *Pollyanna* and *Laddie* were the best-sellers. In 1925 the best-seller list itself had to find place for *An American Tragedy.*

Notes

1. Through this essay I treat this period as one instead of dividing it in August, 1914. The outbreak of the war in Europe shocked American intellectuals but did not immediately become their main preoccupation. Until about the winter of 1916, radical and progressive politics, together with the new literary and philosophical tendencies, get more space than the war in the liberal and literary periodicals.

2. George Santayana, *Winds of Doctrine* (London and New York: Charles Scribner's Sons, 1913), p. 1.

3. *Ibid.,* p. 10.

4. Henry L. Mencken, *The Philosophy of Friedrich Nietzsche* (Boston: Luce and Co., 1918).

5. Irving Babbitt, "Bergson and Rousseau," *Nation,* November 14, 1912, p. 455. One of the more influential of the considerable number of books on Bergson appearing in these years was H. M. Kallen, *William James and Henri Bergson* (Chicago: University of Chicago Press, 1914). There is a very large volume of periodical discussion from 1911.

6. For a helpful review see Frederick J. Hoffman, *Freudianism and the Literary Mind* (Baton Rouge, La.: Louisiana State University Press, 1945). The early impact of Freud and many other foreign influences is clearly recorded in the works of Floyd Dell, one of Freud's important American exponents. Dell deals most specifically with these influences in his retrospective *Intellectual Vagabondage* (New York: George H. Doran Co., 1926).

7. See Lucille C. Birnbaum, "Behaviorism in the 1920's," *American Quarterly,* VII (1955), 15–30, esp. p. 20.

8. Louis Weinberg, "Current Impressionism," *New Republic,* March 6, 1915, pp 124–25.

9. George Santayana, *Winds of Doctrine,* p. 10.

10. James H. Robinson, "A Journal of Opinion," *New Republic,* May 8, 1915, pp. 9–10.

11. An account of all these tendencies in prewar thought, together with a vast bibliography, can be found in two helpful summaries. These are W. Y. Elliott, *The Pragmatic Revolt in Politics* (New York: The Macmillan Company, 1928) and C. E. Merriam and H. E. Barnes, eds., *A History of Political Theories, Recent Times* (New York: The Macmillan Company, 1924).

12. Walter Lippmann, *A Preface to Politics* (New York: M. Kennerley, 1913), p. 200.

13. London: A. Constable and Co., 1908.

14. *E.g.,* Walter Lippmann, *Drift and Mastery* (New York: M. Kennerley, 1914), pp. 249, 274.

15. *E.g.,* January 16, 1915, pp. 6–8; November 6, 1915, p. 1; June 17, 1916, pp. 159–61; July 1, 1916, pp. 211–13.

16. See Daniel Bell, "Marxian Socialism in the United States," in D. D. Egbert and Stow Persons, eds., *Socialism and American Life* (Princeton, N. J.: Princeton University Press, 1952), I, 289–90.

17. Walter Lippmann, *Preface to Politics*, pp. 277–78.

18. See David L. Shannon, *The Socialist Party of America, A History* (New York: The Macmillan Company, 1955). As Shannon and other historians of socialism have pointed out, the apparent revival of the Socialist Party in the big Debs vote of 1920 is misleading. It belongs in the category of protest rather than party success.

19. Harriet Monroe, *A Poet's Life* (New York: The Macmillan Company, 1938), p. 337.

20. Randolph Bourne, "The Immanence of Dostoevsky," *The Dial*, LXIII (1917), 25.

21. In the *New Republic*, November 10, 1917, p. 52.

22. Ezra Pound, "The Audience," *Poetry, A Magazine of Verse*, V (1914–15), 30.

23. See the following helpful autobiographies of Harvard graduates: Malcolm Cowley, *Exile's Return* (New York: W. W. Norton & Company, 1934); Harold E. Stearns, *The Street I Know* (New York: L. Furman, 1935); Van Wyck Brooks, *Scenes and Portraits* (New York: E. P. Dutton & Co., 1954).

24. Brooks, *op. cit.*, pp. 123–48, 210 ff.

25. The same traits that one finds in the ideas of the period characterize much of its social life. Ragtime and the dance craze, the furore over alleged white slave disclosures, in 1913 seem to prefigure the feverishness and the moral divisions of the postwar decade.

26. From a review of Croly's *Progressive Democracy*, which the *Nation* associates with the Bergson influence (April 29, 1915), pp. 469–70.

27. This impression comes from an examination of periodicals and is confirmed by an intensive though brief examination of popular scientific literature by Robert G. Sumpter.

28. Pound to Harriet Monroe, 24 September, 1914, in D. D. Paige, ed., *The Letters of Ezra Pound 1907–1914* (New York: Harcourt, Brace and Co., 1950), p. 10.

Businessmen and the Progressive Movement

ROBERT WIEBE

From 1920 to the end of World War II, historians were preoccupied with progressivism largely in terms of its goals and results. In current historical writing, however, the emphasis has shifted sharply away from goals and outcomes, toward motives and personnel. The prevailing question about progressivism now seems to be: Who were the progressives and why did they become progressive? In *The Age of Reform*, Professor Hofstadter has provided vital clues to the answers to both questions. Professors May and Lasch, in complementary ways, have split the intellectuals away from political progressivism and have raised serious questions about their motivation.

The consequence of such studies is that progressivism seems now to have been much less an ideological movement than had been supposed. As if taking up such cues, other historians have begun to insist that the progressive movement was heavily saturated with the influence of businessmen—not just Professor Hofstadter's professional classes, but working businessmen. The soundest statement of this point of view is made by Professor Robert Wiebe in *Businessmen and Reform*. In ways that parallel Professor May's "The Rebellion of the Intellectuals, 1912–1917," his work also suggests a substantial continuity between the progressive decade and the 1920s.

Robert Wiebe, Professor of History at Northwestern University, is a colleague there of Professor Christopher Lasch. His field of interest is political history between the Civil War and World War I, but he has brought to political history a much broader perspective than most historians of politics possess. His first book was Businessmen and Reform *(1962) and his second is an interpretive survey entitled* The Search for Order, 1877–1920 *(1967). He is also coeditor of* Historical Vistas: Readings in United States History *(2 vols., 1963).*

1

The Cleveland progressives who rallied about Tom Johnson early in the century said that they had captured the city from business and had given it to the people. Breaking through a web of privilege, they had overcome the combined opposition of the newspapers, the Chamber of Commerce and profiteers who milked the city for private gain, in order to provide equitable and humane government. Although their long fight for cheaper urban transportation and a rational property tax justified some exaggeration, their method of exaggerating revealed a particularism in the progressive movement which created a unique problem for businessmen. In their summary, the Johnson forces had excluded support from two Cleveland papers and the work of the Chamber of Commerce for health and housing legislation, urban renewal, and benevolent capitalism.

Early in the progressive era, descriptions of reform acquired a classic form. Progressives, consciously or otherwise, arranged their stories of battle after that ideal type: public men led average Americans against entrenched business privilege to ensure government by and for the people. The simplified version provided a convenient shorthand for proving authenticity, convincing doubters, and communicating with other reformers. But, like any orthodoxy, it could also be a nuisance. Reform-minded politicians such as Roosevelt and Beveridge had incessantly to guard against looking like professional politicians; reform clergymen had to test donations for taints of privilege; and reformers in general had to watch constantly for dubious companions. Well-to-do businessmen especially suffered under these rules. The word "business" automatically connoted special interests, and a profit-seeker, however respect-

REPRINTED BY PERMISSION OF THE PUBLISHERS FROM ROBERT H. WIEBE, *Businessmen and Reform: A Study of the Progressive Movement.* CAMBRIDGE, MASS.: HARVARD UNIVERSITY PRESS, COPYRIGHT 1962, BY THE PRESIDENT AND FELLOWS OF HARVARD COLLEGE.

able in his line, could not easily establish himself as a public man. If, as was very often the case, the reformers saw "business interests" as their ultimate enemy, too many businessmen on the side of reform jeopardized its authenticity as a progressive movement. And if, as was very often the case, the reforming businessmen supported only a portion of a general program, they further weakened their claim as progressives. A crusade belonged to the pure. During the progressive era one either stood with the people or with the interests.

Historians inherited the problems of this orthodoxy whenever they used the essential, yet elusive, term "progressive." The first students of progressivism managed to avoid difficulty by concentrating upon results. Men such as Benjamin DeWitt and Charles Beard, writing in or just beyond the period, relied largely upon a list of particular reforms to describe the movement. And in 1931 Harold U. Faulkner summarized the content school of progressive history with *The Quest for Social Justice*, which traced the outstanding changes of the time with scarcely an interpretation.[1]

Next historians turned to the fascinating gallery of men and women who had dominated the movements which these careful, limited studies detailed. Some of the biographies excluded the broad setting of reform altogether. Others adopted the approach which leading reformers themselves had used. As the autobiographies of Roosevelt and LaFollette had selected events to illuminate their authors, so later biographies, in an effort to recreate personalities, construed the movement to fit the man. Admiring associates of Roosevelt, such as Joseph Bucklin Bishop, arranged his words and claims to present him as the great reformer. Henry F. Pringle, on the other hand, found him wanting in honesty, conviction, humane sensitivity, and detachment from big business. Instead, Pringle elevated Taft for the legislation which had passed during his administration. Claude G. Bowers pictured Beveridge as a reformer because he had fought big business. By implicitly equating progressivism with the preferences for antimonopoly and social justice of Brandeis, Alpheus T. Mason raised LaFollette high among the reformers and dropped Roosevelt.[2]

Three historians broadened this technique to differentiate among factions within the movement. Although John Chamberlain discovered no reformers with the right combination of economic wisdom and intellectual toughness to complete the fight against monopoly capitalism, he recognized LaFollette and a few like him as the most able. Without Chamberlain's reservations, Matthew Josephson also favored the LaFollette group for its honest battle against big business. And in his study of the muckrakers, Louis Filler applied roughly the same criterion—dedication to the strict control of big business—to set off a hard core of journalists who had continued their exposures after magnates had closed all but one of their outlets. Like the biographies, these more incisive studies of the movement did not attempt to define "progressive" and did not search systematically for the participants in reform.[3]

By the 1940's an abundant literature about reform leaders gave historians the confidence to write about progressives as a group. Casual students of the reform era now placed them in the American tradition: they were moral, liberal, democratic, and optimistic; above all, they wanted to salvage the individual from an industrial society.[4] At the same time specialists analyzed the progressive mind. Eric Goldman and Morton G. White, following the general guide of the disenchanted progressive Randolph Bourne, pointed up the corrosive and ill-defined relativism upon which progressive thinkers had relied. David Noble reconstructed a paradox in which progressives had tried to reconcile an inexorable social progress with a man-made leap into utopia. Other intellectual historians tested the reformers against fixed historical definitions of progressive and liberal. Daniel Aaron called the reformers who dominated the early twentieth century "pseudo-progressives," lacking the courage and humane vision necessary to challenge entrenched business privilege. Louis Hartz and Arthur Ekirch, both using variations of Lockean liberalism, arrived at equally uncomplimentary conclusions. Hartz saw the progressive movement as a sham revolt against the American business system by men who shared an all-pervasive Horatio Alger ethos: progressivism illustrated America's irrational Lockeanism. And Ekirch pictured early twentieth-century reformers as statists, illiberal by eighteenth-century standards.[5]

By holding the progressives in place, these historians could detach themselves from many of the reformers' assumptions and walk around the group pointing out foibles and failures. Richard Hofstadter, employing principles from social psychology, greatly extended the range of the historian's freedom. His study of the progressive personality described a half-recognized feeling among members of the urban middle class that big business, organized labor, and political machines threatened their status in American society. With indifferent results, substantial citizens tried to solve America's urban-industrial problems through reforms which rested upon an outmoded set of Yankee-Protestant values. Finally, George Mowry, drawing upon his own findings as well as those of Hofstadter and others, synthesized the recent investigations in a "progressive profile."[6]

Over the years historians had gradually closed the door to the progressive club. The recognized political and social leaders, along with their intellectual spokesmen, comprised its membership, and the common characteristics among these men and women supplied its defining quality. To gain admittance, a latecomer had to pass the progressive-personality test. An examination of Mowry's check list indicates how weak the case is for most reforming businessmen, who did not receive invitations when the club was established. His progressives held optimistic views about mankind and nature which supported their faith in an extensive democracy and a swift, man-made progress. Reform-minded businessmen, insofar as they expressed themselves, distrusted the people, broadly considered, and countered projects for direct democracy with talk about republican restraints. To them social progress was a gradual, delicate process. Mowry's progressives suffered the pangs of status decline. The same held true for a number of businessmen, especially bankers, retailers, and manufacturers in the towns and smaller cities of the South and Midwest, but on balance these men like the country banker Andrew Frame opposed change far more often than they encouraged it. Moreover these townsmen usually did not have the economic security which recent writers have emphasized. On the contrary, both the ideas and impetus for reform came from prospering businessmen on the make, men like Edward Bacon, Herbert Miles, George Reynolds, and George Perkins. And where Mowry's progressives deplored the evil city and idealized rural America, their closest counterparts among businessmen were again the townsmen. The more active urban businessmen had made their peace with the city. The same applies to another trait, a distaste for ostentatious wealth and an attempt to separate good and bad riches: reform-minded businessmen usually did not question how the wealthy had acquired and spent their money. Nor did these businessmen, for all of their booster and boomer spirit, display the missionary zeal of Mowry's progressives.

In a few instances, reform-minded businessmen qualify under his provisions. By and large, they were youthful; they came from a middle-class; they had been standpatters a decade earlier; they considered the new immigrants socially dangerous; they feared organized labor as well as organized capital; and they abhorred the word "class." But they score far higher on Mowry's conservative test.[7] They often doubted man's virtuousness; emphasized the slowness of social progress; believed that leaders, not the masses, initiated that progress; respected the inequalities among men; generally held the judiciary in deep regard; and above all had faith in the fundamental soundness and justice of the American business system. And a glance back through recent literature yields similar results. Reforming businessmen were not the statists Ekirch describes, they had little in common with the patricians whom Aaron discusses, they dreamed none of the utopias which Noble's progressives outlined, they did not subscribe to the optimistic pragmatism of Goldman's reformers, they distrusted the muckrakers, and they considered LaFollette a dangerous radical. By unanimous verdict, then, the large majority of them belong with the enemies of the progressives.

Yet how much light do we cast either upon reform-minded businessmen or upon the progressive period by calling these men who worked diligently for several important progressive causes nonprogressives? And how will we deal with other groups currently outside the progressive pale as we learn more about their roles in reform? We have scant information about the relationship between populism and progressivism. The Democratic party between 1900 and 1910 is a historical blur. If Woodrow Wilson's support in 1916 represented the purest coalition of progressives, as Arthur Link maintains, the movement by then relied largely upon rural, small town America, where Wilson's voting strength lay.

We know very little concerning organized labor and local reform. Hofstadter's provocative suggestions about the legal profession during the reform era remain a challenge. Until we have solved these and similar problems, reforming businessmen can anticipate company in limbo.[8]

The way to reopen the question of the progressives is to start with content rather than with people. Historians generally agree that, despite its diffuseness, the progressive movement did center about certain broad social, political, and economic issues: to provide the underprivileged with a larger share of the nation's benefits; to make governments more responsive to the wishes of the voters; and to regulate the economy in the public interest. Insofar as a man contributed to the solution of these problems, he was a progressive.

Rarely did businessmen try to improve the lot of low-income Americans. With few exceptions they opposed independent unions and fought against labor legislation. Social insurance laws were an anathema, and private welfare capitalism, still in its infancy, affected middle-income employees far more than unskilled workers. Their participation in Americanization programs and their support for prohibition belonged in the realm of social control rather than social meliorism. And in almost all cases those who were more than casual philanthropists had retired from business affairs. The only important contribution which businessmen made to the social welfare movement came as a by-product of their zeal for civic improvement. As they scrubbed and polished their cities, some of them did assist in improving local housing and health codes.

Although businessmen wanted to purify democracy, they opposed extending it. In general they continued the Mugwump tradition, declaiming against local bosses and corrupt legislators, and encouraging civil service. At cries for direct primaries, direct election of senators, or the initiative, referendum, and recall, articulate businessmen took shelter from the mob under principles of regulated democracy.

But questions of economic regulation aroused a very different response: at least one segment of the business community supported each major program for federal control. In this area businessmen exercised their greatest influence on reform and laid their claim as progressives.

II

As a factor in the making of progressivism, businessmen held a number of advantages. They had more money than any other group to invest in the men and causes they liked. Besides wealth, they enjoyed the most extensive organization among private groups in America. And if their profession did not widen social horizons, it extended their vision nationally more naturally than did any other occupation. Before most Americans had found their bearings at the turn of the century, businessmen had ideas about reform and the means to implement them.

But they faced peculiar disadvantages as well. A generalized distrust of "business" and specific complaints about particular groups of business-men gave them a bad reputation during a reform era. Politicians learned that programs identified with business had less than average chances of success, and that too close an affiliation with prosperous businessmen jeopardized their future. Other groups also viewed an avowedly busi-ness campaign with more than normal suspicion. Further weakening their political position, the vigor and abusiveness of their intramural fights both increased their notoriety and consumed their strength.

Finally, businessmen found accommodation even more difficult than did other groups early in the century: they were the most prickly of a sensitive lot. Too accustomed to dominance in their communities, too certain of their superior knowledge in economic affairs, they acted alone rather than compromise with those whom they considered lesser and ignorant Americans. Big businessmen, the first to recognize the wisdom of adjustment, had the most to learn and had not progressed far enough by the end of the era. Moderately prosperous industrialists actually deteri-orated as compromisers during the middle years when organizations such as the NAM and the Illinois Manufacturers' Association said no to almost ever proposal for reform. Although other businessmen dis-played more talent for accommodation than this, the over-all record was poor.

During the first phase of progressivism, their tactical advantages gave businessmen a lead in the debate over national economic reform which often held for several years afterward. Until 1904 business shippers and the carriers monopolized the struggle over rate regulation, and until 1911 they still ranked as the major forces. To 1912 no one except bank-ers had offered systematic proposals for financial reorganization, and no one had equaled the idea behind the Hepburn amendments as a practical alternative to the Sherman Act. Businessmen applied the most persistent pressure for and against tariff reform to the eve of the Payne-Aldrich Act; after that, while professional protectionists continued to uphold the tariff, Republican progressives carried on the businessmen's program for a scientific tariff commission. In these areas, the most serious limita-tions on their power until the Panic of 1907 were internal rivalries and national inertia.

Nineteen hundred and eight was the watershed. The rapid movement of middle-income groups into national reform posed the first important challenges to their leadership, and as hard times took the glamor from reform, businessmen turned increasingly arrogant and rigid. Tariff revisionists, instead of compromising after 1908, gave up their reform movement. Midwestern city bankers entered an alliance with Wall Street behind a politically impossible financial plan. Only the shippers saw their legislative fight to a finish in 1910, and only the businessmen advocating a permissive trade commission offered a new program with a chance of success. Meanwhile, the established business powers in the East had fallen on the defensive within the Republican party. Although still fairly successful in defeating laws which they did not like, they also killed bills with the touch of their name.

These diverse strands formed a peculiar pattern of influence early in the Wilson years. On the one hand, the full range of progressive groups, including newly arrived businessmen from the West and South, were competing for national favors, and the businessmen from the East and Midwest now faced their most complex problems of maneuver and compromise. On the other hand, the more prosperous businessmen, by arriving first and proposing consistently, had so conditioned the debates over economic legislation that their programs continued to set legislative limits well after 1912, when these businessmen lacked the political power to impose them. This was least evident, although not absent, in the case of the Underwood tariff, which depended very little upon general principles; it was most obvious in the case of the Federal Reserve Act, which Congress largely built from the alternatives bankers had already suggested. And both the Federal Trade Commission and the regulation of agricultural exchanges also demonstrated this lingering influence from the formative years. By the time Congress had resolved the issues which established businessmen had once dominated, they had regained sufficient poise and power to act on their own once again. During 1916 they won, among other concessions, the favor of the FTC, the initiation of the Webb-Pomerene bill, and the passage of the Rainey and Kern Acts.

Whether or not businessmen realized it, certain principles of strategy governed their record during the progressive era. Where they rode a wave of other people's hostility, they enjoyed their easiest victories. Entering the twentieth century, almost every articulate American held some grudge againt the railroads: they were either too strong, too arrogant, too expensive, or too irresponsible. Emotions alone never enacted legislation against an ensconced political power. But because of this climate, the determined shippers could depend upon encouragement from a host of middle-income groups not directly involved in questions of freight rates. And a politician looking for a likely reform issue could do no better than support the organized drive for rate regulation.

Where businessmen adopted a conciliatory approach, they maximized their chances of success. In 1913 Senator Owen and Representative Glass assumed that any new financial system would require the approval of the bankers. So inclined, Owen secretly proffered a hand of cooperation to Vanderlip and Benjamin Strong. Vanderlip slapped it away with a vitriolic public letter denouncing everything Congress had thus far done toward a bill. Meanwhile, George Reynolds brought a majority of Midwestern city bankers into an attitude of cooperation toward Congress and impressed this fact time and again upon both Glass and Owen. Disregarding the question of specific influences upon particular portions of the final bill, the Federal Reserve Act most closely approximated the long-standing ambitions of the Midwestern city bankers and bore the least resemblance to the expressed desires of Wall Street.

From 1909 to 1914 the NAM compiled an exceptionally pure record of opposition to reform legislation. Faced with the prospect of measures to limit working hours, reform the tariff, and regulate corporations, the association demanded no laws at all; it received the Eight-Hour Act of 1912, the Underwood tariff, and the Clayton and Federal Trade Commission Acts without appreciably affecting any one of them. Ferdinand Schwedtman, who had repeatedly warned his colleagues that "if we [in the NAM] want to last in politics and in legislative work we must be more constructive," accounted for the one exception. Under his direction the association drew up a model bill for workmen's compensation, which influenced the laws of many states and was also reflected in the federal bill Senator George Sutherland of Utah sponsored.[9]

Where businessmen had the tightest and best established organizations, they enjoyed the greatest opportunities to affect progressive legislation. Big businessmen had organized within the political parties rather than among themselves, and strategic location explained their ability to delay and modify so many reform measures. Through their representatives, they could introduce bills and amendments almost at will, and concrete proposals, as the Wilson years demonstrated, were committing. As the men who filled the party purses, they set boundaries even when they could not dictate legislation. As a result Congress did not attempt to control the insurance companies, pulled teeth from the measures regulating foods and drugs, delayed railroad and tariff laws despite a rising public clamor, and modified both the Clayton and Trade Commission bills toward the wishes of the magnates. Organization also enabled moderately prosperous businessmen to establish their claims early in the century and to keep their demands before Congress. And weakness in organization relegated small businessmen to the cheering sections during most of the progressive era. They applauded antitrust activities, but they did not share in the decisions. Even during the Wilson years, only the country bankers asking for rural credits and the retailers requesting a permissive trade commission exercised a noticeable influence on reform legislation; in both cases these groups were exceptionally well organized for small businessmen, and they profited as well from powerful support outside their ranks.

In all, the business community was the most important single factor— or set of factors—in the development of economic regulation. And a significant portion of this influence supported reform. Until 1908 businessmen deserve Arthur Link's commendation as the "backbone" of the major movements for national regulation, and some, notably the conciliationist city bankers and the shippers in the National Industrial Traffic League, contributed to reform throughout the era.[10] In 1916 the stanchest defenders of the Federal Reserve system were the member bankers, of the Interstate Commerce Commission the shippers, and of the Federal Trade Commission an assortment of merchants and manufacturers. Moderately prosperous businessmen from the Midwestern cities comprised the bulk of the reforming businessmen. After them came the shippers elsewhere in the nation who eventually joined the fight for rate control; a very few big businessmen, such as George Perkins, who contributed to the movement for a trade commission; the country bankers, particularly from the South, who influenced financial legislation during Wilson's administration; and a variety of importers and exporters from the East and South who applied pressure for tariff revision. These men were progressives. They stood apart from the majority of reformers not because they selected (others picked and chose) or because their reforms expressed self-interest (others identified the general welfare with their needs) but because of their narrow public philosophy. Progressive businessmen singularly lacked a grand social vision. Placing reform on a business basis, they represented—to borrow a phrase from Richard Hofstadter—the hard side of progressivism.

III

On the surface the progressive movement had changed businessmen considerably less than they had the movement. They had not untangled their confusion over politics and political action. The close correlation between the roll of the business cycle and the rise and fall of their reform impulses illustrated how much they still longed for stability. After sixteen years their predispositions about American society sounded much the same. And an era of bitter battles had not altered the broad outlines of business disunity.

Yet important, if subtle, changes had occurred in businessmen. Years of discussion about reform had given them a fresh awareness of American society. First reflected in the phenomenal growth of local boosting organizations dedicated to civic improvement, it soon broadened to include national questions as well. Many city associations joined the United States Chamber of Commerce so that they could express themselves on national issues and still have the energy for local problems. A new spirit was abroad when businessmen did not have time for all of their public affairs. They had also grown more sensitive to public criticism, which during the progressive period so often prefaced regulatory legislation. "If businessmen cannot be honest from principle," warned a member of the Memphis Merchants' Exchange, "let them be so through fear of public condemnation."[11] For reasons of prudence and pride, businessmen began to sell themselves along with their products. And this livelier interest in what was happening in America led businessmen to talk increasingly about the nation as a whole rather than about a locality or section.

Years of involvement with the federal government also left a mark. A number of previously strange regulations had become part of life by

1916, and these if nothing else made businessmen more conscious in their daily affairs of the government's existence. From their experiences with government supervision, business leaders had learned to spot more quickly the possible advantages from federal action. In 1905 only Elbert Gary and a very few other magnates had thought to win the Bureau of Corporations to their side; after 1914 businessmen everywhere rushed to cooperate with the Federal Trade Commission. In general the progressive movement had forced them to define more carefully what they wanted.

More alert to the world about them, businessmen gradually acquired a new attitude toward one another. At the turn of the century none of them had talked about a business community. But as wave after wave of business groups matured and entered national affairs, some of their leaders began to discuss the need for a general business spokesman, leading eventually to the U.S. Chamber of Commerce. Although the Chamber fell short of the ideal, the goal remained. The recession of 1914 produced, along with a consensus against reform, an unprecedented number of statements that American business was on trial and that American business would not tolerate such abuse. When disunity returned after 1914, it lacked its former bite. In part businessmen were relaxing after the battles. Most articulate bankers now operated within a common and accepted structure. Shippers had won their legislation, and as long as these controls remained intact, they would assist the railroads in a drive for exclusive national regulation. Recession and fears of postwar dumping had narrowed the differences between the professional protectionists and the revisionists; and as cooperative understandings spread throughout the community, smaller businessmen complained less often about collusion among giant corporations. Moreover, after their experiences with the Sherman and Clayton Acts, many more businessmen had lost faith in a stern antitrust statute. Finally, a deepening aversion to organized labor drew big businessmen and the employer associations closer together in their fight against the unions. Always vague, never binding, their new fellow feeling indicated that after years of debate businessmen recognized each other as kin even if they could not love every brother.

IV

Out of the progressive experience run lines of continuity connecting the business community of that day with the business community of ours. Despite a growing tolerance of organized labor and a broadening conception of the people, the protective ideology has remained substantially the same.[12] Attacks upon private enterprise are un-American, and demands for closer regulation of the economy shameless demagoguery. Although successful businessmen have far greater respect for the power of the federal government, many of them still describe its leadership, financial operations, and services by analogy to a corporation; and "get the government out of business" is still the chamber of commerce war cry. Every four years business spokesmen implore their audience to enter politics, to save America through a businessman's government, and between elections they bemoan the pall of politics over the American economy. The public heroes of businessmen have continued to come primarily from their own community.

If businessmen have used ideology as a buffer against frighteningly rapid change, it has served them well. Beneath a rigid public philosophy, prosperous businessmen in the twentieth century have adjusted to an America in flux more quickly and more effectively than any other segment of society. Thoughtlessly accepting perpetual Republicanism during the progressive era, many business leaders had forgotten to hedge against political mishaps. Since then they have preserved their connections with both parties far more carefully. Even during the darkest days of the New Deal, leading businessmen did not break with important Democrats, and the leverage they retained brought concessions during and after Roosevelt's second administration. Considering the greater stress of the 1930's, their record surpassed that of businessmen from 1910 to 1914. Of course the fact that both parties in an age of mass communication have had to include many more businessmen in their financial base than a Hanna ever required has lightened the task.

A number of business leaders also learned during the progressive years the cost of arrogance toward officeholders. Excepting certain frantic moments of the New Deal, a considerably more suave approach has since characterized their dealings with prominent politicians. Tact has cemented natural alliances between legislators and businessmen back home to procure lucrative government contracts, and between federal commissioners and their charges to regularize regulation within an industry. Again, the deep involvement of many congressmen in business activities and their continuing interest in business-connected jobs upon retirement have eased the problems of diplomacy.

Political tact is only part of a broad canopy which has spread over business affairs. As public relations, born of a concern over progressive attacks, has grown from the ballyhoo of the twenties to the qualitative techniques of our time, it has become increasingly essential in the minds of business leaders and therefore increasingly entwined with business operations. Now no significant policy emerges without a protective coating of public relations. In part this demonstrates the ability of an enterprise to sell its own indispensability. But more important, the expansion of public relations reflects a prudent desire among prominent businessmen to dress well on all occasions so that they will never again stand naked as "interests" or "economic royalists."

This keener appreciation of public forces provides one index to a remarkable success story, the ability of prosperous businessmen to protect their positions of leadership in America's twentieth-century society in transition. Capitalizing upon a sudden worship of productivity in 1917, businessmen comprised most of the "public men" who directed the national mobilization of World War I. Here was the America of Herbert Croly's dreams, a corporate society led by the federal government, only Bernard Baruch had replaced Theodore Roosevelt. After paying for the campaign which elected Warren Harding and a Republican Congress, business leaders held the initiative among the heirs of progressivism early in the twenties.

Rather than frontally attacking the middle-income groups—businessmen, professionals, agriculturalists, and skilled laborers—who had challenged them during the progressive era, big business leaders gradually incorporated or neutralized them. In the late progressive years, big businessmen had started cooperating with erstwhile enemies such as the NAM; during the twenties they joined organizations such as the U.S. Chamber of Commerce and the American Bankers' Association, which they had disdained before. And a more elaborate and permissive federal government, serving as a clearinghouse for business compromise, widened the new communities of interest. Despite continued in-fighting, especially among functional competitors and among those of varying sizes, harmony characterized the business community in this period of prosperity.

Some of the professionals who had made a livelihood from progressivism now found employment with big business. Others, including many teachers and clergymen, discovered anew that their jobs and community standing often depended upon the tolerance of successful businessmen. Through mediators such as Herbert Hoover and Senator Arthur Capper, alert business leaders recognized the wisdom of selective assistance to organized agriculture, a policy which blunted its reform thrust through most of the decade. Following the grim postwar battles which deflated the unions, company paternalism, not skull-cracking, typified labor relations during the 1920's. For a time this approach undermined old unions and forestalled new ones so successfully that most crafts would gladly have accepted a niche within industry, as the Railroad Brotherhoods did, if only their organizations had commanded sufficient respect. One after another, the progressive groups had been brought into a loose and complex system which shared the advantages of industrialism without taking from the most prominent businessmen the important perquisites of leadership. And as this network of relationships materialized, businessmen were also transforming progressive government into a mechanism for self-regulation.

Even economic collapse after 1929 did not destroy the system, despite a widespread belief that "business" was responsible for the worst features of the depression. Considering the pressures of hard times, former progressives remained remarkably passive while successful businessmen worked with President Hoover to strengthen the self-regulatory system of the 1920's. As Hoover turned increasingly negative, more flexible business leaders, well before Franklin Roosevelt's inauguration, proposed the central idea of what would be the National Recovery Administration. Welcoming a change under Roosevelt and the New Deal, they supplied the NRA with its basic substance, the codes. And such men as Edward Filene and John Fahey, reminders of the liberal origins of the U.S. Chamber, ably served the New Deal in minor capacities. When the New Deal after 1935 alienated most successful businessmen, the bulk of the old progressive groups either joined business leaders in protecting the establishment or sought neutral ground. Buttressed by this support and saved by such timely concessions as swift recognition of unionism in Big Steel, prominent business leaders resourcefully defended their power against both the dispossessed and the federal government.

Again a world war enabled business leaders to recoup their losses. By effectively controlling the mobilization process and by winning most of the credit for America's phenomenal wartime productivity, they regained an initiative which they have held through the years of cold war, with its continued emphasis upon productivity and technological advance. Across the nation capitalism and freedom are considered synonymous. Once more prominent businessmen have adjusted rapidly enough to secure their positions of leadership. A prompt acceptance of industrial unions has given labor a larger share of America's plenty without power over broad industrial or national policy. Systematically organized agriculture, which business leaders will not seriously oppose, enjoys latitude in determining the subsidies it will receive but little power in any other area of public policy. By providing Negroes with wider employment and desegregated facilities, major corporations have championed the so-called moderate approach in race relations. Only a greatly enlarged government bureaucracy competes with successful businessmen for national leadership, and this competition is real only to the degree that the two are distinct forces. The great blend of our time has so intermixed business and government that a practical, precise separation of the two is no longer possible.

In spite of the advantages which a dominant economic position and an inside view of technological progress have given business leaders, they have also laid a claim to brilliance by the success of their accommodation. With so few signs of domestic upheaval at the beginning of the 1960's any élite would take pride in the record of America's durable business leadership. In the end, it was these men who benefited most from the progressive movement, which their predecessors once feared would destroy them.

Notes

1. Benjamin DeWitt, *The Progressive Movement* (New York, 1915), pp. 3–5 and *passim;* Charles A. Beard, *Contemporary American History, 1877–1913* (New York, 1918), chaps. x–xiii; Harold U. Faulkner, *The Quest for Social Justice, 1898–1914* (New York, 1931).

2. Robert M. LaFollette, *Autobiography* (Madison, Wis., 1913); Theodore

Roosevelt, *An Autobiography* (New York, 1914); Henry F. Pringle, *Theodore Roosevelt; A Biography* (New York, 1931) and *The Life and Times of William Howard Taft; A Biography* (2 vols., New York, 1939); Claude G. Bowers, *Beveridge and the Progressive Era* (Boston, 1932); Alpheus T. Mason, *Brandeis: A Free Man's Life* (New York, 1946), pp. 365–375 and *passim*.

3. John Chamberlain, *Farewell to Reform* (New York, 1932), pp. 234, 267–269, and *passim*; Matthew Josephson, *The President Makers; The Culture of Politics and Leadership in an Age of Enlightenment, 1896–1919* (New York, 1940); Louis Filler, *Crusaders for American Liberalism* (New York, 1939).

4. See, for example, Samuel E. Morison and Henry S. Commager, *The Growth of the American Republic* (4th rev. ed., 2 vols., New York, 1950), II, chap. xv; Ralph H. Gabriel, *The Course of American Democratic Thought* (2nd ed., New York, 1956), chap. xxv; Merle Curti, *The Growth of American Thought* (2nd ed., New York, 1951), chap. xxiv; Russel B. Nye, *Midwestern Progressive Politics; A Historical Study of Its Origins and Development, 1870–1958* (East Lansing, 1959), pp. 184–189 and *passim*; Carl N. Degler, *Out of Our Past* (New York, 1959), pp. 368–378.

5. Eric F. Goldman, *Rendezvous with Destiny* (New York, 1952); Morton G. White, *Social Thought in America; The Revolt Against Formalism* (New York, 1949); David Noble, *The Paradox of Progressive Thought* (Minneapolis, 1958); Daniel Aaron, *Men of Good Hope; A Story of American Progressives* (New York, 1951), pp. xi–xiv, 245 ff.; Louis Hartz, *The Liberal Tradition in America* (New York, 1955), chaps viii–ix; Arthur A. Ekirch, Jr., *The Decline of American Liberalism* (New York, 1955), chap. xi and *passim*.

6. Richard Hofstadter, *The Age of Reform; From Bryan to F.D.R.* (New York, 1955), chaps. iv–vi; George E. Mowry, *The Era of Theodore Roosevelt, 1900–1912* (New York, 1958), pp. 47–58, chap. v. In a different vein, Samuel P. Hays, *The Response to Industrialism, 1885–1914* (Chicago, 1957), to which this writer is particularly indebted, so thoroughly blends progressivism with the rest of American history in the period that a distinguishable progressive movement no longer exists.

7. Mowry, *Era of Theodore Roosevelt*, pp. 38–45.

8. Arthur S. Link, *Woodrow Wilson and the Progressive Era, 1910–1917* (New York, 1954), pp. 238–241; Hofstadter, *Age of Reform*, pp. 155–163. As an example of the confusion which the word creates for an intelligent, casual student of history, Seymour Martin Lipset writes, "[The] Progressive movement [party?] . . . died away without coming to national power." "The Sources of the 'Radical Right,'" *The New American Right*, Daniel Bell, ed. (New York, 1955), pp. 178–179.

9. F. C. Schwedtman to H. E. Miles, May 29, 1908, U.S. Senate, *Appendix, Lobby*, II, 1671.

10. Arthur S. Link, "What Happened to the Progressive Movement in the 1920's?" *American Historical Review* (New York, Washington), 64:836 (July 1959).

11. *Annual Statement of the Memphis Merchants' Exchange, 1904*, pp. 15–19.

12. See, for example, James W. Prothro, *The Dollar Decade; Business Ideas in the 1920's* (Baton Rouge, 1954); Francis X. Sutton *et al.*, *The American Business Creed* (Cambridge, Mass., 1956).

Introduction to *The Triumph of Conservatism*

GABRIEL KOLKO

The most radical and controversial modern reinterpretation of progressivism is a book published in 1963 by Professor Gabriel Kolko, significantly entitled *The Triumph of Conservatism: A Reinterpretation of American History, 1900–1916.* In this book he leaps beyond previous generalizations about progressivism's broadly middle-class and business orientation. The years of the progressive movement have to be understood, he insists, not as a time when good-natured reform efforts were made by middle-class businessmen and professionals, but instead as the period in which the men who led large and powerful corporations gained control of American politics and the American economy.

In the crisis of the 1890s, according to Professor Kolko's argument, the leaders of large corporations realized that the economy was *too* free, *too* subject to fluctuation, panic, and vicious competition. Armed with this realization, they attempted to use the federal government to *regulate* the economy in their own interests and for their own purposes. The rhetoric of politics may have been a rhetoric of progressive reform, but behind the rhetoric lay a concerted effort by capitalists to use the government to control the economy to insure steady profits and to make long-term industrial planning a possibility. In the introduction to his book, Professor Kolko states his principal argument clearly and forcefully, and also puts his work into a context established by other recent studies of progressivism.

Gabriel Kolko, like Professor Christopher Lasch, is generally regarded as a
"radical" or "New-Left" historian. His field is, in a broad sense, economic history,
but he writes not on the economy as such but on the relationship between economic
and political structures. The resulting subject is what he refers to as "political
economy." He is Professor of History at the State University of New York at Buffalo.
His published books include Wealth and Power in America *(1962),* The Triumph of
Conservatism, 1900–1916 *(1963),* Railroads and Regulation, 1877–1916 *(1965), and*
The Politics of War, 1943–1945 *(1968). Also relevant to the subject at hand is an*
essay of his entitled "Brahmins and Business, 1870–1914," in The Critical Spirit: Essays
in Honor of Herbert Marcuse *(1967).*

*This is a book that is motivated by a concern with the seemingly non-*academic question of "what might have been." All men speculate or dream as they choose, but the value of the speculation depends on the questions asked and on the way they are answered. Speculation of the type prompting this volume has its value only if it leads to the re-examination of what happened—what *really* happened—in the past.

The political or economic history of a single nation, especially during a specific, critical period which has a determining influence on the decades that follow, should be examined with provocative questions in mind. And there is no more provocative question than: Could the American political experience in the twentieth century, and the nature of our economic institutions, have been radically different? Every society has its Pangloss who will reply in the negative. But to suggest that such a reply is mere apologetics would be a fruitless, inaccurate over-simplification. Predominantly, the great political and sociological theorists of this century have pessimistically described and predicted an inexorable trend toward centralization, conformity, bureaucracy—toward a variety of totalitarianism—and yet they have frequently been personally repelled by such a future.

Unless one believes in an invisible, transcendent destiny in American history, the study of men and institutions becomes the prerequisite for discovering how one's question should be answered. The nature of the questions in this study demands that history be more than a reinterpretation of what is already known, in large part because what is known is insufficient, but also because histories of America from the turn of the

REPRINTED BY PERMISSION, FROM GABRIEL KOLKO, *The Triumph of Conservatism: A Reinterpretation of American History, 1900–1916* (NEW YORK: FREE PRESS, 1963), PP. 1–9.

century onwards have all too frequently been obsessed by effects rather than causes. Theories and generalizations based on such an approach have ignored concrete actions and intentions, and for this reason the study of consequences and effects has also been deficient.

Assuming that the burden of proof is ultimately on the writer, I contend that the period from approximately 1900 until the United States' intervention in the war, labeled the progressive era by virtually all historians, was really an era of conservatism. Moreover, the triumph of conservatism that I will describe in detail throughout this book was the result not of any impersonal, mechanistic necessity but of the conscious needs and decisions of specific men and institutions.

There were any number of options involving government and economics abstractly available to national political leaders during the period 1900–1916, and in virtually every case they chose those solutions to problems advocated by the representatives of concerned business and financial interests. Such proposals were usually motivated by the needs of the interested businesses, and political intervention into the economy was frequently merely a response to the demands of particular businessmen. In brief, conservative solutions to the emerging problems of an industrial society were almost uniformly applied. The result was a conservative triumph in the sense that there was an effort to preserve the basic social and economic relations essential to a capitalist society, an effort that was frequently consciously as well as functionally conservative.

I use the attempt to preserve existing power and social relationships as the criterion for conservatism because none other has any practical meaning. Only if we mechanistically assume that government intervention in the economy and a departure from orthodox laissez faire automatically benefits the general welfare can we say that government economic regulation by its very nature is also progressive in the common meaning of that term. Each measure must be investigated for its intentions and consequences in altering the existing power arrangements, a task historians have largely neglected.

I shall state my basic proposition as baldly as possible so that my essential theme can be kept in mind, and reservations and intricacies will be developed in the course of the book. For the sake of communication I will use the term *progressive* and *progressivism*, but not, as have most historians, in their commonsense meanings.

Progressivism was initially a movement for the political rationalization of business and industrial conditions, a movement that operated on the assumption that the general welfare of the community could be best served by satisfying the concrete needs of business. But the regulation itself was invariably controlled by leaders of the regulated industry and directed toward ends they deemed acceptable or desirable. In part this came about because the regulatory movements were usually initiated by the dominant businesses to be regulated, but it also resulted from the nearly universal belief among political leaders in the basic justice of private property relations as they essentially existed, a belief that set the ultimate limits on the leaders' possible actions.

It is business control over politics (and by "business" I mean the major economic interests) rather than political regulation of the economy that is the significant phenomenon of the Progressive Era. Such domination was direct and indirect, but significant only insofar as it provided means for achieving a greater end—political capitalism. *Political capitalism* is the utilization of political outlets to attain conditions of stability, predictability, and security—to attain rationalization—in the economy. *Stability* is the elimination of internecine competition and erratic fluctuations in the economy. *Predictability* is the ability, on the basis of politically stabilized and secured means, to plan future economic action on the basis of fairly calculable expectations. By *security* I mean protection from the political attacks latent in any formally democratic political structure. I do not give to *rationalization* its frequent definition as the improvement of efficiency, output, or internal organization of a company; I mean by the term, rather, the organization of the economy and the larger political and social spheres in a manner that will allow corporations to function in a predictable and secure environment permitting reasonable profits over the long run. My contention in this volume is not that all of these objectives were attained by World War I, but that important and significant legislative steps in these directions were taken, and that these steps include most of the distinctive legislative measures of what has commonly been called the Progressive Period.

Political capitalism, as I have defined it, was a term unheard of in the Progressive Period. Big business did not always have a coherent theory of economic goals and their relationship to immediate actions, although certain individuals did think through explicit ideas in this connection. The advocacy of specific measures was frequently opportunistic, but many individuals with similar interests tended to prescribe roughly the same solution to each concrete problem, and to operationally construct an economic program. It was never a question of regulation or no regulation, of state control or laissez faire; there were, rather, the questions of what kind of regulation and by whom. The fundamental proposition that political solutions were to be applied freely, if not for some other industry's problems then at least for one's own, was never seriously questioned in practice. My focus is on the dominant trends, and on the assumptions behind these trends as to the desirable distribution of power and the type of social relations one wished to create or preserve. And I am concerned with the implementation and administration of a political capitalism, and with the political and economic context in which it flourished.

Why did economic interests require and demand political intervention by the *federal* government and a reincarnation of the Hamiltonian unity of politics and economics?

In part the answer is that the federal government was *always* involved in the economy in various crucial ways, and that laissez faire never existed in an economy where local and federal governments financed the construction of a significant part of the railroad system, and provided lucrative means of obtaining fortunes. This has been known to historians for decades, and need not be belabored. But the significant reason for many businessmen welcoming and working to increase federal intervention into their affairs has been virtually ignored by historians and economists. This oversight was due to the illusion that American industry was centralized and monopolized to such an extent that it could rationalize the activity in its various branches voluntarily. Quite the opposite was true.

Despite the large number of mergers and the growth in the absolute size of many corporations, the dominant tendency in the American economy at the beginning of this century was toward growing competition. Competition was unacceptable to many key business and financial interests, and the merger movement was to a large extent a reflection of voluntary, unsuccessful business efforts to bring irresistible competitive trends under control. Although profit was always a consideration, rationalization of the market was frequently a necessary prerequisite for maintaining long-term profits. As new competitors sprang up and as economic power was diffused throughout an expanding nation, it became apparent to many important businessmen that only the national government could rationalize the economy. Although specific conditions varied from industry to industry, internal problems that could be solved only by political means were the common denominator in those industries whose leaders advocated greater federal regulation. Ironically, contrary to the consensus of historians, it was not the existence of monopoly that caused the federal government to intervene in the economy, but the lack of it.

There are really two methods, both valid, of examining the political control of the economy during the period 1900–1916. One way would be to examine the effects of legislation insofar as it aided or hurt industries irrespective of those industries' attitude toward a measure when it was first proposed. The other approach is to examine the extent to which business advocated some measure before it was enacted and the nature of the final law. Both procedures will be used in this study. The second is the more significant, however, since it points up the needs and nature of the economy and focuses more clearly on the disparity between the conventional interpretation of progressivism and the informal realities. Moreover, it illustrates the fact that many key businessmen articulated a conscious policy favoring the intervention of the national government into the economy. Because of such a policy there was a consensus on key legislation regulating business that has been overlooked by historians. Important businessmen did not, on the whole, regard politics as a necessary evil, but as an important part of their larger position in society. Because of their positive theory of the state, key business elements managed to define the basic form and content of the major federal legislation that was enacted. They provided direction to existing opinion for regulation, but in a number of crucial cases they were the first to initiate that sentiment. They were able to define such sentiment because, in the last analysis, the major political leaders of the Progressive Era—Roosevelt, Taft, and Wilson—were sufficiently conservative to respond to their initiatives.

Although the main view in the business community was for a rationalization of the conditions of the economy through political means, advocates of such intervention, the J. P. Morgan interests being the most notable, were occasionally prepared to exploit the government in an irregular manner that was advantageous as well. The desire for a larger industrial stability did not exclude an occasional foray into government property or the utilization of the government to sanction a business arrangement of questionable legality. Such side actions, however, did not alter the basic pattern. In addition, business advocacy of *federal* regulation was motivated by more than a desire to stabilize industries that had moved beyond state boundaries. The needs of the economy were such, of course, as to demand federal as opposed to random state economic regulation. But a crucial factor was the bulwark which essentially conservative national regulation provided against state regulations that were either haphazard or, what is more important, far more responsible to more radical, genuinely progressive local communities. National progressivism, then, becomes the defense of business against the democratic ferment that was nascent in the states.

Federal economic regulation took two crucial forms. The first was a series of informal détentes and agreements between various businesses and the federal government, a means especially favored by Theodore Roosevelt. The second and more significant approach was outright regulation and the creation of administrative commissions intended to maintain continuous supervision over phases of the economy. We shall examine both forms from the viewpoint of their origins, intent, and consequences; we shall examine, too, a number of movements for regulation that failed to find legislative fulfilment of any sort but that provide insight into the problems and needs of the economy in the Progressive Era.

If business did not always obtain its legislative ends in the precise shape it wanted them, its goals and means were nevertheless clear. In the long run, key business leaders realized, they had no vested interest in a chaotic industry and economy in which not only their profits but their very existence might be challenged.

The questions of whether industrialism imposes narrow limits on the economic and political organization of a society, or on the freedom of men to alter the status quo in some decisive way, have been relatively settled ones for the large majority of social scientists. Max Weber, perhaps more than any social theorist of the past century, articulated a comprehensive framework which has profoundly influenced Western social science to answer such questions in the positive. The bureaucratic nature of the modern state and of modern industry, to Weber, restricted all possibilities for changing the basic structure of modern society. The tendency toward centralization in politics and industry, toward a mechanical impersonality designed to maximize efficiency, seemed to Weber to be the dominant theme in Western society, and the Weberian analysis has sunk deep roots into academic discussions of the problem. The systematic economics of Karl Marx—as opposed to that of "Marxists"—also sustained the argument that the basic trend in capitalist development was toward the centralization of industry. Indeed, such centralization was an indispensable aspect of Western industrialism and could not be circumvented. Both Marx and Weber, one an opponent of capitalism and the other indifferent to it, suggested that industrialism and capitalism, as they saw both develop, were part of the unalterable march of history.

•   •   •

My argument is that neither of the two men, for all their sensitivity and insight, offered much that is of value to understanding the development of capitalism and industrialism in the United States. Indeed, the American experience, I shall try to contend, offers much to disprove the formal theories of probably the two greatest social theorists of the past century. It is perhaps unfair to Marx, who based his case on the conditions existing in England and Western Europe in the mid-nineteenth century, to burden him with American history at the beginning of the twentieth, but he was not terribly modest about its applicability, and any respectable theory should have the predictive value its author ascribes to it. Weber, on the other hand, frequently stated that the United States was the prime example of modern capitalism in the twentieth century, if not the best proof of his theory.

American historians, with some notable exceptions, have tended, without relying on comprehensive theoretical systems of the Weberian or Marxist variety, also to regard the development of the economy as largely an impersonal, inevitable phenomenon. All too frequently they have assumed that concentration and the elimination of competition—business giantism or monopoly—was the dominant tendency in the economy. The relationship between the growth of new competition and new centers of economic power and the legislative enactments of the Progressive Era has been virtually ignored. On the contrary, federal legislation to most historians has appeared to be a reaction against the power of the giant monopoly, or a negative response to the very process of industrialism itself by a threatened middle-class being uprooted from its secure world by corporate capitalism. A centralized economy, historians have asserted, required a centralized federal power to prevent it from damaging the public interest, and the conventional political image of the Progressive Era is of the federal government as a neutral, if not humane, shield between the public and the Morgans, Rockefellers, and Harrimans. Progressivism has been portrayed as essentially a middle-class defense against the status pretensions of the new industrialists, a defense of human values against acquisitive habits, a reassertion of the older tradition of rural individualism.

Recent historians have, for the most part, assumed monopoly was an economic reality concomitant with maximum efficiency even where, as I shall show, it was little more than a political slogan. For it is one thing to say that there was a growth of vast accumulations of corporate power, quite another to claim that there existed a largely monopolistic control over the various economic sectors. Power may be concentrated, as it was, but the extent of that concentration is crucial. Historians of the period have too often confused the power of corporate concentration with total monopoly. The distinction is not merely important to American economic history, it is vital for the understanding of the political history of the period. And to the extent that historians have accepted the consensus among contemporaries as to the inevitable growth of monopoly at the turn of the century, they have failed to appreciate the dynamic interrelationship between politics and economics in the Progressive Era.

I shall be accused of oversimplifying what historians have written about the Progressive Era, and with some justice. But I believe it can be stated that although there are important and significant monographic works or histories of specific phases of progressivism which provide evidence to disprove aspects of such a comprehensive interpretation, no other theory of the nature of the Progressive Era has, in fact, yet been offered. And even most of the critical historians have accepted the traditional view of progressivism as a whole. No synthesis of the specific studies disproving what is, for better or worse, the conventionally accepted interpretation among historians of the Progressive Period has been attempted. Nor has there really been a serious effort to re-examine the structural conditions and problems of the economy during the period and to relate them to the political and especially the detailed legislative history of the era. And it is here, more than any other place, that a new synthesis and a new interpretation are required.

Yet the exceptional historical works that have raised doubts about specific phases of the larger image of progressivism are suggestive in that they indicate that the time for reinterpreting the Progressive Era and the nature, character, and purpose of progressivism, is opportune. The work of the Handlins, Louis Hartz, and Carter Goodrich, to name only a few, in showing the *dependence* of business on politics for government aid and support until the Civil War, suggests that the unity of business and politics was still a relatively fresh memory by the end of the nineteenth century. Sidney Fine has pointed out how many businessmen treated laissez faire and Social Darwinian doctrine gingerly when it was to their interest to have the government aid them. William Miller has shown that the background and origins, and hence the status, of the triumphant industrialists were respectable and at least well-to-do, implicitly raising questions about the status conflict between the allegedly old élite and the new. John Morton Blum has expressed doubts as to the radicalism of Theodore Roosevelt, whom he has portrayed as a progressive conservative, but ultimately a conservative. And, perhaps more than anyone else, Arthur S. Link has critically dissected the history of the Wilson Administration in a manner that forces the historian to doubt whether the conventional usage of the term "progressive" really describes the New Freedom.

Although other monographs and studies can be cited, there are still too many loose ends in the traditional view of the Progressive Period, and no synthesis. More important, there has been no effort to study the entire period as an integrated whole. The very best work, such as Link's, deals with presidential periods, but the movements for legislative enactments ran through nearly all the administrations and can only be really understood in that context. For without such a comprehensive view, the origins and motives behind the legislative components of the Progressive Period cannot be fully comprehended, assuming that there is some correlation between intentions or purposes and results. And although historians have increasingly been puzzled by the growing incompatibility of the specific studies with the larger interpretation, they have not been able to reconcile or explain the disparities. The Progressive Era has been treated as a series of episodes, unrelated to one another in some integrated manner, with growing enigmas as the quantity of new research into the period increases. The Progressive Party was one incident, the Food and Drug Act another, the conservation movement yet one more event.

In this study I shall attempt to treat the Progressive Era as an interrelated and, I hope, explicable whole, set in the context of the nature and tendencies of the economy.

•   •   •

Progressives and the Business Culture of the 1920s

PAUL W. GLAD

I find this article perfectly insipid and useless

Professor Gabriel Kolko's provocative account of the "triumph of conservatism" is not likely to persuade a majority of historians in the near future—though it does have a considerable appeal to younger historians who are committed to various versions of the "new" radicalism. But his is only one of many streams of reinterpretation that are forcing a new look at the 1920s. In the following essay on the survivals of progressivism in the "business culture" of the decade after World War I, Professor Paul W. Glad follows some of these leads. Instead of assuming that progressivism "died" and then trying to perform an historical autopsy, he assumes that it survived and attempts to map out the kinds of choices that were available to men still bound to a progressive stance.

Professor Glad's conclusion is that because of the political defeats of the 1920s, progressivism as a political movement was fragmented, but it still remained a vital force in other ways and channelled men into a variety of new tactical options, such as attempting to find progressive values in the "business culture" itself, organize "independent" voters, regain control of one of the major parties, or foster third-party politics. All these activities amounted, according to him, to more than mere gestures of persistence. They constituted a decade of a "process of renewal" for progressivism.

Paul W. Glad is a specialist in the political history of the early twentieth century, and is especially expert on the political career of William Jennings Bryan. He is Professor of History at the University of Wisconsin. His most important book is The Trumpet Soundeth: William Jennings Bryan and His Democracy, 1896–1912 *(1960). He is also the editor of* William Jennings Bryan: A Profile *(1968), and* The Dissonance of Change, 1929 to Present *(1970).*

The decade of the 1920s—the era of Red Grange, Jack Dempsey, and the Babe—was a decade of contests. Flagpole sitters vied with one another. Marathon dancers stumbled about in agonizing competition. Thousands of Americans, some of them sincerely interested in the cause of world tranquillity, drafted elaborate essays in contending for the Bok Peace Prize. In January 1924 journalist William Hard announced still another contest. Writing in the *Nation* he informed his readers that "I herewith offer a lock of Senator [Henrik] Shipstead's hair to the person who will provide the best and most useful answer to the question: 'What is "progressivism"?' "[1]

Men and women who responded to Hard's query doubtless experienced greater difficulty in coming up with an answer than they would have had a decade earlier. Those who identified themselves as progressives were, as a group, much less confident of their position in 1924 than they had been in the period before the war. Nevertheless the question touched off a lively discussion (in which one contestant demanded Senator Reed Smoot's scalp instead of Shipstead's hair)[2] and that discussion in a rough way suggested most of the possible approaches to an analysis of progressivism.

Hard himself anticipated and rejected one approach. He refused to consider any attempt to classify progressive individuals and blocs or to define progressivism in terms of specific proposals or specific legislation. In explaining why he thought an emphasis on individuals and programs inadmissible, he pointed to members of both houses of Congress who had associated themselves with the progressive cause. Some of them had opposed the veterans' bonus; others had come out in favor of it. Senators William E. Borah and Robert M. La Follette opposed a high tariff,

REPRINTED BY PERMISSION, FROM *Journal of American History*, 53 (JUNE 1966), 75–89.

but Middlewesterners such as Smith W. Brookhart and Lynn J. Frazier were trying to secure a higher tariff on wheat. Senators Borah and Shipstead vigorously opposed bureaucracy; Senator George W. Norris, on the other hand, endorsed large scale government activity in the buying and selling of farm products. Any definition based upon legislation unanimously supported or opposed by progressives would be misleading.

What Hard wanted was a definition that would "lay down the philosophic difference between 'progressivism' and 'conservatism.' " The prize, he insisted, would go to that entry which would "clearly show to every citizen of the United States whether he is a progressive or a conservative." The Baltimore *Evening Sun* contended that a search for such a definition could only result in confusion. Instead of engaging in philosophical speculation, Hard should examine the actual behavior of progressives in real life.³ Representative Henry T. Rainey also took a behaviorist approach when he wrote that "A progressive is a Republican who thinks his district is going Democratic."⁴

Most of those who responded to Hard's question, however, manifestly believed that progressivism rested upon certain fundamentals, whether such fundamentals were derived from the study of economics, history, political theory, ethics, or religion. While definitions did not come easily, a majority of those who regarded themselves as progressives in the 1920s clearly believed that there was such a thing as progressivism and that there was something about progressivism which made it different from the prevailing business culture of the time.

To understand such an attitude, and why participants in Hard's contest had so much trouble in coming up with a satisfactory definition, the historian must first examine the ingredients of progressivism in the prewar period. Then he must turn his attention to how progressivism fared in a time of change. The progressive movement was nothing if not pluralistic, and its very diffuseness should be a warning against a narrow conception of it. The problems which aroused the progressive conscience were broad social, political, and economic problems. Whatever may have been their differences in status and interest, progressives wanted to provide the underprivileged with the means of achieving human dignity. Whatever their differences in political influence and power, progressives wanted to make the institutions of government more responsive to the needs of all citizens. Whatever their differences in occupation and wealth, progressives believed that the nation's economy should serve the public interest. Programs and methods varied, but insofar as anyone shared in these broad aspirations he was to that extent a progressive.⁵

Men who identified themselves as progressives characteristically interlarded their speeches and writings with phrases which gave the movement some of its moral overtones. When Theodore Roosevelt stood at Armageddon in 1912, for example, he battled for the Lord. He offered wise and fearless leadership in "a movement of truth, sincerity, and wisdom." He proposed "to raise aloft a standard to which all honest men can repair." His approach to national problems was one of "understanding and good faith." Primary elections were necessary, he said, because "largely under the influence of special privilege in the business world, there have arisen castes of politicians who do not represent the people, but who make their bread and butter by thwarting the wishes of the people." In demanding the recall of judicial decisions his purpose was to emancipate the courts "from a position where they stand in the way of social justice." Recognizing that "the first charge on industrial statesmanship of the day is to prevent human waste," he wanted to "shape conditions so that a greater number of the small men who are decent, industrious, and energetic shall be able to succeed, and so that the big man who is dishonest shall not be allowed to succeed at all." Progressives, he said, "stand for the rights of the people." The main purpose of the movement was "to place the American people in possession of their birthright, to secure for all the American people unobstructed access to the fountains of measureless prosperity which their creator offers them."[6]

To an important degree, then, the progressive style inhered in the way leaders of the movement talked about themselves and their beliefs. The field of politics has never been without its spreadeagle orators, but progressives had a way of investing grandiloquent phrases with deep significance. Their rhetoric brought catharsis and reassurance. It satisfied their need for a sense of forward motion and their need for a sense of mastery. Progressives wanted to believe that God was in his heaven and that all would be right with the world. Reform rhetoric served still another and perhaps more important function: it provided progressives with a consciousness of unity. Programs might be diffuse and difficult to reconcile. In the first decade of the twentieth century the progressive idiom brought reformers into sympathetic partnership with one another.

Times changed. The disintegration of the Bull Moose party, the shattering impact of World War I, and the triumph of normalcy severely tested the progressives' faith. Throughout the years of change they asked themselves what was going wrong. As early as 1914 Theodore Roosevelt thought that the country had grown "sick and tired" of reform, and he wrote to William Allen White that "the dog returned to its vomit."[7] A year later, Henry J. Allen, White's friend and fellow progressive, predicted "a good many years of standpattism." He believed "that the humanitarian movements that have been thriving during the last fifteen years are going to experience a slump."[8] By 1920 White himself was writing: "What a God damned world! Starvation on the one hand, and indifference on the other, pessimism rampant, faith quiescent, murder met with indifference; the lowered standard of civilization faced with universal complaisance, and the whole story so sad that nobody can tell it."[9]

Nevertheless, the progressives persisted in their efforts to tell the

story of the decline which they felt so keenly. In 1926 editor Paul U.
Kellogg conducted a symposium in the pages of the *Survey*, printing
some twenty-three answers to Frederic C. Howe's famous question:
"What has become of the pre-war radicals?"[10] Newton D. Baker contributed a perceptive analysis to that symposium. In the first place, he
suggested, progressives had achieved many of the things for which they
had contended. In particular he cited the reform of municipal government which he said had made the American city "freer from bossism,
more responsive to popular control and more efficient than it used to
be." Second, Baker argued that some progressive reforms, such as the
initiative, referendum, and recall, had proven less valuable in practice
than their proponents had thought they would be. Third, he blamed
progressives for failing to unite in a common effort during the postwar
period. "When the war was over," wrote Baker, "real liberal cooperation would have captured the future for the world, but every radical
and every liberal, apparently, had his own theory or his own grievance,
and the conservative reaction marched through the liberal ranks, which
were broken into fragments by their own dissensions." Fourth, the war
itself had destroyed both "physical property and faith in human institutions." Finally, "the experience of the Russian people under a degrading
despotism, with radicals in the saddle, [had] tempered the welcome of
radical ideas in other parts of the world."[11]

To Baker's five points Hard added a sixth, which some historians
would consider more important than all the others combined.[12] Hard
confessed that he had once thought that a radical was a person who
wished to prevent the state from "throwing its weight—its coercion—
into the scales in favor of the powerful against the weak." Radicals, he
had believed, wanted to elect "legislators who would not give undue
and excessive tariffs and franchises to manufacturers and investors." They
were men who wanted to choose "executives who would not use their
administrative powers to check the growth of new expression in political
philosophy, in literature, in motion pictures." They were men who hoped
to select "judges who would not use the rod of the injunction to repeal
the constitutional rights of strikers." But Hard had discovered that instead of weakening the power of the state, radicals were "trying to
strengthen the power of the State to enslave the manager and the capitalist." It was a vain attempt. "At Washington," wrote Hard, "we see
bureau after bureau, commission after commission, founded by the
energies of 'radicals' and dominated now—and used against 'radicals'—
by 'reactionaries.' "[13]

Whether or not Hard was correct about the origin of bureaus and
commissions, he saw more clearly than did most of his contemporaries
the crucial relationship between businessmen and reform. While generalizations about businessmen are risky, it is safe to say that in the area
of economic regulation they did much to shape what has traditionally
been regarded as progressive legislation. An important segment of the

business community supported a scientific tariff commission; another cooperated in the development of the Federal Reserve System; still another had a hand in passing the Federal Trade Commission Act and the Clayton Act.[14] During the war crisis, moreover, businessmen entered into the government service as never before, and they received in turn unprecedented support from government agencies. All this did not necessarily mean that businessmen had become progressive, but it did mean that businessmen were to exercise a profound influence on the operations of regulatory commissions and offices in the 1920s. It was this influence which Hard saw and deplored.

If businessmen succeeded in molding progressive programs to their own ends, they also succeeded in adapting progressive rhetoric to their own uses. In 1913, a year after the founding of the Chamber of Commerce of the United States, President Harry A. Wheeler described his organization. It was, he said, "officered by the most virile life of the community, interested not only in the upbuilding of commerce but in the purification of civic life." Such groups, indeed, constituted "but the expression of national progress and prosperity."[15] Even the National Association of Manufacturers employed the idiom; sections of its first platform, drawn up in 1920, read like a progressive tract:

> We have no claim for public consideration, save the nature of the service we render to the social organization. The efficient direction and continuous improvement of the means, conditions and quality of industrial production, is our social obligation. This involves not only the advancement of the art of manufacture, but the progressive development of all its human relations. Without this, industry cannot successfully perform its function nor make its contribution to social welfare.[16]

Politicians also joined the purveyors of progressive rhetoric. Herbert Hoover won a large following among progressives in part because he talked like one of them. But Hoover was not unique in this respect. In 1920 White wrote Warren G. Harding to explain why he was reluctant to support the Republican candidate. Harding replied that he did not believe there was a fundamental difference between the so-called reactionary and the progressive. He assumed that in essentials White was "a red-headed reactionary" while he himself was "a white-haired progressive." The world was in constant motion, and Harding did not expect it to stand still. He had always been a "rational progressive." Then to make his point with what must have seemed to him proof positive he wrote: "My printing office is filled with the latest devices which demand and hand of men have produced for carrying on that business, and I think that fact should be significant to you."[17]

Businessmen and their political allies tended to identify progress with technological development. Charles F. Kettering of General Motors warned that "There are no places where anyone can sit and rest in an industrial situation."[18] Nevertheless before the period of prosperity came to an end, spokesmen for business believed that industrial and commercial advance had brought progress in other areas as well. Merle Thorpe, editor of *Nation's Business,* thought he saw a new era in human relations taking shape in 1928. That new era would come when businessmen developed a "modern 'law merchant' " out of their dealings with one another. It would be a system of equity—as distinguished from legality —and it would be "a contribution to society worthy of the best in American business."[19]

When businessmen assumed control over progressive programs, and when they employed the progressive idiom in articulating their views, advocates of reform saw themselves floundering in disarray. Progressive sentiment had by no means disappeared by the decade of the 1920s; on the contrary, Senator Albert J. Beveridge and others thought it was "increasing by leaps and bounds."[20] But progressives faced the problem of converting that sentiment into an effective political force. Some, such as White and William E. Dodd, professor of history in the University of Chicago, chose to work within the two major parties. Others looked toward the creation of another third party.[21]

The third-party men had begun to discuss possibilities for a new organization of progressives early in 1919, and out of their discussions came the Committee of Forty-Eight.[22] So named because its founders hoped to establish connections in all forty-eight states, the committee took upon itself the task of constructing a new party. It was not an easy task. Labor groups, socialists, the Non-Partisan League, and other dissidents expressed an interest in the committee's activities, thereby compounding the difficulties standing in the way of agreement. Amos Pinchot, a member of the executive committee and one of the principal philosophers of the movement, thought that a proper approach would be "to get up a coalition between all of the groups that are being exploited, declare war against the common enemy and unite upon a short, vigorous platform."[23]

For a time optimism prevailed. "The third party movement is going along fast," wrote Pinchot in April 1920, and he predicted that "a presidential ticket will be put in the field in July." With a good candidate —such a man as Frank Walsh or Frazier—Pinchot looked forward to polling four or five million votes. Of course he did not expect to win in 1920. "That is what makes the situation promising for 1924," he exulted, "for if there were a chance of electing a president this year, the new party would probably find itself breaking its neck to get votes and letting fundamentals slide."[24]

What were those fundamentals which Pinchot thought so important? He and his friend George Record, an adroit politician from New Jersey who also happened to be a disciple of Henry George, carried on long, earnest conversations in the effort to clarify their views and to formulate strategy. In July 1920, when it seemed that La Follette might head up the new party, Pinchot made bold to write to the great Wisconsin progressive. Admitting that he felt "like a sign painter giving Leonardo advice," Pinchot suggested that "the great issue is no longer that of preventing the abuse of power by the privileged class." As he and Record saw it, "the great issue now is to take away the power itself." To accomplish that objective, "we must deprive the privileged class of its present control over transportation and the great natural resources, such as coal, iron ore, oil, etc., which are the raw materials of industry and the sources of energy." Control over transportation and the sources of energy had led to monopoly. With competition stifled the privileged class could fix prices and exploit labor. The short, vigorous platform that Pinchot and Record urged was a platform that called for government ownership and operation of railways and government ownership (with perhaps private operation under a leasing agreement) of natural resources.[25]

Whatever hopes they may have had for such a program in 1920, Pinchot and Record met defeat when the Committee of Forty-Eight held a convention in Chicago together with representatives from farmer and labor organizations. The labor radicals dominated the meetings and formed the Farmer-Labor party, the kind of class party that Pinchot and Record had hoped to avoid. The Pinchot-Record group had sought to abolish privilege through government ownership of transportation and resources. They had never advocated socialism, but socialists had flocked to their committee assuming it represented socialism under another name. "It is obvious," concluded Record in one of the great understatements of the campaign, "that we have never gotten our idea over. . . ."[26] The fiasco at Chicago, commented a writer in the *Nation*, was but a demonstration of the fact that "When a group of liberals set out, with admirable logic and clearly defined propaganda, to collect other liberals, they end up by finding that what they have collected are not liberals at all, but radicals, because the radical happens to be more active, crosser about abuses, and much more easily collectable." He went so far as to doubt that there were any liberals, i.e. progressives, left in America, "with the exception of the clear-thinking and precise expounders of the doctrine of abolition of economic privilege, who are now ensconced in lonely majesty of thought behind the desks at 48 headquarters."[27]

For his part, Pinchot gave up even that sanctuary. He and Record, convinced that the Forty-Eighters were hopeless, resigned from the executive committee. The heart of the problem, grumbled Pinchot, was that "the committee of 48 cannot possibly get anywhere under the leadership of men who don't understand the difference between socialism and individualism and who naturally drift into socialism every time George and I turn our backs."[28] But the two opponents of economic privilege did not give up their ideas. Throughout the decade of the 1920s they carried on a running dialogue which reinforced their basic convictions and left them more than ever committed to their program of restoring competition through government ownership of transportation and resources.[29]

From time to time Pinchot and Record sent out feelers to political leaders testing their readiness to join in the fight against monopoly.[30] The results of such sampling were invariably disappointing. "The Progressive movement in this country is in a most discouraging state," wrote Record to La Follette in 1923. Despite the good showing which progressives had made in the congressional elections of 1922, no one had yet come forward with a fundamental program. The progressives in Congress could not even "agree among themselves on a program of palliatives."[31] When Pinchot talked to Senators Smith W. Brookhart and Borah, he found that "these statesmen (if that is the right term) were not quite ready to throw down the gauntlet to privilege," although they were "heartily in favor of all things in the public interest, especially their own candidacy for the presidency of the United States." Pinchot could only conclude that "we cannot find leadership among those who are in high office" because "the 'ins' have too much to risk." Nevertheless he was "not at all discouraged," he assured his friend, Patrick Henry Callahan, head of the Louisville Varnish Company and one of the versatile operators of the prohibition era. He suggested that if Callahan would ship him "in a blue Standard Oil barrle [sic] a little of your unflagging enthusiasm and courage, we will be better than new."[32]

Whatever the contents of that barrel may have done to bolster his spirits, Pinchot continued to search in vain for a leader who would take up his cause. La Follette, himself, failed the Pinchot-Record group. During the campaign of 1924 Pinchot urged the Progressive candidate to show the people "not only that they are ruled by plutocracy, not only how they are ruled by plutocracy, not only what things give plutocracy the power to rule us, but also, how we can take the power-giving things away from plutocracy and restore power to the public."[33] La Follette did emphasize that the great issue was monopoly control of both government and industry, but not until just before election day did he outline a plan for dealing with monopoly. Pinchot saw a parallel between the Progressive campaign of 1924 and the Progressive campaign of 1912: like Theodore Roosevelt, La Follette in effect said to the voters, "I don't know how I am going to do the job, but put me in and I'll show you." To Pinchot the campaign was "a discouraging reminder that T. R. and La Follette were not out primarily to do the big job but to get in."[34]

Once more Record and Pinchot returned to the task of refining their views. At the close of the era of prosperity they were whistling essentially the same tune they had piped at the beginning of the decade. That few progressives, to say nothing of Americans in general, listened to their song is beside the point. More important, the Pinchot-Record criticism revealed the discord within the progressive chorus. Musical metaphors aside, businessmen had cooperated with the agencies of economic regulation and they had appropriated progressive rhetoric. They had, in consequence, forced those who were dissatisfied with babbitt progressivism to examine their own ideas and to articulate them precisely. As the Pinchot-Record experience suggests, however, precise articulation of ideas did not produce the unity which was essential if progressives were to achieve effective political organization.

An alternative to creating an independent third party was available. Having formulated his response to the business culture of the 1920s, a progressive might also choose to work within one of the two established parties. Yet those who attempted to use either the Democratic or the Republican party as a vehicle for progressive reform fared little better than Pinchot and Record. Franklin D. Roosevelt provides a case in point. Attempting to rally Democrats around some liberal statement of principles, he failed repeatedly in his efforts to build a progressive coalition. Not until the era of prosperity had passed did he succeed.[35]

Less conspicuous than the labors of Roosevelt were those of Dodd, who also sought a formula for progressive unity. An admirer of Woodrow Wilson and one of the most important of Wilson's early apologists, the professor recognized the Democratic party for what it was, "a curious combination of progressiveness and reaction." Nevertheless in 1920 he predicted that if the Democrats did not recapture the presidency "we shall go straight to an industrial imperialism that for actual power will make the Germans of 1914 look like thirty cents."[36] The hope of the country, he believed, rested in the agrarian South and West—sections which the Democratic party could control.

Adhering to his agrarian convictions as the years passed, Dodd thought he saw a new American feudalism taking shape. Wilson had been destroyed at Paris by attacks from home, and Wilsonian progressivism had given way "to a new regime that would save business if nothing else." When farmers sought to reverse the trend toward oblivion and isolation, "business turned upon them with anger and fear." Would American farmers become peasants? Many of them already had, said Dodd, "peasantry, an American peasantry already jeered at all over the country as morons and yokels . . . dirty, ill clad men and women, millions of them producing the foodstuffs for the great country of Washington and Jefferson." But if farmers became peasants, city-dwellers could hardly escape a similar fate. As Dodd read his history it offered both a warning and a remonstrance. This was not the time for "complacent big-city politics"; it was not the time for "empty heads in high office with mere vetoes for their weapons. Is it peasantry for the farmers and feudalism in the world of industry and business?" Dodd asked. "Southern men and western leaders might well take stock of their resources and seek a new deal in the politics of the time."[37]

Taking a discriminating look at the prominent men of both parties who might unite West and South in agrarian partnership against an expanding business civilization, Dodd was ready to break with his party if a sectional alliance could be effected.[38] But not many of Dodd's friends thought such an alliance possible. "Can farmers and workingmen do anything in the presence of the steel helmeted giant of modern business?" asked Charles A. Beard. "I have my doubts, alas!"[39] And Josephus Daniels wrote that the country had become urban-minded: "the trend of business has been to a great degree towards the cities and city ways so that America has unconsciously been virtually transformed." Only by defeating the Republican party, thought Daniels, could progressives defeat the "big interests."[40]

Confronted with a choice between Hoover and Alfred E. Smith in 1928, Dodd thought that it was "a case of both great parties putting their heads in the sand." That Hoover had betrayed Wilson was bad enough. Even worse were his "stupid speeches about the tariff" and his department's assistance to "all the big trusts."[41] And Dodd thought that Smith knew "little of the old America." The Democratic candidate was "tied to a great church, which may or may not rule him" and was "the favorite of Tammany Hall, which may or may not guide him."[42] Charging that the policies of the last few years had concentrated wealth, built enormous cities, and disrupted "the old American life," the professor escaped to Europe at the height of the campaign.[43]

While Smith attracted widespread support from liberal groups, Dodd was not the only progressive to deplore his candidacy. White also viewed the New Yorker as a threat to American ideals. The product of a city "maggot-eaten with saloons" in the days of his youth, Smith had gained political prominence under the aegis of a vicious political machine and he had acquired the Tammany mind.[44] As much as White agreed with Dodd about Tammany Hall and its candidate, however, the Kansas editor saw Smith's opponent in an entirely different light: Hoover symbolized the ultimate triumph of the progressive cause. As early as 1920 White had thought that Hoover was moving in a liberal direction.[45] By 1927 he regarded the secretary of commerce as the only man in the cabinet who had "an acute and practical knowledge of what the Wall Street fellows are trying to put over." More than any other one man, Hoover had "tried earnestly and sincerely and all the time to checkmate the Wall Street crowd."[46]

Yet White was less troubled about business influences in American life than were some other progressives. He refused to join Pinchot's fight against monopoly, for he disliked forcing the issue of public ownership.[47] Not that the American economic system was perfect. It had obvious faults, but White did not believe "that you can take away the profit motive from American industry and make it work at all." In a generation or two, perhaps, the system would deal fairly with all men.[48]

During the 1920s, then, White overcame whatever antagonism he might have felt toward the business culture that dominated the period. Strongly influenced by Harvard economist Thomas Nixon Carver, he began to think that a new reign of virtue had already begun. After all, prosperity carried within itself "the germs of social justice."[49] If business-men had labored to combine the progressive mystique with programs that would benefit business, White worked hard to combine the busi-ness mystique with progressivism. When he was finished he had pro-duced a strong case for Hoover's election. Hoover, he explained to a skeptical Harold L. Ickes, believed in prosperity because out of pros-perity would come "that just and equitable relation between labor and capital which will permit a larger distribution of the rewards of industry to labor." Beyond this, the Sage of Emporia was convinced that Hoover would realize "a spiritual gain out of this material thing we call pros-perity."[50] Progressive goals would be achieved automatically in a prosper-ous society. Through such rationalization the progressivism of White survived a period of doubt and uncertainty.

Different as they were in their points of view—and divergent as they were in the causes they espoused—Pinchot and Record, Dodd and White all pasted the progressive label on their ideas and their activities. Nor were theirs the only ideas and activities that bore the label in the 1920s. That Hard never received the definition he called for in 1924 should hardly surprise anyone. Perhaps part of the difficulty confronting those who try to analyze progressivism lies in the temptation to search for ideological, or class, or behavioral unity among progressives. Unity of some sort is necessary for partisan political action, and progressives of the 1920s never reached sufficient agreement to assure either the success of an independent third party or the control of a major party. Yet, as Herbert Croly astutely observed in 1928, progressives were "not obliged to identify the welfare of their ideal with the fortunes of one political party." Progressivism, he argued, was not necessarily political in its methods. Its future depended less upon the capture of political power than it did upon the energy, capability, and open-mindedness with which progressives sought to improve economic and social processes. As inde-pendent voters they could exert pressure on all parties without com-mitting themselves irrevocably to any.[51] Croly recognized that progres-sivism had disintegrated as a movement or series of movements. It had not disappeared, however, for it had passed back into the hands of individual reformers. Progressivism had, in other words, returned to the source of its vitality, and the process of renewal had only begun when Black Thursday signalled the arrival of the Great Depression.

Notes

1. William Hard, "What is Progressivism?" *Nation*, CXVIII (Jan. 9, 1924), 27.
2. *Nation*, CXVIII (Feb. 13, 1924), 160.
3. *Ibid.*
4. *Ibid.*, 161.
5. Robert H. Wiebe, *Businessmen and Reform* (Cambridge, 1962), 211.
6. Theodore Roosevelt, "A Confession of Faith," address before the national con-vention of the Progressive party, Chicago, Aug. 6, 1912, reproduced in Herman Hage-

dorn, ed., *The Works of Theodore Roosevelt* (20 vols., New York, 1926), XVII, 254, 256, 260, 264, 266, 277, 287.

7. Roosevelt to White, Nov. 7, 1914, William Allen White Papers (Manuscript Division, Library of Congress).

8. Allen to White, Oct. 14, 1915, *ibid.*

9. White to Ray Stannard Baker, Dec. 28, 1920, *ibid.* Hundreds of similar statements from progressives could be added. See George W. Anderson to Baker, Oct. 19, 1920; John S. Phillips to Baker, Dec. 20, 1920; Walter Lippmann to Newton D. Baker, Aug. 12, 1921, Newton D. Baker Papers (Manuscript Division, Library of Congress); Albert J. Beveridge to A. E. Van Valkenburg, June 16, 1916; Beveridge to George H. Lorimer, June 24, 1916; Beveridge to William Fortune, Aug. 6, 1920, Albert J. Beveridge Papers (Manuscript Division, Library of Congress); Hiram W. Johnson to William Jennings Bryan, Sept. 14, 1920, William Jennings Bryan Papers (Manuscript Division, Library of Congress); William E. Dodd to [Claude?] Kitchin, Jan. 27, 1918 (not sent); James Franklin Jameson to Dodd, May 12, 1920; Carl Becker to Dodd, June 17, 1920, William E. Dodd Papers (Manuscript Division, Library of Congress).

10. "Where Are the Pre-War Radicals?" *Survey*, LV (Feb. 1, 1926), 556–66; Frederic C. Howe, *The Confessions of a Reformer* (New York, 1925), 195.

11. "Where Are the Pre-War Radicals?" 556–57.

12. An extended treatment of the point which Hard made may be found in Gabriel Kolko, *The Triumph of Conservatism: A Reinterpretation of American History, 1900–1916* (New York, 1963).

13. "Where Are the Pre-War Radicals?" 559.

14. Kolko, *Triumph of Conservatism*, 242–47, 257–67; Wiebe, *Businessmen and Reform*, 129–41, 147–49; Harry A. Wheeler, "Fair Play and the National Spirit," *Nation's Business*, I (Aug. 15, 1913), 5–6. Samuel P. Hays has shown that businessmen were active on a local level as well as on a national level. Hays, "Politics of Reform in Municipal Government in the Progressive Era," *Pacific Northwest Quarterly*, 55 (Oct. 1964), 157–69. See also "Achievements of Commercial Organizations," *Nation's Business*, III (Jan. 15, 1914), 10.

15. Wheeler, "Fair Play and the National Spirit," 5.

16. Leaflet, "National Association of Manufacturers Platform for American Industry, Adopted in Convention, New York, May 18, 1920," pp. 1–3. How businessmen developed the idea of progress has been discussed in James Warren Prothro, *The Dollar Decade* (Baton Rouge, 1954), 43, 86–87.

17. Harding to White, Aug. 12, 1920, White Papers.

18. Charles F. Kettering, "Keep the Consumer Dissatisfied," *Nation's Business*, XVII (Jan. 1929), 31.

19. Merle Thorpe, "Out of Industry—Justice," *Nation's Business*, XVI (May 1928), 9.

20. Beveridge to George B. Baker, May 4, 1920; J. Edward Cassidy to Beveridge, May 4, 1922, Beveridge Papers; Charles W. Bryan to William Jennings Bryan, Nov. 28, 1922; William Jennings Bryan to Jonathan M. Davis, March 5, 1924, Bryan Papers; Claude Bowers to Dodd, July 30, 1926, Dodd Papers; William S. Culbertson to White, Nov. 17, 1922, Sept. 4, 1923; White to Beveridge, Nov. 25, 1922; White to Sheffield Ingalls, Aug. 4, 1924; Charles M. Sheldon to White, July 9, 1926. White Papers; George Henry Payne, "Where Shall the Progressives Go?" *Forum*, LXXII (July 1924), 110–13.

21. George L. Record to Gifford Pinchot, April 21, 1919, Amos Pinchot Papers (Manuscript Division, Library of Congress).

22. J. A. H. Hopkins to Amos Pinchot, Feb. 4, 15, 1919, *ibid.*; Nathan Fine, *Labor and Farmer Parties in the United States, 1828–1928* (New York, 1928), 363–64, 389–94; Kenneth Campbell MacKay, *The Progressive Movement of 1924* (New York, 1947), 54–60.

23. Amos Pinchot to James H. Maurer, March 23, 1920, Pinchot Papers.

24. Pinchot to Francis J. Heney, April 26, 1920, *ibid.*

25. Pinchot to Robert La Follette, June 25, 1920, *ibid.* See also Pinchot to James H. Maurer, Feb. 4, 1920; Pinchot to Henry Delbarre, June 28, 1920, *ibid.*

26. Record to Pinchot, Aug. 27, 1920, *ibid.*; Allen McCurdy, "The Forty-Eighters' Position," *Nation*, CXI (July 31, 1920), 126–27.

27. Swinburne Hale, "What Has Happened to the Forty-eighters?" *Nation*, CXI (Aug. 28, 1920), 243.

28. Pinchot to A. W. Ricker, Jan. 21, 1921, Pinchot Papers. See also Pinchot to

Lincoln Steffens, Oct. 6, 1920; J. A. H. Hopkins to Pinchot, Nov. 20, 1920; Pinchot to Hopkins, Nov. 26, 1920; Record to Hopkins, Dec. 2, 1920; Arthur Wray to Pinchot, Dec. 10, 1920; A. W. Ricker to Record, Dec. 16, 1920, *ibid.*

29. Record to Pinchot, Feb. 16, 1928; Pinchot to Robert F. Wagner, May 30, 1930; Record, undated memorandum sent to Pinchot, Nov. 22, 1928, *ibid.*

30. Record to Pinchot, Sept. 7, 1921; Pinchot to La Follette, April 5, 1922; Pinchot to Grenville S. MacFarland, Feb. 14, March 19, 1923; Pinchot to William Randolph Hearst, June 12, 1923; Hopkins to Pinchot, June 14, 1923; Pinchot to Augustus O. Stanley, Victor Murdock, Henry McCracken, Royal Meeker, John Dewey, E. P. Costigan, and White, June 16, 1923, *ibid.*

31. Record to Robert La Follette, March 26, 1923, *ibid.*

32. Pinchot to Callahan, April 10, 1923, *ibid.*

33. Pinchot to La Follette, June 28, 1924, *ibid.*

34. Pinchot to Gilson Gardner, Nov. 26, 1924, *ibid.*

35. Frank Freidel, *Franklin D. Roosevelt: The Ordeal* (Boston, 1954), 199–228. Arthur Link has pointed out to the author that Woodrow Wilson, Louis D. Brandeis, and others also sought to work out a statement of principles early in the decade.

36. Dodd to Newton D. Baker, April 28, 1920, Dodd Papers.

37. Dodd to A. M. Loomis, March 6, 1926; Baccalaureate address delivered at George Peabody College, Nashville, Tennessee, June 7, 1927, *ibid.* See also William E. Dodd, "Shall Our Farmers Become Peasants," *Century Magazine*, 116 (May 1928), 30–44.

38. Dodd to Angus McLean, July 14, 1926; Dodd to Frank O. Lowden, May 7, Oct. 16, 1927; Dodd to Thomas J. Walsh, Aug. 4, 1927; Dodd to Daniel C. Roper, July 21, 1927; Dodd to Hugh MacRae, Aug. 4, 1927, Dodd Papers.

39. Beard to Dodd, May 12, 1928, *ibid.*

40. Daniels to Dodd, April 30, 1928, *ibid.*

41. Dodd to Herman H. Horn, June 26, 1928, *ibid.*

42. Dodd to Daniel C. Roper, June 5, 1928, *ibid.*

43. Dodd to Frank O. Lowden, Aug. 14, 1928, *ibid.*

44. Ms. of a speech by White at Independence, Kansas, Oct. 19, 1928, White Papers. See also White to Franklin D. Roosevelt, Feb. 11, 1928; White to James L. Murray, July 17, 1928; White to Hubert Work, July 19, 1928; White to John A. Ryan, July 20, 1928; White to Henry J. Allen, July 21, 1928; White to J. C. Rochester, Oct. 18, 1928; White to Julian S. Mason, Nov. 13, 1928, *ibid.*; *Nation*, CXXVII (Aug. 15, 1928), 148; Gordon Russell, "The Demise of a Progressive: William Allen White, 1920–1928" (Master's thesis, University of Maryland, 1964), 126–55.

45. White to Gifford Pinchot, Dec. 3, 1920, White Papers.

46. White to Rodney Elward, July 14, 1927, *ibid.*

47. White to Amos Pinchot, June 20, 1923, *ibid.*

48. White to Laurence Todd, Nov. 26, 1927, *ibid.*

49. Thomas Nixon Carver to White, [March or April?] 1928; Carver to White, May 14, 1928; White to Carver, May 18, 1928; White to Borah, May 2, 1928; White to Hoover, May 2, 1928, *ibid.* See also Thomas Nixon Carver, *The Present Economic Revolution in the United States* (Boston, 1925); Carver, *This Economic World and How It May Be Improved* (Chicago, 1928), esp. 70–109 of the latter work.

50. White to Ickes, Nov. 23, 1928, White Papers.

51. Herbert Croly, "The Progressive Voter: He Wants to Know!" *New Republic*, LV (July 25, 1928), 243, 246. See also George W. Norris to Oswald Garrison Villard, June 19, 1928; Norris to John Dewey, Dec. 27, 1930, George W. Norris Papers (Manuscript Division, Library of Congress).

PART II
The World and the War

Progressivism and Imperialism:
The Progressive Movement and
American Foreign Policy,
1898–1916

WILLIAM E. LEUCHTENBURG

The twin themes suggested by recent studies of progressivism are, first, that progressivism was not nearly so liberal, democratic, and anti-corporate as many of its participants and most of its early historians had believed; and, second, that the break between the prewar and postwar decades was not nearly so sharp and clean as had been supposed. If these twin arguments are valid, then they must somehow cover not only domestic events and policies, but also American foreign policy between 1900 and 1929.

Before the new interpretations can stand securely, three related points must be established: that progressives were committed to a foreign policy of jingoist expansion that undercut their claim to be called humanitarian liberals; that progressives viewed World War I not as a challenge to their labors, but as an *opportunity* of one sort or another; and that the same policies of expansionism that characterized the progressive period continued to control diplomacy during the 1920s. In the following essay, Professor William E. Leuchtenburg takes up the first of these points and argues convincingly that "the Progressives . . . ardently supported the imperialist surge."

William E. Leuchtenburg, Professor of History at Columbia University, is a leading student of twentieth-century politics and of the "New Deal" period in particular. Professor Leuchtenburg's published books include The Perils of Prosperity 1914–1932 *(1958),* Franklin D. Roosevelt and the New Deal *(1963), and* Franklin D. Roosevelt: a Profile *(1967). He has also published an extremely interesting essay that bears on the present subject, entitled "The New Deal and the Analogue of War,"* in Change and Continuity in Twentieth-Century America *(1964).*

*No distinction is more revered by the American historian than that be-*tween domestic and foreign affairs, and in few periods of our history has that distinction been more religiously observed than in the Progressive era. The Theodore Roosevelt who fought the trusts, defied the special interests, and stood at Armageddon to battle for the Lord and the Theodore Roosevelt who preached jingoism and "took" Panama have been divorced on grounds of incompatibility.[1]

The leaders of the Progressive movement, we are given to understand, welcomed Roosevelt's aid in fighting the railway kings and the coal barons, but dissented vigorously from his imperialism and chauvinism. The Progressives were deeply disturbed by Roosevelt's racism, and even more by such episodes as the acquisition of the Canal Zone, but accepted his leadership because of his avowed hostility to corporation control of American life. George Norris' biographer represents the prevailing attitude in asserting that "Western progressives . . . had never adhered to the big-stick doctrines of Roosevelt."[2]

The thesis of this article is that the Progressives, contrary to the orthodox accounts, did not oppose imperialism but, with few exceptions, ardently supported the imperialist surge or, at the very least, proved agreeably acquiescent. The majority of the Progressive members of Congress voted for increased naval expenditures and for Caribbean adventures in imperialism. At no time did the Republican insurgents in the Taft administration take issue with Dollar Diplomacy, even when the Progressives were searching for campaign issues in 1912. Not until after the 1912 elections did they concern themselves actively with foreign affairs, and then it was not to combat imperialism but to urge the use of American force in Mexico and an increase in armaments. By 1916

REPRINTED BY PERMISSION, FROM *Mississippi Valley Historical Review*, 39 (DECEMBER 1952), 483–504.

the Progressive party had forsaken its program of domestic reform to condemn the foreign policy of the Wilson administration, and a fondness for a "strong" foreign policy was an important cause of the death of the party. Moreover, the ideological content and the motivation of imperialism and progressivism had much in common, a relationship made explicit in the writings of Herbert Croly.

Senator Albert J. Beveridge of Indiana epitomized the two interlocking forces, although his imperialistic views were unquestionably more fervently held than those of the average Progressive. One of the most eloquent orators of the period, he made the keynote speech at the Progressive convention of 1912 in Chicago. Beveridge's fame as an orator started with his declamatory avowal of American imperialism in the Spanish-American War, and he maintained this enthusiasm for imperialism throughout the Progressive era. "The opposition tells us we ought not to rule a people without their consent. I answer, the rule of liberty, that all just governments derive their authority from the consent of the governed, applies only to those who are capable of self-government," he told an enthusiastic Indianapolis meeting in 1898.

> The proposition of the opposition makes the Declaration of Independence preposterous, like the reading of Job's lamentations would be at a wedding, or an Altgeld speech on the Fourth of July. . . . Cuba not contiguous? Porto Rico not contiguous? The Philippines not contiguous? Our navy will make them contiguous! . . . Dewey and Sampson and Schley have made them contiguous, and American speed, American guns, American heart and brain and nerve will keep them contiguous forever.[3]

No member of the Senate in the first decade of this century contributed more to the Progressive movement than Senator Beveridge. He sponsored the bill for federal meat inspection and carried the fight against the bitter opposition of the slaughterhouses. He fought a long, courageous, abortive campaign to end child labor in America. In the 1910 campaign in Indiana he urged federal control of railways, the eight-hour day, and the regulation of trust capitalization. It was Beveridge who managed the insurgent revolt against the Payne-Aldrich tariff. He walked out of the Republican party with the Progressives in 1912, and he fought against the drift toward reconciliation after the election, even accepting the hopeless assignment of Progressive candidate for the Senate in 1914.

Yet his faith in America's imperialist mission continued to be just as strong as his belief in economic reform, and Beveridge's imperialism ultimately proved his undoing as a Progressive. Many of the reforms dearest to Beveridge, which the Republican party had opposed and Roosevelt had shunned, were pushed through Congress by Woodrow Wilson, and Beveridge could have little quarrel with the President's domestic program, but by 1914 he was bitterly opposed to him. Wilson should have recognized Huerta, for Mexico needed a strong man, and the repeal of the Panama tolls was a "fatal blunder." "The Progressive Party in Congress will be solid against the repeal."[4] In 1916 he lashed into Wilson for refusing to use arms to support American investments in China, for his proposal to withdraw from the Philippines, and, strangely, for not increasing the tariff to meet new European competition. Beveridge, faced with the necessity to choose between progressivism and imperialism for the first time, chose the latter. By 1920 he was crying out against " 'Organized labor's assault on American institutions!' " interspersing speeches against the League of Nations with demands for the repeal of the excess profits tax. Inflation was caused by the draining of money to Europe through foreign propaganda and the unreasonable demands of labor unions for higher wages.[5] Once more Beveridge's views on domestic and foreign policy had merged, and this new outlook persisted until his death.

At the outbreak of the Spanish-American War few men saw any conflict between social reform and democratic striving at home and the new imperialist mission; indeed, the war seemed nothing so much as an extension of democracy to new parts of the world, and few political figures exceeded the enthusiasm of William Jennings Bryan for the Spanish War.[6] As the war continued and its consequences were realized, as the dream of *Cuba libre* gave way to the realities of Aguinaldo's insurrection, a few of the Progressives, like Hazen Pingree and Jane Addams, joined the anti-imperialist forces, but, first and last, it was the conservatives who bore the burden of the anti-imperialist campaign.

In late March, 1899, William Allen White explained the Emporia *Gazette's* support of the war. "Only Anglo-Saxons can govern themselves. . . . It is the Anglo-Saxon's manifest destiny to go forth as a world conqueror,"[7] he observed. Years later he wrote of this time:

> And we in Emporia, and "Our Charley" in Washington, thought we were free to spout and jower and jangle about the atrocities of the "brute Weyler" without in the slightest affecting the reality of our lives. We were as little boys making snoots across the fence, throwing rocks into the next yard, but innocent of the fact that we were starting wars that would last far into the next century, threaten all that we loved and wreck much that we cherished.[8]

"Though I hate war *per se,*" wrote Elizabeth Cady Stanton, "I am glad that it has come in this instance. I would like to see Spain . . . swept from the face of the earth."[9]

A few of the Progressives, and many of the older generation of radicals like Henry Demarest Lloyd, joined forces with the anti-imperialists, but it was conservative Republicans like Thomas B. Reed, Democrats like Grover Cleveland and Bryan, frequently for partisan ends, businessmen like Andrew Carnegie, and Mugwumps like Carl Schurz who provided the bulk of the leadership. "The Republicans who joined the anti-imperialist movement were, almost without exception, Republicans of the older generation. . . . The anti-imperialists made great efforts to attract labor support, but, on the whole, were unsuccessful."[10] The one important political figure who persistently linked the fight for progressivism with the struggle against imperialism was the ineffective Silver Republican, Senator Richard Pettigrew of South Dakota, and he was retired from office in 1900, partly because of his anti-imperialist views.[11]

Theodore Roosevelt's accession to the presidency brought the new imperialist movement to full flower, and, in all of his foreign ventures, in Santo Domingo, Panama, the Far East, in building a greater American fleet, Roosevelt had the support of a majority of the Progressives. "I confess that the half-hearted criticism I hear of the way of the administration with Panama provokes in me a desire to laugh," Jacob Riis noted. "I am not a jingo; but when some things happen I just have to get up and cheer. The way our modern American diplomacy goes about things is one of them."[12] Gifford Pinchot warmly admired Roosevelt's policy in Panama,[13] while Oscar Straus, the Progressive candidate for governor of New York in 1912, helped prepare the dubious legal defense of Roosevelt's course with Panama, with his concept of a "covenant running with the land." As John Bassett Moore observed cynically to Straus, it was "indifferently, a question of the 'covenant running with the land' or a question of the 'covenant running (*away!*) with the land'!!"[14] When Bryan negotiated a treaty of indemnity and apology with Colombia, the Progressives were outraged. The Colombians, said Senator Joseph L. Bristow heatedly, were "a lot of blackmailers." As for the contention that Roosevelt had acted immorally in Panama, "there could be no greater slander pronounced against the Government and nothing more unjust, and in my opinion it borders on treason."[15] The final word on the Progressive position on Panama was had by George Norris over forty years later, when he ruefully observed:

> Often those years I followed him [Roosevelt] when I had some doubts as to the righteousness of his course. . . . Yet he built the Panama Canal after other governments and a great corporation had spent a vast amount of money and had failed in their efforts. He threw his heart into the construction of this waterway, whose long useful service has caused the struggle for it to be forgotten; but during its progress the means by which the Panama Canal was accomplished in some respects seem doubtful to me. *I followed him step by step in that fight.* Doubts assailed me at the time, and I have since reached the conclusion that our government's decision to establish the new republic of Panama, which in reality prevented Colombia from defending her own territory with her army, was open to argument.[16]

The Progressives were scarcely less cooperative in promoting American hegemony in the Caribbean and defending Roosevelt's big stick diplomacy there. On the Platt amendment Senators Beveridge and Jonathan P. Dolliver voted with the majority, and the Silver Republicans, Pettigrew and

Henry M. Teller, cast the only dissenting Republican votes.[17] Roosevelt's action in taking over the customhouse of the Dominican Republic received the approval of Senators Beveridge, Moses E. Clapp, Dolliver, and Robert M. La Follette, with not a single Progressive senator voting against the treaty.[18] By March, 1907, Charles Joseph Bonaparte, who prosecuted the trusts under Roosevelt and was to be a bitter foe of George W. Perkins in 1916, could sound a popular note in praising the President's skill in "promoting the peace of Central America, in staying civil strife in Cuba, in discouraging rebellion in Santo Domingo."[19]

Bonaparte also shared with a great many Progressives Roosevelt's enthusiasm for a big navy, a viewpoint of inestimable advantage for a secretary of the navy. When Roosevelt appointed him to this post in 1905, Bonaparte assured him: "It is perhaps proper to say, in this connection, that I am in hearty sympathy with your frequently expressed views as to the importance and, indeed, necesssity of a very strong and very efficient Navy to the United States."[20] The antinavy bloc in Congress was led not by the Progressives but by the conservative Eugene Hale in the Senate and the conservative Theodore Burton in the House, and their main supporters were likewise conservatives.[21]

The first uprising of the insurgents against Nelson W. Aldrich occurred not over the Payne-Aldrich tariff, but on behalf of Roosevelt's request for four new battleships in 1908 against the outspoken opposition of the Old Guard. Led by Senator Beveridge, two fifths of the Republicans deserted Aldrich in a debate featuring repeated attacks on the leadership of the Old Guard. The debate, which ended in the compromise on two battleships, badly shook Aldrich's domination of the Senate. "The Senate oligarchy is in a bad way," reported the *Saturday Evening Post*. "It is tottery and wobbly at the knees. Its members do not know just what it was that hit them, but they do know that they have been hit hard."[22] On the final vote on the Piles amendment for four battleships, which was defeated 50 to 23, Beveridge, William E. Borah, and Jonathan Bourne voted with the big navy minority against Aldrich, W. Murray Crane, Thomas C. Platt, and other Old Guard leaders. Senator Weldon B. Heyburn expressed the general sentiment of the debate in observing: "I care nothing for the poetic idea of turning swords into plowshares and spears into pruning hooks. This is a business proposition." On this occasion two of the Progressives, Clapp and Joseph M. Dixon, voted against navalism, and Clapp launched a brilliant, bitter attack on Beveridge for raising false issues "that the public might be prejudiced."[23]

The degree to which the majority of the Progressives were bound to Roosevelt's foreign policy is indicated in a letter of Brand Whitlock's:

I have your note asking me if I could help you with a letter against wasting $32,000,000 on two more useless battleships. I am not sure that anything I can say on that subject will be of any use in stopping the construction of battleships; if it would I would say a great deal, for, of course, it is all but a part of the vast and amazing superstition of war. . . . I suppose that as long as there are some nations in the world who want to go to war, and so long as there are commercial interests that will keep up revolutions in Mexico and Central and South America, we shall need a navy and army to do police duty and keep the peace in this hemisphere, for which, under the Monroe Doctrine, I suppose we are responsible; but I know of no reason for going beyond this need.[24]

Whitlock was an intelligent, eloquent critic of Roosevelt's foreign policy who once observed that "Thayer can see the megalomania which afflicted Garibaldi but cannot see it when the same symptoms are repeated in Roosevelt."[25] Yet even the hostile Whitlock accepted reluctantly the obligations of "police duty" and the Monroe Doctrine, and from these premises much could follow.

In March, 1909, Theodore Roosevelt gave way to his heir apparent, William Howard Taft, and for the next four years the Progressives were confronted by the phenomenon of Dollar Diplomacy. Philander C. Knox, who had prosecuted the Northern Securities case, directed the new Caribbean policy, while Willard D. Straight, who in 1914 was to found the *New Republic* "to explore and develop and apply the ideas which had been advertised by Theodore Roosevelt when he was the leader of the Progressive party,"[26] fostered Dollar Diplomacy in the Orient. The liberal character of Straight's Oriental diplomacy, which attempted to force American capital to go into China where it did not care to enter, rests on the nice distinction between territorial integrity and economic hegemony, and the dubious assumption that the investments of Edward H. Harriman, who allegedly asserted he could buy Congress and, if need be, the judiciary, would be more beneficial to the Chinese people than French and Russian capital. Ultimately, Straight ended up attempting to raise a foreign loan to crush the Chinese revolution, on the assumption that what China needed was a dictator. The British and Germans were unsympathetic, and Straight was forced to allow the Chinese people to determine their own political destiny.[27]

From the days of the Payne-Aldrich tariff dispute, the rift between the insurgents and Taft grew wider, and Taft was beleaguered by a Progressive bloc which at times opposed him on purely ideological grounds, on occasion out of personal spite, but at no time because of disagreement with Taft's Dollar Diplomacy. While the Progressives were meeting in Chicago in 1912 to establish their third party, Taft was landing American marines in Nicaragua, but no word of condemnation for Taft's foreign policy appears in the Progressive platform of 1912. Instead, the platform stated:

> It is imperative to the welfare of our people that we enlarge and extend our foreign commerce. In every way possible our federal government should co-operate in this important matter. Germany's policy of co-operation between government and business has in comparatively few years made that nation a leading competitor for the commerce of the world. . . . The Panama Canal, built and paid for by the American people, must be

used primarily for their benefit. . . . American ships engaged in coastwise trade shall pay no tolls.

Roosevelt's speech to the Progressive convention called for building a larger navy,[28] and Frank Munsey assured his readers that "The new Progressive party believes in a navy that will insure peace, that will give us a rightful position among the powers of the world, and that will make the Monroe Doctrine an actuality."[29]

The two issues of foreign policy which did affect the Progressive bolt of 1912 were the arbitration treaties and Taft's Mexican policy, both of which earned the ire of Theodore Roosevelt, and with Taft's prosecution of United States Steel, brought about the final break between Roosevelt and Taft. "Describing the treaties as an outrage, born of some very 'sloppy thinking,' Roosevelt furiously set about to destroy them. He wrote innumerable letters to [Henry Cabot] Lodge, chairman of the Senate Foreign Relations Committee, corresponded with [Elihu] Root, and indirectly reached [Albert B.] Cummins and Borah."[30] In a series of articles in the *Outlook*, starting on May 20, 1911, Roosevelt lashed out at the arbitration treaties with thinly veiled references to Taft. We should not indulge in "amiable sentimentality"; it is "our duty not to indulge in shams, not to make believe we are getting peace by some patent contrivance which sensible men ought to know cannot work"; "to speak of it as silly comes far short of saying what should be said."[31] When the treaties reached the Senate floor, the Progressive forces were divided, Borah, Bourne, Bristow, and Cummins voting for the crippling amendment to exclude from arbitration questions affecting the admission of aliens to the United States or any question involving the Monroe Doctrine, while Clapp and John D. Works voted against it, a courageous act on the part of Senator Works, who came from the alien-conscious state of California.[32] Roosevelt denounced as "flabby" Taft's firm action in refusing to intervene on behalf of American oil interests in Mexico.[33] "Of all the misconduct of the Administration," Roosevelt concluded, "no misconduct had been greater than that relating to foreign affairs."[34]

The campaign of 1912 offered the Progressives another excellent opportunity to attack Taft's Dollar Diplomacy, but they were strangely silent. Scarcely had the election returns of November, 1912, been counted, however, than they began their attack on Woodrow Wilson and a movement started within the Progressive party to return to the Republican fold at almost any price. The Progressives were embarrassed by Wilson's commendable record in domestic affairs, and as Wilson drove through one reform after another in 1913 it became clear that their only choice was between joining forces with Wilson or maintaining their party organization intact with a more radical approach to domestic problems; there were no grounds for choosing the Republicans over the Wilson administration. Instead, they chose to fight it out with the administration on

foreign policy. For the first time in the history of the Progressive movement foreign affairs determined the line of direction, and by 1916 the Progressives were completely absorbed with foreign policy issues and their
movement was moribund.

On July 11, 1914, Roosevelt announced the new direction of the party
when he resigned as contributing editor to the *Outlook* to devote his
time to opposing the Wilson administration for its foreign policy which
had "meant the abandonment of the interest and honor of America."[35] In
later years Roosevelt indicated that his violent turn against the administration was over Wilson's indifference to the plight of Belgium, but in
September, 1914, Roosevelt was urging American neutrality with respect
to Belgium. "Of course it would be folly to jump into the gulf ourselves
to no good purpose; and very probably nothing that we could have done
would have helped Belgium."[36] The main grievances of Roosevelt and the
Progressives with Wilson were originally not over the European war at
all, but over the treaty of apology and indemnity with Colombia, Bryan's
cooling off treaties, and the "mushy amiability" of Wilson in withdrawing
from Mexico and agreeing to arbitration by the ABC powers.[37]

Borah announced a "last ditch" fight against Wilson's bill to repeal the
Panama Canal tolls, and on the vote for final passage, Borah, Bristow,
Clapp, Cummins, La Follette, Miles Poindexter, and Works all voted in
opposition, with only Asle J. Gronna and Norris voting with the Wilson
administration.[38] Mexico was an even hotter issue. In March, 1915, Walter
A. Johnson, New York state chairman of the Progressive party, asserted
in an interview in the New York *Sun* that Wilson, instead of following
the policy of "watchful waiting" in Mexico, should follow the sterling
example of Theodore Roosevelt in the Perdicaris case in Morocco by
sending warships and issuing an ultimatum.[39] A few months later Dr. H.
Nelson Jackson, chairman of the Progressive party of Vermont, issued a
statement to the Burlington *Free Press:*

> While hundreds of Americans were being murdered, their wives and
> daughters outraged, their property destroyed, and have received no pro-
> tection from our spineless, psalm-singing administration, thousands of our
> citizens thought that President Wilson was locked in his study praying
> and planning for peace and good will to this beloved country of ours, but
> in the past few weeks they suddenly realized that his time had been taken
> up otherwise, with courting. . . . Oh! God give us a leader that will keep
> our country in the exalted position made possible by such leaders as
> Washington and Abraham Lincoln and that will make Americans feel no
> matter where they go, no matter where they invest their capital, that they,
> their families, and their properties will be respected and protected, and
> above all that our dear flag will be honored among all nations.[40]

In December, 1914, the Progressives issued a statement completely
omitting the progressive planks of the 1912 platform and concentrating
on demands for a higher protective tariff, a far cry from the insurgency
of 1909 and a clear bid for amalgamation with the Republican party.
By the fall of 1915 domestic issues had almost completely disappeared

from the Progressive program, and the one issue that was hammered home in Progressive publications and meetings was the need for military preparedness. On September 25, 1915, Victor Murdock, the Kansas radical who was chairman of the National Committee of the Progressive party, wrote Walter Johnson:

> I was greatly gratified to find this view [the necessity for maintaining the Progressive party] confirmed at a dinner given by Mr. Perkins to me at the Manhattan Hotel here on Wednesday evening. . . . There was straight-out, complete candor in the addresses made by all of them, and an absence of boast and fustian. They were in favor of holding the line, facing forward and throwing themselves into the campaign of 1916 with uncompromising aggression, behind a ticket and platform which will challenge the sense and patriotism of the nation.
> The strong notes sounded were for military and economic preparedness. The men present favored insuring peace for the nation by placing us in a position to command respect and for an adjustment of the tariff under the Progressive plan of a tariff commission to meet the abnormal selling campaign by Europe which will follow inevitably the cessation of hostilities abroad.[41]

Not only had foreign policy become a key issue, but it had been linked by now with the need for high tariff walls, a prophecy of the economic policy of Warren G. Harding and Herbert Hoover.

In December Chairman Murdock issued a statement emphasizing the main points of the Progressive party program:

> The Progressive Party proposes to bring, first of all, a constructive program for business ills, the proposal of a sane protective tariff policy and a demand for social justice and for straight-out preparedness both on the military side and the industrial and economic sides. The Progressive Party's policy of 1912 for a tariff commission with broad powers has already the endorsement of the whole country and must be enacted into law if the industrial invasion from Europe after the war is to be forestalled.[42]

On January 11, 1916, the Progressive National Committee, meeting in Chicago, issued a statement, adopted unanimously, condemning the Wilson administration for its failure "to deal adequately with National honor and industrial welfare."

> The Wilson administration has repudiated the faith of our forefathers which made the American flag the sufficient protection of an American citizen around the world. It has suffered American men, women and children to be slaughtered in Mexico and on the high seas, American property to be destroyed and American liberty to travel and trade to be subject to the arbitrary and lawless coercion of foreign belligerents. . . . We need a reawakening of our elder Americanism, of our belief in those things that our country and our flag stands for.

At their national convention in 1916 the Progressive party, which had had only a few sentences on foreign policy in its 1912 platform, devoted almost its entire platform to preparedness, Americanism, and the excoriation of the Wilson program on Mexico and the European war. The Progressives demanded a regular army of 250,000 men, compulsory universal military training, and "a navy restored to at least second rank in battle efficiency." When Roosevelt refused the nomination, the party turned to Charles E. Hughes, who Roosevelt told them stood for "clean-cut, straightout Americanism," and the party decided to support him, because only he could "serve the two vital causes of Americanism and Preparedness."[43]

For many it was a hard choice. The Republican platform of 1916, as the *New Republic* observed, was a "stupidly, defiantly and cynically reactionary document." "The Republican party of 1916 does not differ in any essential respect from that portion of the party which nominated Mr. Taft. . . . They have revised none of their professed principles; they have dismissed none of their objectionable leaders; they have not by a single act or declaration betrayed a leaning toward liberalism, such as would make an honest Progressive welcome reunion."[44] When Raymond Robins of Illinois, chairman of the national convention, heard Roosevelt tell him that "Mr. Hughes would answer the preparedness, Americanism and progressive demands of our party," Robins dissented. On June 26, at a meeting of the Progressive National Committee, Robins announced: "At this hour, if I had to vote or declare my sentiments, I should declare for Woodrow Wilson and vote for him."

Robins sounded out the other Progressive leaders. Hiram W. Johnson, Gifford Pinchot, and James R. Garfield all told him that the only hope was to go back to the Republican party and support Hughes, Pinchot explaining it was necessary because of "this national crisis." Soon Robins was announcing his support of Hughes, in part because "we must develop a national mind that will comprehend our social, industrial and military unpreparedness. It must appreciate the domestic injury and national danger that lies in our lack of a definite foreign policy." He further asserted his warm support of compulsory military training, the Oriental Exclusion acts, and "our obligations under the Monroe Doctrine."[45]

In the campaign of 1916 the Progressive party frankly announced its abandonment of its earlier political ideals. On June 26, 1916, the National Committee, after listing recent important gains in progressive legislation, which it termed "national advance," observed that the war had brought

> an issue deeper than national advance, the issue of national unity and the nation's existence, of Americanism and of Preparedness. The Progressive Platform of 1916, therefore, placed foremost as our immediate need preparedness in arms, industry and spirit. . . . The Progressive National Committee recognizes that such are now the issues that immediately confront the country and *looks only to the duty that arises therefrom.*[46]

The Republican and Progressive platforms of 1916 were almost identical, except that Lodge could not get the Republicans to accept the provision for universal service.[47] Partly out of political desperation, partly out of loyalty to Roosevelt, in large part because of their views on foreign affairs, the mass of the Progressives supported Hughes, although the

Republicans made no pretense of progressivism and Wilson had enacted much of the Progressive platform. The 1916 campaign was the last presidential election the Progressive party entered; imperialism and militarism had replaced the old liberal formulas of protest, and within a year the party was dead.

How does one account for the wide divergence between Progressive principle and practice, between a concern for democratic processes at home and a disregard of them abroad, for antagonism to financial empires in America and encouragement of them overseas, for the destruction of American progressivism in the interest of imperialism, militarism, and Americanism?

In the first place, many Progressives were able to convince themselves that there was no conflict at all, that their domestic and foreign policies were two sides of the same coin. The Spanish-American War was not merely a struggle to bring freedom to Cuba and end Spanish tyranny but a crusade for principle against the greed of Wall Street interests opposed to the war. "Cuba is free and she thanks President Roosevelt for her freedom," wrote Jacob Riis. "But for his insistence that the nation's honor was bound up in the completion of the work his Rough-Riders began at Las Guasimas and on San Juan Hill, a cold conspiracy of business greed would have left her in the lurch, to fall by and by reluctantly into our arms, bankrupt and helpless, while the sneer of the cynics that we were plucking that plum for ourselves would have been justified."[48] "We will have this war for the freedom of Cuba in spite of the timidity of the commercial interests," Roosevelt told a Gridiron dinner.[49] We must save the "wretched Cubans" from Spain, Roosevelt averred, and then noted, "It would be a splendid thing for the Navy, too."[50]

Compulsory military training was likewise a phase of progressivism. "The proposed continental army is utterly undemocratic; it denies to the patriotic man of small means the chance to train which it gives to his well-to-do brother," Roosevelt asserted.[51] Compulsory universal military training, agreed Raymond Robins, "will do more in one generation to break down class and section prejudice, develop disciplined, vigorous and efficient citizenship, and to unify the diverse groups of our national life in a vital Americanism than all other forces combined." As opposed to this Progressive program, Robins added, the Democrats, in opposing universal training, offer only "a state-dominated militia with its menace of shiftless incompetence, spoils politics and organized snobbery as a national defense force, at a time of world peril."[52]

Secondly, it is impossible to understand the acquiescence of many Progressives in the imperialist movement without realizing the remarkable hold that Theodore Roosevelt had on his followers. Norris' testimony that "often those years I followed him when I had some doubts as to the righteousness of his course" is not an isolated instance. To many American liberals "Roosevelt was . . . [by 1912] something more than

a revered political leader. He was gradually becoming a minor deity."[53]
Years later, William Allen White described his first meeting with
Roosevelt:

> I met Theodore Roosevelt. He sounded in my heart the first trumpet call
> of the new time that was to be. . . . I had never known such a man as he,
> and never shall again. He overcame me. And in the hour or two we spent
> that day at lunch, and in a walk down F Street, he poured into my heart
> such visions, such ideals, such hopes, such a new attitude toward life and
> patriotism and the meaning of things, as I had never dreamed men had.[54]

Even after Roosevelt had deserted the Progressives and helped disrupt
the movement, even after he had had the obtuseness to suggest Lodge as
the standardbearer, Harold Ickes could see only George Perkins as the
Iago of the movement and had no harsh words for Roosevelt.[55]

Thirdly, the attitude of the Progressives toward the American Negro
made them more receptive to American imperialism. They readily
accepted the notion that the little brown brother was a ward of the
United States, not fit for self-government, because they regarded the
southern Negro as a ward when they did not think of him as a corrupt
politician attempting to sell his vote to the highest bidder at Republican
conventions. The Progressive party plan with respect to the Negro,
wrote Roosevelt, was "to try for the gradual re-enfranchisement of the
worthy colored man of the South by frankly giving the leadership of
our movement to the wisest and justest white men of the South."[56]
Despite the fact that the Negro vote in Maryland was credited with
giving Roosevelt his margin of victory over Taft in the 1912 primaries,
he persisted in his aim to make the Progressive party a lily white party
in the South, with Senator Dixon, his national campaign manager, publicly disavowing a Progressive organization in South Carolina because
of its Negro membership and the convention refusing to seat any
southern Negro delegates, despite the dissent of Jane Addams.[57] W. A. D.
Venerable, head of the Colored Men's National Progressive Association,
denounced the Progressive party for holding the Negro unfit for suffrage
in the South, and, immediately after the convention, his organization
announced for Wilson in the 1912 elections.[58]

Nor was this policy limited to the Progressive party. At the American Socialist Congress in 1910, over a third of the delegates, led by
Victor Berger, favored legislation against Asiatic immigration. Ernest
Untermann, the Socialist candidate for governor of Idaho, asserted: "The
question as to what race shall dominate the globe must be met as surely
as the question of what class shall own the world. We should neglect
our duty to the coming generation of Aryan peoples if we did not do
everything in our power, even today, to insure the final race victory
of our own people." Both Robert Hunter of the National Executive
Committee of the Socialist party and Adolph Germer of the Miners'
Union attacked foreign and Negro labor as hostile to unionism, and

Untermann stated, " 'we should be false to our Socialist agitation if we insisted first on doing away with the race prejudice.' "[59]

Hostility toward and contempt for Oriental labor, in particular, was an avowed part of the Progressive campaign of 1912, a legacy of its trade union support and the sectional attitudes of the west coast which made an unsympathetic attitude toward Oriental nations a concomitant part of the outlook of many Progressives. The *Progressive Bulletin*, the official organ of the party, attacked Wilson in 1912 because he "prefers Chinese immigrants to white," and inquired whether "the Chinese are more desirable immigrants than the white people who dig our ground?" The first two points listed on Roosevelt's "labor record" in the 1912 campaign were "renewing the Chinese Exclusion Act and extending its provisions to the island territory of the United States," and "prohibiting the employment of Mongolian labor on irrigation works."[60] Nor did the Progressives always view southern European labor with favor. "These hearty 'hunkies' and 'dagoes' feel that they are working to make America rich and that their services should be appreciated, but are they?" asked the leading Progressive magazine on the west coast. "Are they not rather displacing the American of forty-five to fifty, when otherwise, he would work on until sixty without showing the white feather?"[61]

Most important, imperialism and progressivism flourished together because they were both expressions of the same philosophy of government, a tendency to judge any action not by the means employed but by the results achieved, a worship of definitive action for action's sake, as John Dewey has pointed out,[62] and an almost religious faith in the democratic mission of America. The results of the Spanish-American War were heartily approved not merely because the war freed subject peoples from tyranny, but because, since the United States was the land of free institutions, any extension of its domain was *per se* an extension of freedom and democracy. It was an age that admired results, that was not too concerned with fine distinctions and nice theories. The Progressives, quite apart from sharing in the general excitement of middle-class America in the rise of the United States as a world power and the sense of identity with the nation which imperialism afforded in a time of national stress, admired anyone who could clean up the slaughterhouses or link two great oceans, who could get a job done without months of tedious debate and deference to legal precedents.

The Progressives believed in the Hamiltonian concept of positive government, of a national government directing the destinies of the nation at home and abroad. They had little but contempt for the strict construction of the Constitution by conservative judges, who would restrict the power of the national government to act against social evils and to extend the blessings of democracy to less favored lands. The real enemy was particularism, state rights, limited government, which would mean the reign of plutocracy at home and a narrow, isolationist concept of national destiny abroad, which would deny the democratic mission of America and leave the brown peoples pawns of dynastic wars and colonial exploitation.

No writer better demonstrates the close link between progressivism and imperialism, with the concept of the Hamiltonian state and the democratic mission, than Herbert Croly, whose *The Promise of American Life* (1909) influenced the Progressive movement more profoundly than any other work. Roosevelt was more deeply moved by Croly's book than by anything he had read since the early Alfred T. Mahan. A few months after his return from Africa, Roosevelt was preaching the "New Nationalism" of Croly in his Osawatomie address and the war against the Old Guard was on in earnest.

"The American nation, just in so far as it believes in its nationality and is ready to become more of a nation, must assume a more definite and a more responsible place in the international system," wrote Croly. ". . . In spite of 'old-fashioned democratic' scruples and prejudices, the will to play that part for all it was worth would constitute a beneficial and a necessary stimulus to the better realization of the Promise of our domestic life."[63] We should shun the Jefferson administration's policy of basing "its international policy not upon the firm ground of national interest, but on the treacherous sands of international democratic propagandism."[64]

The first task of a truly national foreign policy was to develop hemispheric solidarity, and Croly left no doubt of what he meant by "a stable American international system."

> In all probability no American international system will ever be established without the forcible pacification of one or more centers of disorder. . . . In short, any international American political system might have to undertake a task in states like Venezuela, similar to that which the United States is now performing in Cuba. . . . The United States has already made an effective beginning in this great work, both by the pacification of Cuba and by the attempt to introduce a little order into the affairs of the turbulent Central American republics.[65]

Our work was greatly simplified by the fact that the political condition of Mexico, under the dictatorship of Diaz, had "become more stable and more wholesome," and "any recrudescence of revolutionary upheavals in Mexico would enormously increase the difficulties and perils of the attempt."[66]

The Spanish-American War was a great boon to the American people for it ushered in the Progressive era.

> Not until the end of the Spanish War was a condition of public feeling created, which made it possible to revive Hamiltonianism. That war and its resulting policy of extra-territorial expansion, so far from hindering the process of domestic amelioration, availed, from the sheer force of the national aspirations it aroused, to give a tremendous impulse to the work of national reform . . . and it indirectly helped to place in the Presidential

chair the man who, as I have said, represented both the national idea and
the spirit of reform. The sincere and intelligent combination of those two
ideas is bound to issue in the Hamiltonian practice of constructive national
legislation.[67]

Bryan's campaign of 1900, on the other hand, Croly continued, was
composed of two disastrous mistakes. "In seeking to prevent his countrymen from asserting their national interest beyond their own continent,
he was also opposing in effect the resolute assertion of the national interest in domestic affairs. He stamped himself, that is, as an anti-nationalist,
and his anti-nationalism has disqualified him for effective leadership
of the party of reform."[68]

Far from being isolated movements, our international mission and our
domestic reform program were interlocking forces, and frequently one
and the same thing, Croly concluded, for "it is entirely possible that
hereafter the United States will be forced into the adoption of a really
national domestic policy because of the dangers and duties incurred
through her relations with foreign countries."[69]

As Felix Frankfurter observed, "Unlike almost all American prewar
writers on politics (with the notable exception of Captain Mahan, because
of his special interest in navalism) Croly saw the American situation with
its international implications."[70] He did more than that. He provided
an intelligible rationale for the union of progressivism and imperialism,
ordering the apparently unrelated events of the Roosevelt administration
into a coherent political system and contending that imperial ventures
were an important phase of the new religion of national reform, steps
toward the fulfillment of the promise of American life.

The attitude of the Progressives toward imperialism explains much
about the basic character of the Progressive movement. Despite the
evangelical aura about the 1912 convention, the movement was not an
attempt to remold the world anew, to discard the old system for a
new society. The Progressives were completely a part of American life,
accepting the traditional values and ideals, cherishing the aspirations
of middle-class America, including the new sense of delight in the rise
of the United States as a world power. Although a few leaders like
Jane Addams saw the movement as an aspect of a broad humanitarian
philosophy, the most influential spokesmen thought not in terms of
universals but of providing remedies for certain specific political abuses
and economic ills. Insofar as they thought in more general terms, they
were concerned less with the rights of *all* men, with universal brotherhood, than with the promise of *American* life. They were interested
not only in a more equitable division of the pie but in a larger pie to
divide, and consequently saw nothing incongruous in supporting American investments abroad in the interest of expanded markets while condemning the same businesses at home for excessive profits and sub-
standard wages. The same group of men who could tear the Repub-

lican party asunder because of a discriminatory tariff in 1909 could outdo the Old Guard in arguing for protectionism in 1916 when they feared foreign goods would undercut the home market.

In the final analysis the Progressive movement suffered from a contradiction between humanistic values and nationalist aspirations, which, if not inherent, had certainly beset other democracies from the time of the wars of the French Revolution. In arguing for a positive national government, the followers of Croly ultimately lost sight of the distinction between the state as an instrument and the state as an end. The consequences were not only the endorsement of an imperialistic foreign policy but the death of the Progressive party in the interest of their nationalist zeal.

Notes

1. Insofar as any link has been made between the domestic and foreign aspects of the Progressive period, it has been to present a tableau of Theodore Roosevelt, the warrior, brandishing a big stick at American corporations on the one hand and foreign potentates on the other.

2. Alfred Lief, *Democracy's Norris* (New York, 1939), 155.

3. Claude G. Bowers, *Beveridge and the Progressive Era* (Boston, 1932), 73–76.

4. *Ibid.,* 448.

5. *Ibid.,* 511–12.

6. Merle Curti, *Bryan and World Peace,* Smith College *Studies in History* (Northampton), XVI, Nos. 3–4 (1931), 117 ff.

7. Walter Johnson, *William Allen White's America* (New York, 1947), 111.

8. *The Autobiography of William Allen White* (New York, 1946), 305–306.

9. Merle Curti, *Peace or War: The American Struggle, 1636–1936* (New York, 1936), 171.

10. Fred H. Harrington, "The Anti-Imperialist Movement in the United States, 1898–1900," *Mississippi Valley Historical Review* (Cedar Rapids), XXII (September, 1935), 218–19. See also Fred H. Harrington, "Literary Aspects of American Anti-Imperialism, 1898–1902," *New England Quarterly* (Baltimore, Portland), X (December, 1937), 650–67. The support given by organized labor to various imperialist ventures may be traced in John C. Appel, "The Relationship of American Labor to United States Imperialism, 1895–1905" (Ph.D. dissertation, University of Wisconsin, 1950).

11. Cf. Richard Pettigrew, *Imperial Washington* (Chicago, 1922); William G. Carleton, "Isolationism and the Middle West," *Mississippi Valley Historical Review,* XXXIII (December, 1946), 379. Even Senator Pettigrew favored war with Spain, "because I believe it will put us on a silver basis." Arthur W. Dunn, *From Harrison to Harding . . . 1888–1921,* 2 vols. (New York, 1922), I, 232. There was a close tie, in fact, between the jingoes and the silverites. Julius W. Pratt, *Expansionists of 1898* (Baltimore, 1936), 242 ff.

12. Jacob A. Riis, *Theodore Roosevelt, The Citizen* (New York, 1903), 384, 385.

13. Cf. Gifford Pinchot, *Breaking New Ground* (New York, 1947).

14. Oscar S. Straus, *Under Four Administrations; From Cleveland to Taft* (Boston, 1922), 175, 176.

15. *New York Times,* October 14, 1914, p. 10; Claudius O. Johnson, *Borah of Idaho* (New York, 1936), 191 ff.

16. *Fighting Liberal; The Autobiography of George W. Norris* (New York, 1945), 145–47 (italics supplied).

17. *Cong. Record,* 56 Cong., 2 Sess., 3151–52.

18. *Ibid.,* 59 Cong., 2 Sess., 3917.

19. Charles J. Bonaparte, "Two Years of a Government That Does Things," *Outlook* (New York), LXXXV (March 16, 1907), 600.

20. Joseph B. Bishop, *Charles Joseph Bonaparte* (New York, 1922), 100.

21. Curti, *Peace or War*, 220.

22. *Saturday Evening Post* (Philadelphia), CLXXX (May 23, 1908), 18–19.

23. *Cong. Record*, 60 Cong., 1 Sess., 5291, 5284, 5274.

24. Brand Whitlock to General Isaac R. Sherwood, February 26, 1913, Allan Nevins (ed.), *The Letters and Journal of Brand Whitlock*, 2 vols. (New York, 1936), I, 158–159.

25. Whitlock to Albert J. Nock, June 14, 1916, *ibid.*, 195.

26. Walter Lippmann, "Notes for a Biography," *New Republic* (New York), LXIII (July 16, 1930), 250.

27. Herbert Croly, *Willard Straight* (New York, 1924), 422 ff.

28. Chicago *Record-Herald*, August 7, 1912, p. 5.

29. Frank A. Munsey, "The New Progressive Party—What It Is and Why It Is," *Munsey's Magazine* (New York), XLVII (August, 1912), 678.

30. George E. Mowry, *Theodore Roosevelt and the Progressive Movement* (Madison, 1946), 187 ff.

31. See particularly Theodore Roosevelt, "The Peace of Righteousness," *Outlook*, XCIX (September 9, 1911), 66 ff.

32. *Cong. Record*, 62 Cong., 2 Sess., 2954–55.

33. Mowry, *Theodore Roosevelt and the Progressive Movement*, 307.

34. *Ibid.*, 187 ff.

35. *Outlook*, CVII (July 11, 1914), 569.

36. Theodore Roosevelt, "The World War: Its Tragedies and Its Lessons," *ibid.*, CVIII (September 23, 1914), 169–78.

37. New York *Times*, June 25, 1914, p. 2.

38. *Cong. Record*, 63 Cong., 2 Sess., 10247–48. This is not to say that the Wilson administration was free from imperialist manifestations. Indeed, the degree to which Woodrow Wilson was involved with American imperialist aspirations makes the attitude of the Progressives all the more remarkable. The relation of the New Freedom to American foreign policy merits further study, but it necessarily lies outside the scope of this short paper.

39. *Progressive Opinion* (New York), I (March 27, 1915), 7.

40. *Ibid.*, II (January, 1916), 3.

41. *Ibid.*, II (October 2, 1915), 2.

42. *Ibid.*, II (December 4, 1915), 3.

43. Progressive Party, National Committee, *The Progressive Party; Its Record From January to July, 1916* (New York, n. d.), 6 ff.

44. *New Republic*, VII (June 17, 1916), 160.

45. Progressive Party, National Committee, *Progressive Party; Its Record From January to July, 1916*, pp. 102 ff.

46. *Ibid.*, 112 ff.

47. Mowry, *Theodore Roosevelt and the Progressive Movement*, 348.

48. Riis, *Theodore Roosevelt, The Citizen*, 383.

49. Arthur W. Dunn, *Gridiron Nights* (New York, 1915), 70 ff.

50. Theodore Roosevelt to Henry C. Lodge, August 3, 1897, Henry C. Lodge (ed.), *Selections from the Correspondence of Theodore Roosevelt and Henry Cabot Lodge, 1884–1918*, 2 vols. (New York, 1925), I, 268.

51. *Progressive Opinion*, II (December 4, 1915), 6.

52. Progressive Party, National Committee, *Progressive Party; Its Record From January to July, 1916*, pp. 121 ff.

53. Mowry, *Theodore Roosevelt and the Progressive Movement*, 243.

54. *Autobiography of William Allen White*, 297.

55. Harold L. Ickes, "Who Killed the Progressive Party?" *American Historical Review* (New York), XLVI (January, 1941), 306–37.

56. Theodore Roosevelt, "The Progressives and the Colored Man," *Outlook*, CI (August 24, 1912), 911.

57. "Official Minutes of the (Provisional) Progressive National Committee," Theodore Roosevelt Collection (Widener Library, Harvard University, Cambridge); George E. Mowry, "The South and the Progressive Lily White Party of 1912," *Journal of Southern History* (Baton Rouge, Lexington), VI (May, 1940), 237–47.

58. Chicago *Record-Herald*, August 6, 1912, p. 1; August 9, 1912, p. 2. See also the

attack on the action of the convention in "No Square Deal," *Independent* (New York), LXXIII (August 15, 1912), 391–93.

59. William E. Walling, *Progressivism—And After* (New York, 1914), 377–81.

60. *Progressive Bulletin* (New York), I (September 16, 1912), 5. At the same time, however, the *Bulletin* attacked the nativism of the Republican party.

61. *California Outlook* (Los Angeles and San Francisco), XII (February 10, 1912), 5. William Allen White recalled that "of course, I read the popular pseudo-sciences of the day, such as 'Anglo-Saxon Superiority,' by Edmond Demolins." *Autobiography of William Allen White*, 326.

62. John Dewey, *Characters and Events*, 2 vols. (New York, 1929), I, 91.

63. Herbert Croly, *The Promise of American Life* (New York, 1909), 289.

64. *Ibid.*, 290.

65. *Ibid.*, 302–303.

66. *Ibid.*, 301, 303.

67. *Ibid.*, 169.

68. *Ibid.*, 157.

69. *Ibid.*, 310.

70. Felix Frankfurter, "Herbert Croly and American Political Opinion," *New Republic*, LXIII (July 16, 1930), 248.

The War Machine

SAMUEL HABER

Professor William Leuchtenburg's examination of the progressives' attitudes toward foreign policy resulted in a mild critique of the "contradiction between humanistic values and nationalist aspirations." His essay was published in 1952, when the critical reinterpretation of the progressive movement was just getting under way. A more severe examination of the relationship between progressivism and World War I is contained in Professor Samuel Haber's *Efficiency and Uplift: Scientific Management in the Progressive Era, 1890–1920*, published in 1964. His general argument is that important strains in the progressive movement were influenced by the system of "scientific management," pioneered by Frederick W. Taylor. Taylor's system, which became known as "Taylorism," was—from a mid-twentieth-century vantage point—inhuman and undemocratic. But it did attract such "progressive" intellectual leaders as Herbert Croly, Louis Brandeis, and Walter Lippmann.

In general, then, Professor Haber's book is part of the general discovery of embarrassing skeletons in the progressive closet of ideology and motivation. In the present chapter on "The War Machine," he argues that with the onset of war, two related things happened. First, progressive leaders began to look at the war as an opportunity for expanding reform, and adopted industrial efficiency as a slogan. Second, the movement for scientific management itself became more concerned with the promotion of "industrial democracy" as part and parcel of the program of efficiency. The implications of Professor Haber's argument are clear: to many progressives, if not to most, the war seemed a blessing and not a defeat because it created a national demand for disciplined, regulated efficiency. The great concern for industrial efficiency in the 1920s and the enthusiasm for Herbert Hoover's powers as an "engineer" were not new phenomena, then, but were natural extensions of fads and movements that had their beginnings during the progressive years.

Samuel Haber is Associate Professor of History at the University of California at Berkeley. He received his B.A., M.A., and Ph.D. degrees at Berkeley, where he was trained in the very productive seminars of Professor Henry F. May. Professor May's influence shows subtly but strongly in Professor Haber's book entitled Efficiency and Uplift *(1964).*

It is sometimes said that World War I killed progressivism, that reform-
ers put aside reform to fight the War to End Wars and then found that
they had lost their winning combination, and for some time to come
could score only sporadically. There is much to be said for this view,
especially if one concentrates on the legislative achievements of the years
during and after the war. But a look beyond the *Congressional Record*
to the sequence of popular attitudes suggests some changes in this picture. The war appears as an occasion when important progressive principles were put into service rather than pushed aside. In fact, the absence
of legislative milestones of reform can be seen, in part, as a characteristic
of a period when administration superseded legislation—in itself a dream
of many reformers in the prewar years. In the Overman and Lever
Acts, Congress placed the most important problems of the country in
the hands of administrative agencies set up by the President. Senator
Brandegee offered an ironical amendment to the Overman Act, providing that "if any power, constitutional or not, has been inadvertently
omitted from this bill, it is hereby granted in full."[1]

The administrative arm of the government was suddenly, almost reck-
lessly, enlarged. Washington was glutted with dollar-a-year-men, and
these were outnumbered by the professors, the engineers, the "college-
bred." The term "white collar" came into use.[2] Wesley Clair Mitchell,
who had just moved from Columbia University to the Division of Planning and Statistics of the War Industries Board, conveyed the exuberance of these new administrators in a letter to his wife: "Indeed I am
in a mood to demand excitement and to make it up when it doesn't offer
of itself. I am ready to concoct a new plan for running the universe at

REPRINTED BY PERMISSION, FROM SAMUEL HABER, *Efficiency and Uplift:*
Scientific Management in the Progressive Era, 1890–1920 (CHICAGO: UNIVERSITY
OF CHICAGO PRESS, 1964), PP. 117–133.

any minute. . . ."[3] Petty politics had been thrust aside, and it seemed that a new industrial regime had taken its place.

The War Industries Board marshaled the resources of the country through a system of priorities and price-fixing. The War Labor Board, backed by threats of government seizure and warnings of "work or fight," moved to put an end to class conflict. When the Smith and Wesson plant at Springfield rejected a Labor Board ruling, it was commandeered. When the machinists at Bridgeport refused to obey, they were confronted with the draft. This was the type of "positive government" which the *New Republic* had been talking about for so long.[4] A surprising number of reformers and radicals called it socialism or the first steps toward socialism.[5]

The United States found a singleness of purpose similar to the Union Sacrée of France and the Burgfriede of Germany during the early years of the war. "The supreme test of the nation has come," Wilson announced. "We must speak, act, and serve together."[6] This was much like the spirit of civic unity which had carried Galveston to commission government after its great tidal wave and Dayton to the city manager system after its disastrous floods. Where singleness of purpose was accepted, questions of efficiency usually became important, and the analogy between society and the machine became more agreeable.

Even John Dewey, who had spent a good part of his early career explaining the shortcomings of the mechanical analogy, inadvertently fell under its spell. The image of the machine lay beneath the peculiar distinction between "force" and "violence" upon which Dewey built his argument against pacifism and his eventual justification of American entry into the war. Force, he said, was the energy necessary for the accomplishment of social ends. Violence was simply force used wastefully. Law, then, became "a method for employing force economically, efficiently, so as to get results with the least waste." Following this logic, it was sensible to oppose all use of violence but silly to oppose all use of force. Of course, it is a machine, in particular, which works only through the application of force. The hidden mechanical analogy helped make the argument powerful. Other forms and characteristics of human organization—voluntary agreement and co-operation, and the fundamental contrast between compulsion and choice—were neglected. Having once taken this ground, Dewey, when he condemned persecution of the opponents of the war, could only argue that the government's strong-arm tactics were, in this case, inefficient.[7]

Efficiency became a patriotic duty. Conservatives often presented their criticism of the Wilson war effort in terms of efficiency; and liberals, for their part, insisted that efficiency was a liberal thing.[8] This was complicated by the fact that Germany had popularly been considered the paragon of efficiency. Before America entered the war, propagandists for the Allies had advanced an image of German inhumanity derived from her supposed machine-like efficiency. However, once America was in the war, efficiency became a necessary virtue and, like many virtues, it was decontaminated of "Prussianism."[9]

Industrial efficiency, especially in the armament industries, was an urgent matter. Taylor's advocacy of unrestrained production became common sense. In wartime England, interest in scientific management boomed, and by 1916 even the Fabian Society offered its conditional endorsement. In France, Clemenceau ordered that Taylor's principles be applied in military plants. One patriotic Taylorite began to worry that the spread of Taylorism abroad might mean that the United States would be outstripped in the industrial world.[10]

In America, a Conservation Division in the War Industries Board was charged with cutting out unnecessary uses of labor, materials, and capital. Standardization agreements eliminated styles and sizes, thus placing strict limits on consumers' choices and giving production problems precedence over sales problems.[11]

Yet even in these seemingly favorable circumstances there was no great run on scientific management. "We could not sell scientific management thirty years ago," complained a prominent member of the Taylor Society; "we can hardly sell it today."[12] There were new installations—most notably that at the Winchester Repeating Arms Company. However, some previously Taylorized plants weakened their system to take advantage of the new business opportunities. On a cost-plus contract, all costs, including the costs of waste, were less pressing than the demand for whopping production.[13]

Another reason for the lack of impressive advances of scientific management in private industry lay in the exodus of Taylorites from commercial work to government service. All of the officers and a large part of the membership of the Taylor Society went to work for Uncle Sam.[14] Many found their place in the Ordnance Department, where scientific management had already gained a foothold, as a result of the running battle to Taylorize the arsenals. Others were drawn to the Shipping Board and the Emergency Fleet Corporation. (Shipping was the first industry which the government was empowered to take over and run as a unit.)

The Taylorites gathered to discuss the problems of war production amid widespread criticism of what were alleged to be the lax war policies of the administration. The call for centralized power and control,[15] a frequent refrain among the critics of Wilson's wartime policies, was now heard at the Taylor Society meetings. "There is nothing to do," remarked Ernest Hopkins, president of Dartmouth College and a good friend of scientific management, "except to make a complete democratic move, to commandeer everything and everybody and every resource of this country for the common purpose."[16] Henry P. Kendall, manager of a model Taylor factory, deplored the fact that Wilson did not understand the principles of organization. The time had come for an "organization of experts with complete responsibility." America should break with tradition and set up "a single machine," "the most efficient, democratic autocracy."[17]

But the very bluntness of these demands for control from the top produced, as a reflex action, a "democratic" counterargument which stressed the importance of "response from below." Morris L. Cooke, who had often talked about the need for decisive leadership, now led those Taylorites who thought that things might be going too far toward high-handed assertions of authority. What is most significant, however, is that even the Taylorites who stressed the importance of "response from below" accepted a hierarchy of authority and initiative, as well as a unity of interest, in their "democratic" concept of organization. The disagreement could therefore be construed somewhat innocuously as a matter of emphasis. "My own feeling," said Cooke, "is that we should have the maximum of decentralization that is consistent with a strong and able and far-sighted central control."[18]

Even before the Armistice, public interest turned from the problems of the "war machine" to those of "reconstruction." To most progressives, it seemed that there had never been a time more favorable for serious reform. The war, Wilson told the nation, was "a peoples' war" which would bring "a full and unequivocal acceptance of the principle that the interest of the weakest is as sacred as the interest of the strongest"; it would bring "the final triumph of justice and fair dealing."[19] William Allen White announced that the back of the profit system was broken,[20] and Charles M. Schwab of U.S. Steel described the coming new order as "a world for the workers, a world in which mere possession will no longer rule, a world which will yield honor not to those who have but to those who serve."[21] The journals of reform declared that progressivism would go forward.[22] This was seconded by the pro-war socialists, who saw the wartime "collectivism" as a step leading to the further "conscious organization of society."[23]

There were many plans of "reconstruction."[24] Almost all of them, with the important exception of that of the American Federation of Labor, made much of the idea of worker participation in management. Before the war, industrial democracy (as worker participation in management was often called) had been linked with the audacious proposals of Brandeis, Croly, and Lippmann but also with the prudent system of industrial representation set up by John D. Rockefeller, Jr., at the Colorado Fuel and Iron Company.[25] During the war, the growth of workers' representation programs as a means of extra-union collective bargaining had been encouraged by the War Labor Board's policy of maintaining the status quo in industry while insisting on collective bargaining.[26] However, it was not until the months following the Armistice that the notion of industrial democracy took hold of a large and zealous following. On May 20, 1919, President Wilson sent a message to Congress which proposed "the genuine democratization of industry, based upon a full recognition of the right of those who work, in whatever rank, to participate in some organic way in every decision which directly affects their welfare or the part they are to play in industry."[27]

The great variety of programs of industrial democracy were animated *motives* by a great variety of motives. Some advocates wanted a Christian capitalism, some wanted to fight off the trade unions, and others wanted a new social order. Fundamentally, these programs were of two kinds: those which seemed to challenge the traditional source of authority in the factory and those which left it intact, and perhaps even strengthened it.

The most popular primer of the second group was John Leitch's *Man to Man*.[28] Reading the book today, without the assumptions of 1919, one finds it difficult to understand how so many thoughtful men could have taken Leitch so seriously. How, for example, Justice Oliver Wendell Holmes could have dropped his much-vaunted skepticism and written to Harold Laski: "I read John Leitch's *Man to Man*. . . . It gave me more hopefulness than anything I have read. He talks as one who had applied his ideas and succeeded in making employers and employees work together heartily."[29] Leitch simply presented a literal-minded application of Brandeis' rhetorical pronouncement that the nineteenth century had been the century of political democracy and the twentieth would be the century of industrial democracy. He transferred the apparatus of a modified American constitution to the factory. There was a "House of Representatives," usually elected by a meeting of all employees below the rank of foreman; a "Senate," consisting of superintendents and foremen; and a "Cabinet," composed of executive officers and presided over by the president. There were speakers of the House, presidents of the Senate, legislative committees, bills passed, Roberts' Rules of Order followed, etc. Of course, this was closer to Alexander Hamilton's ideal government than to Brandeis'. Leitch wished to have the worker see his employer, and the employer see himself, as the executive of the workers' best interest. Yet one wonders whether this insistence that the government of the shop under his system was just like the government of the country, fostered loyal workers or disloyal citizens. In any event, Leitch assured his readers that the adoption of his plan would increase efficiency, end strikes, and further the Americanization of the immigrant worker. His program seemed to appeal especially to those who were just coming to accept the existence of the large, permanent working class of large-scale industry but who longed for the old, supposedly harmonious, employer-worker relationship of small-scale enterprise; a relationship which, as Leitch's title indicates, was man-to-man.[30]

Of quite a different order was that variety of industrial democracy which challenged the rights of ownership and sometimes placed limits on the powers of management. This was the industrial democracy that shaped the Plumb plan[31] for the railroads and looked to Mary Parker Follett's *The New State*[32] rather than Leitch's *Man to Man* for guidance. Characteristically, Miss Follett placed industrial democracy in a broad frame. It was but one of the applications of the "Group Principle," which was to serve as the basis for the reorganization of all society. Only in later years did she turn her attention fully to the factory and become one of the leaders in the field of industrial administration.

Mary Parker Follett was a Boston settlement worker and friend of the Brandeis family; a gifted, well-to-do, well-educated woman who found in the settlement house a door to a wider world. Her book, *The New State*, was first published in December, 1918, and soon ran through four printings. It contained most of the fashionable notions to be expected of an up-and-coming serious thinker of that day. Here was the "New Psychology" (which Miss Follett credited to McDougall's social psychology, Freud, and behaviorism), as well as Roscoe Pound's sociological jurisprudence. Allusions to the Bergsonian *élan vital* were included, along with Hegelian patter from the works of T. H. Green, Bosanquet, and the British idealist school. (There is something intriguing about a high-minded, deeply religious New England spinster repeatedly propounding the fundamental importance of "the law of interpenetration.") Finally, the book finished off with generous helpings from the functionalist and anti-state doctrines of the political pluralists, Leon Duguit, J. N. Figgis, and Harold Laski.

Miss Follett pointed this odd mixture of doctrines toward a new concept of democracy, political and industrial. She attacked representative government, the "fictitious democracy" which spoke in terms of equal rights, consent of the governed, and majority rule, and proposed the "true democracy," which was to be based on the "group process."[33] This process was characterized by "integration" rather than domination or the compromise of differences.[34] It was not opposed to aristocracy; it included aristocracy. This was an aristocracy of function, rather than of birth or property, which found its justification in expert service to the group. The war, Miss Follett declared, had taught the startling spiritual truth of unity. Now the task at hand was to convert this sentiment into a system of organization, into a "cooperative collectivism." This was the New State, to be compounded of small neighborhood groups (the Social Unit of Wilbur Phillips), occupational groups (of the guild socialists), and factory groups (the "industrial democracy" idea).[35]

Miss Follett was trying to reassert the primacy of community, to establish more open yet more intense relationships between men than modern social institutions seemed to afford. The group meant fellowship, co-operation, altruism, and increased creative force, but also increased discipline. It stood opposed to the uncontrolled individual and the unprincipled class; against egoism, conflict, the scramble for power and wealth. The "group process" somehow made the traditional distinctions between ruler and ruled, powerful and powerless, public and private, consent and compulsion, irrelevant.[36]

When Miss Follett wrote that "every department of our life must be controlled by those who know most about that department, by those who have most to do with that department," she attacked the rights of property. At one point, she proposed state ownership and "producers' control" of industry. This, apparently, did not mean workers' control but the application of the group process to the factory. This "group process" which was to create harmony—by integration, interpenetration, compenetration, etc.—meant guidance by the expert and did not mean "the rule of numbers." The functional principle attacked the rights of property but left other rights vulnerable as well. It beckoned toward popular participation through "groups" but clearly not toward popular rule within "groups" or by "groups."[37]

Under orthodox Taylorism the worker's participation in management, if it could be called that, had been restricted to his understanding orders and the bonus system. In cases of insubordination or repeated failure, the "shop disciplinarian" in the planning department would take the matter in hand. When Brandeis and others suggested that the workers might accept scientific management more readily if some form of worker consultation were to be used, the reply was that no one could install scientific management "and simultaneously participate in a debating society or risk the results of unfavorable decisions by a well-meaning but uninformed board of arbitration."[38]

There had been, however, even in the prewar period, a few Taylorites who had departed from this view.[39] These unorthodox Taylorites were responding to the opposition of organized labor, trying to overcome the objections of otherwise sympathetic reformers, or simply yielding to the ambiguous democratic enthusiasms of the era. An important influence upon these Taylorites was Professor Robert F. Hoxie's investigation of scientific management, conducted on behalf of the Commission on Industrial Relations. Hoxie had concluded that scientific management was a major step forward in industrial progress but that it held immediate dangers for the worker and in the long run spelled the doom of craft unionism. Many of the friends of scientific management, therefore, decided that the workers needed the protection of some sort of democratic control. Even some of the model Taylor shops cautiously introduced elected shop committees with limited authority.[40]

During the war, the many Taylorites in the Ordnance Department and Emergency Fleet Corporation were confronted by all manner of industrial democracy programs.[41] Industrial democracy proved to be harmless, if not helpful. When the Taylorites returned from war, what had previously been the dissenting view became the view of the majority. The Society became a rostrum for the ideas of industrial democracy.[42] A speech in vigorous defense of the powers of the executive and the need for maintaining the discipline of management found but few supporters, and met chiefly hostile reactions from the audience, at a Taylor Society meeting.[43] Morris L. Cooke proposed "industrial institutes," joint councils of workers and managers, to discuss production problems. And when Lenin called for the adoption of the techniques of Taylorism as part of a policy of centralization of authority in Russian factories, Taylorites were gratified by the references to scientific management but objected to "the spirit of the super-boss and the industrial autocrat" in his program.[44]

Changes within the body of ideas which went to make up the Taylor system also left it susceptible to the notions of industrial democracy. Some influential writers on management had begun to examine Taylor's psychological assumptions and find them unfashionable. By 1919, the differential piece rate, through which Taylor had first presented his new vision for the factory, had "ceased to be a major principle." The differential piece rate, it must be remembered, was Taylor's method for securing the co-operation of the worker and giving him an incentive for hard work. With its decline, other possible sources of incentive and discipline became of interest. Even before the war, one prominent defender of the Taylorite orthodoxy began to speak of "the type of discipline which wells up from beneath and is at least partially self-enforcing." The claims that worker participation in management led to increased output gave it new drawing power.[45]

For the public at large, the drawing power of industrial democracy lay partly in its vagueness. The boom in the shop committee programs owed much to those who thought of them as substitutes for the trade unions, those who thought of them as supplements to the trade unions, and those who thought of them as the basis for a new social order. During the war, the AFL had recommended that its unions take part in the shop committees which were being set up in war industries. The locals, however, were often openly hostile to these programs. They feared that the shop committees would usurp their functions as agents of collective bargaining and would be used to break the unions. The craft unions, moreover, for which only a fraction of the workers were eligible, were put in a difficult position with respect to the companies' programs of "factory solidarity." At the 1919 Convention, the AFL condemned the shop committee system and began its fight to unionize the steel industry where Rockefeller-type plans were in force.[46]

The opponents in the steel strike of 1919 laid waste to the middle ground of which many reformers were so fond. The steel companies made it clear that their shop committees eliminated the need for unionism, and the AFL insisted that unions would replace the shop committees. For many advocates of industrial democracy, this turn of events was the signal for retreat. At the Taylor Society, however, there was little sign of distress. The optimistic belief that there was no necessary conflict between industrial democracy and trade unionism was reaffirmed. Morris L. Cooke went so far as to suggest that the Taylor Society should actively support both industrial democracy and the trade unions, not in order to strengthen the bargaining power of the worker, but rather to lay the basis for the national planning of the future. This would require national unions; shop committees unaffiliated on a national basis would not do.[47]

The postwar discussions of industrial democracy at the Taylor Society were much like the wartime debates on centralization and decentralization. Even the most ardent partisans of the shop councils had no intention of destroying hierarchy in the factory. Ordway Tead, who brought the teachings of Miss Follett and the guild socialists to the Taylorites, pointed out that there "must be executive direction which employs a high order of intelligence. There must be unified control and there must be the machinery which secures prompt decisions and assures prompt carrying out of decisions."[48] The over-all significance of industrial democracy for the Taylor Society was twofold: first, it provided a way station for many Taylorites en route to an acceptance of the trade union, and second, it provided a pattern for the absorption of democratic criticism within Taylor doctrine.

The discussions of industrial democracy were encouraged by the enthusiasm for new ideas and new measures so common in the first months after the Armistice. "Certain it is that the old order has passed never to return and that a new day is here," declared a speech to a meeting of Taylorites.[49] This was the kind of fervor which inspired the reorganization of the Taylor Society after the war. In place of the somewhat informal arrangements of the prewar days, a substantial organization was set up to support more ambitious activities and to carry the message of Taylorism to the country. An important change was the creation of the post of managing director, to conduct the Society's affairs. This, now the most influential office, was given to Harlow S. Person, who had served as president before the war. Person was neither an engineer nor a businessman but a college professor with a strong interest in the social consequences of Taylorism. The office of president became something of an honorary position. And E. W. Clark and Company, a Philadelphia banking house with close ties to the Taylor family, supplied the treasurer and probably underwrote any deficits.[50]

Moreover, when the work of the Taylor Society was redefined in the light of war experience, new undertones of radicalism were heard. "The businessmen as a class," Person reported, "failed to measure up to the reputations which they brought with them from private industry." The businessman's talents could not be transferred from the very specific conditions in which he had achieved his success. Therefore, there was a great need for "trained managers with universal and adaptable managerial principles, free and able to organize and direct enterprises— national, state, municipal or private—wherever at any moment or in any emergency their services may be in demand." Taylorism would serve as the foundation of the new profession of "transferable administrators" or "engineer-administrators." For it was the only unified system of management which applied the methods of the exact sciences and incorporated the findings of the other sciences as well.[51]

Many members of the Taylor Society saw themselves as peculiarly fitted to act as disinterested spokesmen for the community at large. They were dedicated to greater production—the sustenance of an advancing America. In the factory, these "engineer-administrators" stood between the owners and the workers. Beyond the factory, they might muster their forces to hold the balance of power in the conflict of industrial classes and bring a return to productive efficiency. By 1919, many prominent Taylorites had moved closer to labor and were apt to present efficiency as a criticism of existing institutions. The *Bulletin of the Taylor Society* sided with the workers in the bituminous coal strike of 1919 and later supported the eight-hour shift in the steel industry. When the *Dial* published the series of Veblen essays which were later to form the book, *The Engineers and the Price System*, the *Bulletin* reprinted an excerpt with favorable comment. It gave prominence to an open letter from one of its members that condemned the waste of private control of the power industry and recommended a plan of government ownership.[52]

The Taylorites had absorbed some of the social concerns of the progressive era and included them in their program. "Our profession," declared Cooke, "that of industrial engineering, has come of age at a time when the interests of society and not the interests of individuals is the master test. This is one advantage which our profession has over all others, and it carries with it a very deep significance."[53]

Notes

1. Quoted in Frederick L. Paxson, *America at War* (Boston: Houghton Mifflin, 1939), p. 226.

2. Charles Earle Funk, *Heavens to Betsy! And Other Curious Sayings* (New York: Harper, 1955), p. 29.

3. Quoted in Lucy Sprague Mitchell, *Two Lives: The Story of Wesley Clair Mitchell and Myself* (New York: Simon & Schuster, 1953), p. 299.

4. "Springfield and Bridgeport," *New Republic*, XVI (Sept. 14–21, 1918), 185–86, 216–17.

5. William Dean Howells, "Editor's Easy Chair," *Harper's Monthly*, CXXXVI (April, 1918), 756; Charles Nagel, "The Growth of Socialistic Influence," *Speeches and Writings of Charles Nagel, 1900–28*, ed. Otto Heller (New York: Putnam, 1931), I, 64–67; *American Labor Year Book, 1917–1918*, ed. Alexander Tractenberg (New York: Rand School of Social Science, 1918), pp. 40–42. For H. L. Gantt's appraisal, see "Tool Power, Not Wealth Supplies Sinews of War," [*Philadelphia*] *Public Ledger*, April 10, 1917, p. 14. For similar observations on European experience see Albert Bushnell Hart, "The War and Democracy," in *Problems of Readjustment after the War* (New York: D. Appleton, 1915), pp. 19–20; "Practical Socialism in War Time," *American Review of Reviews*, LIII (June, 1916), 730–31; Alvin Johnson, "Socialism of Modern War," *Unpopular Review*, IX (January, 1918), 139–53.

6. *Americanism: Woodrow Wilson's Speeches on the War*, ed. Oliver Marble Gale (Chicago: Baldwin Syndicate, 1918), p. 50.

7. Dewey's argument is found in his *Character and Events* (New York: Holt, 1929), II, 567, 636–41, 782–89. Morton White presents a sharp critique from a different angle in his very helpful book, *Social Thought in America: The Revolt against Formalism* (Boston: Beacon Press, 1957), pp. 161–68, chap. xiii.

8. George Harvey, "Wanted a Leader: Can Pacifists Win the War?" *North American Review*, CCVII (March, 1911), 321–29, and "Constructive Criticism," *ibid.*, CCVIII (August, 1918), 161–68; Warren G. Harding, "Causes of Our War Delay," *Forum*, LIX (Jan. 26, 1918), 661–66; "Is the Administration Staggering under the Burdens Assumed?" *Current Opinion*, LXIV (February, 1918), 80–82. For liberal views see William Hard, "Victory for Efficiency," *New Republic* XII (Aug. 11, 1917), 40–42, "Efficiency and the 'He-Man,'" *ibid.*, XIV (March 9, 1918), 165, and "Efficiency and Slackers," *ibid.* (March 16, 1918), pp. 201–3.

9. Compare, for example, the reports of Edison's trip to Germany with later accounts of that country. Allen Louis Benson, "Edison Says Germany Excels Us," *World To-Day*, XXI (November, 1911), 1356–60; "What Edison Learned in Germany," *Literary Digest*, XLIV (June 1, 1912), 1156–57; "Made in Germany," *Scientific American*, CV (Dec. 16, 1911), 550; Robert H. Davis and Perley Poore Sheehan, *Efficiency: A Play in One Act* (New York: Doran, 1917); Fletcher Durell, "Germany from the Efficiency Standpoint," *National Efficiency Quarterly*, I (May, 1918), 18 ff.; Herbert F. Small, "The Legend of German Efficiency," *Unpopular Review*, VII (April, 1917), 230.

10. Horace Bookwalter Drury, *Scientific Management: A History and Criticism* (3d ed., New York: Columbia University Press, 1922), pp. 189–90; George H. Seldes, "American Efficiency in England," *Bellman*, XXII (Feb. 3, 1917), 122–23; Sidney Webb and Arnold Freeman, *Great Britain after the War* (London: Allen & Unwin, 1916), chap. viii; H. S. Person, "Opportunities and Obligations of the Taylor Society," *Bull. Taylor Soc.*, IV (February, 1919), 5; Frank Barkley Copley, *Frederick W. Taylor: Father of Scientific Management* (New York: Harper, 1923), I, xxi; H. K. Hathaway, "Discussion," *Bull. Taylor Soc.*, III (March, 1917), 6. As of 1917, the foreign countries with the most numerous applications of scientific management were Russia, Japan, France, England, and Canada, in that order. C. Bertrand Thompson, *The Theory and Practice of Scientific Management* (Boston: Houghton Mifflin, 1917), p. 39.

11. Bernard M. Baruch, *American Industry in the War* (New York: Prentice-Hall, 1941), chap. v.

12. Morris L. Cooke, "Discussion," *Bull. Taylor Soc.*, IV (April, 1919), 7.

13. R. G. Scott, "Discussion," *ibid.*, VI (December, 1921), 232.

14. *Ibid.*, IV (February, 1919), 1.

15. "Call for a War Lord," *Literary Digest*, LVI (Jan. 26, 1918), 10–11; "Cerebral Congestion at Washington," *Nation*, CV (Dec. 27, 1917), 708; "The Conduct of the War," *Independent* (Dec. 29, 1917), pp. 577–78; "The Conduct of the War," *New Republic*, XIII (Dec. 8, 1917), 136–38; Joseph Henry Odell, "Passing of the Buck in Washington," *Outlook*, CXVIII (Feb. 13, 1918), 241–43.

16. Ernest Martin Hopkins, "Discussion," *Bull. Taylor Soc.*, IV (April, 1919), 17. The minutes of this discussion were not published until 1919. Hopkins had been interested in scientific management since the Dartmouth College Conference in 1911. He became a pioneer in "employment management," and during the war held a position on the War Labor Policies Board.

17. Henry P. Kendall, "Discussion," *ibid.*, pp. 18, 19.

18. Morris L. Cooke, "Discussion," *ibid.*, pp. 5, 7.

19. "Address delivered in New York at the opening of the Fourth Liberty Loan Drive," Sept. 27, 1918, in *Americanism: Woodrow Wilson's Speeches on the War*, pp. 130–36. In private, Wilson expressed views which might be considered socialistic. He thought the world was going to change radically after the war. Governments would have to do many things which had hitherto been left to individuals and corporations. The government would have to take over such things as water power, the coal mines, and the oilfields. Ray Stannard Baker, *Woodrow Wilson* (New York: Doubleday, Doran, 1939), VIII, 241–42. Theodore Roosevelt advocated compulsory peacetime industrial service for young men and women. John M. Blum, *The Republican Roosevelt* (Cambridge, Mass.: Harvard University Press, 1954), p. 158.

20. Quoted in William J. Ghent, *The Reds Bring Reaction* (Princeton, N.J.: Princeton University Press, 1923), p. 3.

21. Quoted in Charles W. Wood, *The Great Change: New America as Seen by Leaders in American Government, Industry, and Education Who Are Remaking Our Civilization* (New York: Boni & Liveright, 1919), p. 125.

22. "The Aim of Reconstruction," *Nation*, CVII (Nov. 9, 1918), 545; "The Meaning of Reconstruction," *New Republic*, XVII (Dec. 14, 1918), 182–83; Edward T. Devine, "Nation Wide Drive for Social Reconstruction," *Survey*, XLI (March 1, 1919), 784–85; Thorstein B. Veblen, "The Modern Point of View and the New Order," *Dial*, LXV–LXVI (Oct. 19, 1918–Jan. 25, 1919), 19–24, 75–82, 289–93, 349–54, 409–14, 482–88, 543–49, 605–11; Frederick M. Davenport, "The Spirit of Political Reconstruction in America," *Outlook*, CXXI (Jan. 8, 1919), 61–62; D. Joy Humes, *Oswald Garrison Villard* (Syracuse, N.Y.: Syracuse University Press, 1960), pp. 129–30.

23. Algie M. Simons, *The Vision for Which We Fought* (New York: Macmillan, 1919). See views of Walter Lippmann, Algie M. Simons, John Spargo, J. G. Phelps Stokes, and William English Walling in "Socialists and the Problem of War: A Symposium," *The Intercollegiate Socialist*, V (April–May, 1917), 7–27. In addition, there is an interesting series of articles by Harry W. Laidler: "War Collectivism and Wealth Conscription," *ibid.*, VI (April–May, 1917), 4–7, " 'State Socialism' in War Time," *ibid.* (February–March, 1918), pp. 11–18, "War Time Control of Industry," *ibid.*, VII (October–November, 1918), 11–14, and "Washington and the Coming Reconstruction," *ibid.* (December–January, 1918–19), 8–11.

24. Among them was that of the National Catholic War Council (with the official sanction of the Catholic hierarchy) which pleased and displeased many by its "socialistic" proposals, and that of the AFL, which pleased and displeased many by its non-socialistic proposals. The Catholic program recommended a legal minimum wage, compulsory sickness insurance, labor participation in management, profit-sharing, and "considerable modifications" in income distribution and in "the present system." Raymond E. Swing, "The Catholic View of Reconstruction," *Nation*, CVIII (March 29, 1919, 467–68; "Catholic Reconstruction," *Survey*, XLI (Feb. 22, 1919), 727; Ralph M. Easley, "Radicals Mislead Churches about Labor," *National Civic Federation Review*, IV (March 25, 1919), 3–4; "Practical vs. Visionary Program," *ibid.* (Jan. 25, 1919), p. 10.

25. "John D. Rockefeller, Jr., Puts over His Industrial Peace Plan with the Colorado Miners," *Current Opinion*, LIX (December, 1915), 415–16; John D. Rockefeller, Jr., "There's a Solution for Labor Troubles," *System*, XXX (August, 1916), 115–21.

26. William L. Stoddard, *The Shop Committee* (New York; Macmillan, 1919), chap. ii.

27. Woodrow Wilson, *War and Peace: Presidential Messages, Addresses, and Public Papers (1917–1924)*, ed. Ray Stannard Baker and William E. Dodd (New York: Harper, 1927), I, 488.

28. *Man to Man: The Story of Industrial Democracy* (New York: B. C. Forbes, 1919).

29. *The Holmes-Laski Letters: The Correspondence of Mr. Justice Holmes and Harold J. Laski, 1916–1935*, ed. Mark DeWolfe Howe (Cambridge, Mass.: Harvard University Press, 1953), I, 212.

30. Leitch, pp. 70, 228, chaps. vii and viii.

31. Glenn E. Plumb, "Let the Workmen Run the Railroads," *Independent*, XCIX (Aug. 30, 1919), 288–89, and "Should Labor Participate in Management?" *Ann. AAPSS*, LXXXVI (November, 1919), 222–26.

32. Mary Parker Follett, *The New State*, introduction by Lord Haldane (4th imp., New York: Longmans Green, 1923). For information on her life and writings see *Dynamic Administration: The Collected Papers of Mary Parker Follett*, ed. Henry C. Metcalf and L. Urwick (New York: Harper, 1940), esp. pp. 9–29.

33. Follett, *New State*, pp. 5, 173, chaps. xvi–xxi.

34. She lists "good words": integrate, interpenetrate, compenetrate, compound, harmonize, correlate, co-ordinate, interweave, reciprocally relate or adapt or adjust, etc. *Ibid.*, p. 39.

35. *Ibid.*, pp. 117–21, 139, 158, 175, 239, 324–30, chap. v.

36. *Ibid.*, pp. 42, 47, 141, 189, 276.

37. *Ibid.*, pp. 7, 142, 145, 328.

38. Frank Bunker Gilbreth, *The Primer of Scientific Management* (New York: D. Van Nostrand, 1912), pp. 48, 86; Frederick W. Taylor, "Shop Management," *Trans. ASME*, XXIV (1902–3), 1393–94; Louis D. Brandeis, "Organized Labor and Efficiency," *Survey*, XXVI (April 22, 1911), 148–51; Meyer Bloomfield, "Scientific

Management: Cooperative or One-Sided," *ibid.*, XXVIII (May 18, 1912), 312–13; Frank T. Carlton, "Scientific Management and the Wage Earner," *Journal of Political Economy*, XX (October, 1912), 834–45.

39. The most radical departure was that of Robert G. Valentine, "Scientific Management and Organized Labor," *Bulletin of the Society for the Promotion of the Science of Management*, I (January, 1915), 3–9. Also see chapter III in this book, above. In addition, see Morris L. Cooke, "Who Is Boss in Your Shop," pp. 167–85; Horace B. Drury, "Scientific Management and Progress," *Bull. Taylor Soc.*, II (November, 1916), 7; H. S. Person, "The Manager, the Workman, and the Social Scientist," *ibid.*, III (February, 1917), 4–5.

40. Robert Franklin Hoxie, *Scientific Management and Labor* (New York: D. Appleton, 1915), pp. 123–39, and "Scientific Management and Labor Welfare," *Journal of Political Economy*, XXIV (November, 1916), 833–54; Alvin Johnson, "Hoxie's Scientific Management and Labor," *New Republic*, (Dec. 4, 1915), 127. Alvin Johnson, *Pioneer's Progress* (New York: Viking Press, 1952), presents important background information on the Hoxie report. Milton J. Nadworny, *Scientific Management and the Unions: 1900–1932* (Cambridge, Mass.: Harvard University Press, 1955), pp. 94–95, chap. vi; Mary Barnett Gilson, *What's Past Is Prologue: Reflections on My Industrial Experience* (New York: Harper, 1940), chap. x.

41. "Vigilans," "Industrial Democracy at Rock Island," *Nation*, CIX (Sept. 13, 1919), 366–67; Dean Acheson, "Rock Island," *New Republic*, XXIII (Aug. 25, 1920), 358–61; John A. Fitch, "Manufacturing for Their Government," *Survey*, XLII (Sept. 13, 1917), 846–47; Horace B. Drury, "Labor Policy of the Shipping Board," *Journal of Political Economy*, XXIX (January, 1921), 1–28. Paul H. Douglas and French E. Wolfe, "Labor Administration in the Shipbuilding Industry during War Time," *Trade Unionism and Labor Problems: Second Series*, ed. John R. Commons, (New York: Ginn, 1921), pp. 318–20, 347–48.

42. Keppelle Hall, "The New Day," *Bull. Taylor Soc.*, IV (June, 1919), 5–7; George D. Babcock, "Discussion," *ibid.* (December, 1919), p. 25; Felix Frankfurter, "Discussion," *ibid.*, pp. 13, 14, 16; Henry W. Shelton, "Discussion," *ibid.*, pp. 45–46.

43. John E. Otterson, "Industrial Relations," *ibid.*, pp. 34–43, and the "Discussion," following.

44. Morris L. Cooke, *An All American Basis for Industry* (Philadelphia: Morris L. Cooke, 1919), pp. 13–15; [H. S. Person], "Comment," *Bull. Taylor Soc.*, IV (June, 1919), 2.

45. Ordway Tead, *Instincts in Industry: A Study of Working Class Psychology* (Boston: Houghton Mifflin, 1918), pp. 50–51, 54–55, and "Problems of Incentives and Output," *Ann. AAPSS*, LXXXIX (May, 1920), 170–79; H. S. Person, "The Opportunities and Obligations of the Taylor Society," *Bull. Taylor Soc.*, IV (February, 1919), 3; "Comment," *ibid.*, V (April, 1920), 49; Bertrand Thompson, *The Theory and Practice of Scientific Management* (Boston: Houghton Mifflin, 1917), p. 168.

46. *Trade Unionism and Labor Problems: Second Series*, ed. John R. Commons, pp. 319–20, 345, 346–48.

47. William F. Willoughby, "American History," *American Year Book, 1919*, ed. Francis G. Wickware (New York: D. Appleton, 1920), pp. 24–26; John B. Andrews, "Labor and Labor Legislation," *ibid.*, pp. 458–59; Samuel Crowther, "The Fetish of Industrial Democracy," *World's Work*, XXXIX (November, 1919), 23–27; compare this with his earlier "What I Found British Labor Planning," *System*, XXXVI (July, 1919), 35–38. See also Elmer H. Fish, "Some Dangers in the Shop Committee," *Industrial Management*, LVIII (September, 1919), 205; Albert W. Atwood, "Industrial Democracy and Human Nature," *Saturday Evening Post*, CXCIV (Aug. 20, 1921), 21; Henry S. Dennison, "The President's Industrial Conference," *Bull. Taylor Soc.*, V (April, 1920), 82, 90; Morris L. Cooke, "Discussion," *ibid.*, p. 91.

48. Ordway Tead, "The Technician's Point of View," in *New Tactics in Social Conflict*, ed. Harry W. Laidler (New York: Vanguard Press, 1926), p. 123.

49. Keppelle Hall, *loc. cit.*, p. 5.

50. *Bull. Taylor Soc.*, IV (April, 1919), supp. 1–6.

51. Person, "Opportunities and Obligations," pp. 3, 4, 6–7.

52. Keppelle Hall, *loc. cit.*, p. 5; Henry H. Farquhar, "Positive Contributions of Scientific Management," *Bull. Taylor Soc.*, IV (October, 1919), 24; Person, "Opportu-

nities and Obligations," p. 5; [H. S. Person], "Comment," *Bull. Taylor Soc.*, IV (August, 1919), 2, 27; Cooke, *An All American Basis for Industry*, p. 2, and "Discussion," *Bull. Taylor Soc.*, IV (October, 1919), 47, 49, 50; *ibid.*, V (April, 1920), 49; Walter N. Polakov, "Open Letter," *ibid.*, IV (October, 1919), 49–50.

53. Morris L. Cooke, "Discussion," *Bull. Taylor Soc.*, V (June, 1920), 128.

The Legend of Isolationism in the 1920s

WILLIAM APPLEMAN WILLIAMS

A basic and influential assault on the inherited view of the 1920s is made by Professor William Appleman Williams in the following essay, first published in 1954. His point, as his title suggests, is that the decade was not nearly so dominated by "isolationism" in foreign policy as most historians had believed. But this simple point has important implications. He argues that there was a considerable amount of continuity in American foreign policy between the Treaty of Versailles and the extended involvements in the world of the 1950s. Indeed, this continuity stretched well back into the nineteenth century and was a principal theme of American history.

But in Professor Williams' view, continuity does not preclude change. What happened after 1919 was simply that American techniques of expansion became much more subtle. Overt "imperialism"—which Professor Williams calls a much abused word—was more or less abandoned in favor of a more euphemistic "internationalism," promoted primarily by corporate influences on the State Department. However, even this new subtlety was not a product of the twenties, but rather represented the triumph of a style developed during the last years of the nineteenth century.

William Appleman Williams has been one of the most controversial historians of recent years. During his years as a teacher at the University of Wisconsin, he developed a distinctive approach to American foreign policy, an approach that has been identified somewhat inaccurately as the "Williams school" or the "Wisconsin school." He is currently Professor of History at Oregon State University. His books include American-Soviet Relations, 1917–1947 *(1952),* The Contours of American History *(1961),* The Tragedy of American Diplomacy *(1962),* The Great Evasion *(1962), and* The Roots of the Modern American Empire *(1969).*

The widely accepted assumption that the United States was isolationist from 1920 through 1932 is no more than a legend. Sir Francis Bacon might have classed this myth of isolation as one of his Idols of the Market-Place. An "ill and unfit choice of words," he cautioned, "leads men away into innumerable and inane controversies and fancies."[1] And certainly the application of the terms *isolation* and *isolationism* to a period and a policy that were characterized by vigorous involvement in the affairs of the world with consciousness of purpose qualifies as an "ill and unfit choice of words." Thus the purpose of this essay: on the basis of an investigation of the record to suggest that, far from isolation, the foreign relations of the United States from 1920 through 1932 were marked by express and extended involvement with—and intervention in the affairs of—other nations of the world.

It is both more accurate and more helpful to consider the twenties as contiguous with the present instead of viewing those years as a quixotic interlude of low-down jazz and lower-grade gin, fluttering flappers and Faulkner's fiction, and bootlegging millionaires and millionaire bootleggers. For in foreign policy there is far less of a sharp break between 1923 and 1953 than generally is acknowledged. A closer examination of the so-called isolationists of the twenties reveals that many of them were in fact busily engaged in extending American power. Those individuals and groups have not dramatically changed their outlook on foreign affairs. Their policies and objectives may differ with those of others (including professors), but they have never sought to isolate the United States.

This interpretation runs counter to the folklore of American foreign relations. Harvard places isolationism "in the saddle." Columbia sees

REPRINTED BY PERMISSION, FROM *Science & Society*, 18 (WINTER 1954), 1–20.

"Americans retiring within their own shell." Yale judges that policy "degenerated" into isolation—among other things.[2] Others, less picturesque but equally positive, refer to a "marked increase of isolationist sentiment" and to "those years of isolationism." Another group diagnoses the populace as having "ingrained isolationism," analyzes it as "sullen and selfish" in consequence, and characterizes it as doing "its best to forget international subjects." Related verdicts describe the Republican party as "predominantly isolationist" and as an organization that "fostered a policy of deliberate isolation."[3]

Most pointed of these specifications is a terse two-word summary of the diplomacy of the period: "Isolation Perfected."[4] Popularizers have transcribed this theme into a burlesque. Their articles and books convey the impression that the Secretaries of State were in semi-retirement and that the citizenry wished to do away with the Department itself.[5] Columnists and commentators have made the concept an eerie example of George Orwell's double-think. They label as isolationists the most vigorous interventionists.

The case would seem to be closed and judgment given if it were not for the ambivalence of some observers and the brief dissents filed by a few others. The scholar who used the phrase "those years of isolationism," for example, remarks elsewhere in the same book that "expansionism . . . really was long a major expression of isolationism." Another writes of the "return to an earlier policy of isolation," and on the next page notes a "shift in policy during the twenties amounting almost to a 'diplomatic revolution.' " A recent biographer states that Henry Cabot Lodge "did not propose . . . an isolationist attitude," but then proceeds to characterize the Monroe Doctrine—upon which Lodge stood in his fight against the League of Nations treaty—as a philosophy of "isolation." And in the last volume of his trilogy, the late Professor Frederick L. Paxton summed up a long review of the many diplomatic activities of the years 1919–1923 with the remark that this was a foreign policy of "avoidance rather than of action."[6]

But a few scholars, toying with the Idol of the Market-Place, have made bold to rock the image. Yet Professor Richard Van Alstyne was doing more than playing the iconoclast when he observed that the "militant manifest destiny men were the isolationists of the nineteenth century." For with this insight we can translate those who maintain that Lodge "led the movement to perpetuate the traditional policy of isolation." Perhaps William G. Carleton was even more forthright. In 1946 he pointed out that the fight over the League treaty was not between isolationists and internationalists, and added that many of the mislabeled isolationists were actually "nationalists and imperialists." Equally discerning was Charles Beard's comment in 1933 that the twenties were marked by a "return to the more aggressive ways . . . [used] to protect and advance the claims of American business enterprise." All these interpretations were based on facts that prompted another scholar to change his earlier conclusion'and declare in 1953 that "the thought was all of keeping American freedom of action."[7]

These are perceptive comments. Additional help has recently been supplied by two other students of the period. One of these is Robert E. Osgood, who approached the problem in terms of *Ideals and Self-Interest in American Foreign Relations*.[8] Though primarily concerned with the argument that Americans should cease being naïve, Osgood suggests that certain stereotypes are misleading. One might differ with his analysis of the struggle over the Treaty of Versailles but not with his insistence that there were fundamental differences between Senators Lodge and William E. Borah—as well as between those two and President Woodrow Wilson. Osgood likewise raises questions about the reputed withdrawal of the American public. Over a thousand organizations for the study of international relations existed in 1926, to say nothing of the groups that sought constantly to make or modify foreign policy.

Osgood gives little attention to this latter aspect of foreign relations, a surprising omission on the part of a realist.[9] But the underlying assumption of his inquiry cannot be challenged. The foreign policy issue of the twenties was never isolationism. The controversy and competition were waged between those who entertained different concepts of the national interest and disagreed over the means to be employed to secure that objective. Secretary of State Charles Evans Hughes was merely more eloquent, not less explicit. "Foreign policies," he explained in 1923, "are not built upon abstractions. They are the result of practical conceptions of national interest arising from some immediate exigency or standing out vividly in historical perspective."[10]

Historian George L. Grassmuck used this old-fashioned premise of the politician as a tool with which to probe the *Sectional Biases in Congress on Foreign Policy*. Disciplining himself more rigorously in the search for primary facts than did Osgood, Grassmuck's findings prompted him to conclude that "the 'sheep and goats' technique" of historical research is eminently unproductive. From 1921 to 1933, for example, the Republicans in both houses of Congress were "more favorable to both Army and Navy measures than . . . Democrats." Eighty-five percent of the same Republicans supported international economic measures and agreements. As for the Middle West, that much condemned section did not reveal any "extraordinary indication of a . . . tendency to withdraw." Nor was there "an intense 'isolationism' on the part of [its] legislators with regard to membership in a world organization."[11] And what opposition there was seems to have been as much the consequence of dust bowls and depression as the product of disillusioned scholars in ivory towers.

These investigations and correlations have two implications. First, the United States was neither isolated, nor did it pursue a policy of isolationism from 1920 to 1933. Second, if the policy of that era, so generally accepted as the product of traditional isolationist sentiment, proves non-isolationist, then the validity and usefulness of the concept when applied to earlier or later periods may seriously be challenged.

Indeed, it would seem more probable that the central theme of American foreign relations has been the expansion of the United States. Alexander Hamilton made astute use of the phrase "no entangling alliances" during the negotiation of Jay's Treaty in 1794, but his object was a *de facto* affiliation with the British Fleet—not isolation.[12] Nor was Thomas Jefferson seeking to withdraw when he made of Monticello a counselling center for those seeking to emulate the success of the American Revolution. A century later Senator Lodge sought to revise the Treaty of Versailles and the Covenant of the League of Nations with reservations that seemed no more than a restatement of Hamilton's remarks. Yet the maneuvers of Lodge were no more isolationist in character and purpose than Hamilton's earlier action. And while surely no latter-day Jefferson, Senator Borah was anything but an isolationist in his concept of the power of economics and ideas. Borah not only favored the recognition of the Soviet Union in order to influence the development of the Bolshevik Revolution and as a check against Japanese expansion in Asia but also argued that American economic policies were intimately connected with foreign political crises. All those men were concerned with the extension of one or more aspects of American influence, power, and authority.

Approached in this manner, the record of American foreign policy in the twenties verifies the judgments of two remarkably dissimilar students: historian Richard W. Leopold and Senator Lodge. The professor warns that the era was "more complex than most glib generalizations . . . would suggest"; and the scholastic politician concludes that, excepting wars, there "never [was] a period when the United States [was] more active and its influence more felt internationally than between 1921 and 1924."[13] The admonition about perplexity was offered as helpful advice, not as an invitation to anti-intellectualism. For, as the remarks of the Senator implied, recognition that a problem is involved does not mean that it cannot be resolved.

Paradox and complexity can often be clarified by rearranging the data around a new focal point that is common to all aspects of the apparent contradiction. The confusion of certainty and ambiguity that characterizes most accounts of American foreign policy in the twenties stems from the fact that they are centered on the issue of membership in the League of Nations. Those Americans who wanted to join are called internationalists. Opponents of that move became isolationists. But the subsequent action of most of those who fought participation in the League belies this simple classification. And the later policies of many who favored adherence to the League casts serious doubts upon the assumption that they were willing to negotiate or arbitrate questions that they defined as involving the national interest. More pertinent is an examination of why certain groups and individuals favored or disapproved of the League, coupled with a review of the programs they supported after that question was decided.

Yet such a re-study of the League fight is in itself insufficient. Equally important is a close analysis of the American reaction to the Bolshevik Revolution. Both the League Covenant and the Treaty of Versailles were written on a table shaken by that upheaval. The argument over the ratification of the combined documents was waged in a context determined as much by Nikolai Lenin's *Appeal to the Toiling, Oppressed, and Exhausted Peoples of Europe* and the Soviet *Declaration to the Chinese People* as by George Washington's Farewell Address.[14]

Considered within the setting of the Bolshevik Revolution, the basic question was far greater than whether or not to enter the League. At issue was what response was to be made to the domestic and international division of labor that had accompanied the Industrial Revolution. Challenges from organized urban labor, dissatisfied farmers, frightened men of property, searching intellectual critics, and colonial peoples rudely interrupted almost every meeting of the Big Four in Paris and were echoed in many Senate debates over the treaty. And those who determined American policy through the decade of the twenties were consciously concerned with the same problem.

An inquiry into this controversy over the broad question of how to end the war reveals certain divisions within American society. These groupings were composed of individuals and organizations whose position on the League of Nations was coincident with and part of their response to the Bolsheviks; or, in a wider sense, with their answer to that general unrest, described by Woodrow Wilson as a "feeling of revolt against the large vested interests which influenced the world both in the economic and the political sphere."[15] Once this breakdown has been made it is then possible to follow the ideas and actions of these various associations of influence and power through the years 1920 to 1933.

At the core of the American reaction to the League and the Bolshevik Revolution was the quandary between fidelity to ideals and the urge to power. Jefferson faced a less acute version of the same predicament in terms of whether to force citizenship on settlers west of the Mississippi who were reluctant to be absorbed in the Louisiana Purchase. A century later the anti-imperialists posed the same issue in the more sharply defined circumstances of the Spanish-American War. The League and the Bolsheviks raised the question in its most dramatic context and in unavoidable terms.

There were four broad responses to this reopening of the age-old dilemma. At one pole stood the pure idealists and pacifists, led by William Jennings Bryan. A tiny minority in themselves, they were joined, in terms of general consequences if not in action, by those Americans who were preoccupied with their own solutions to the problem. Many American businessmen, for example, were concerned primarily with the expansion of trade and were apathetic toward or impatient with the hullabaloo over the League.[16] Diametrically opposed to the idealists were the vigorous expansionists. All these exponents of the main chance did not insist upon an overt crusade to run the world, but they were united on Senator Lodge's proposition that the United States should dominate world politics. Association with other nations they accepted, but not equality of membership or mutuality of decision.

Caught in the middle were those Americans who declined to support either extreme. A large number of these people clustered around Woodrow Wilson, and can be called the Wilsonites. Though aware of the dangers and temptations involved, Wilson declared his intention to extend American power for the purpose of strengthening the ideals. However noble that effort, it failed for two reasons. Wilson delegated power and initiative to men and organizations that did not share his objectives, and on his own part the President ultimately "cast in his lot" with the defenders of the status quo.[17]

Led by the Sons of the Wild Jackass, the remaining group usually followed Senator Borah in foreign relations. These men had few illusions about the importance of power in human affairs or concerning the authority of the United States in international politics. Prior to the world war they supported—either positively or passively—such vigorous expansionists as Theodore Roosevelt, who led their Progressive Party. But the war and the Bolshevik Revolution jarred some of these Progressives into a closer examination of their assumptions. These reflections and new conclusions widened the breach with those of their old comrades who had moved toward a conservative position on domestic issues. Some of those earlier allies, like Senator Albert J. Beveridge, continued to agitate for an American century. Others, such as Bainbridge Colby, sided with Wilson in 1916 and went along with the President on foreign policy.

But a handful had become firm anti-expansionists by 1919.[18] No attempt was made by these men to deny the power of the United States. Nor did they think that the nation could become self-sufficient and impregnable in its strength. Borah, for example, insisted that America must stand with Russia if Japan and Germany were to be checked. And Johnson constantly pointed out that the question was not whether to withdraw, but at what time and under what circumstances to use the country's influence. What these men did maintain was that any effort to run the world by establishing an American system comparable to the British Empire was both futile and un-American.

In this they agreed with Henry Adams, who debated the same issue with his brother Brooks Adams, Theodore Roosevelt, and Henry Cabot Lodge in the years after 1898. "I incline now to anti-imperialism, and very strongly to anti-militarism," Henry warned. "If we try to rule politically, we take the chances against us." By the end of the First World War another generation of expansionists tended to agree with

Henry Adams about ruling politically but planned to build and maintain a similar pattern of control through the use of America's economic might. Replying to these later expansionists, Borah and other anti-expansionists of the nineteen-twenties argued that if Washington's influence were to be effective it would have to be used to support the movements of reform and colonial nationalism rather than deployed in an effort to dam up and dominate those forces.

For these reasons they opposed Wilson's reorganization of the international banking consortium, fearing that the financiers would either influence strongly or veto—as they did—American foreign policies. With Senator Albert B. Cummins of Iowa they voted against the Wilson-approved Webb-Pomerene Act, which repealed the anti-trust laws for export associations. In the same vein they tried to prevent passage of the Edge Act, an amendment to the Federal Reserve Act that authorized foreign banking corporations.[19] Led by Borah, they bitterly attacked the Versailles Treaty because, in their view, it committed the United States to oppose colonial movements for self-government and to support an unjust and indefensible status quo. From the same perspective they criticized and fought to end intervention in Russia and the suppression of civil liberties at home.[20]

Contrary to the standard criticism of their actions, however, these anti-expansionists were not just negative die-hards. Senator Cummins maintained from the first that American loans to the Allies should be considered gifts. Borah spoke out on the same issue, hammered away against armed intervention in Latin America, played a key role in securing the appointment of Dwight Morrow as Ambassador to Mexico, and sought to align the United States with, instead of against, the Chinese Revolution. On these and other issues the anti-expansionists were not always of one mind, but as in the case of the Washington Conference Treaties, the majority of them were far more positive in their actions than has been acknowledged.[21]

Within this framework the key to the defeat of the League treaty was the defection from the Wilsonites of a group who declined to accept the restrictions that Article X of the League Covenant threatened to impose upon the United States. A morally binding guarantee of the "territorial integrity and existing political integrity of all members of the League" was too much for these men. First they tried to modify that limitation. Failing there, they followed Elihu Root and William Howard Taft, both old-time expansionists, to a new position behind Senator Lodge. Among those who abandoned Wilson on this issue were Herbert Hoover, Calvin Coolidge, Charles Evans Hughes, and Henry L. Stimson.

Not all these men were at ease with the vigorous expansionists. Stimson, for one, thought the Lodge reservations "harsh and unpleasant" and later adjusted other of his views.[22] Hoover and Hughes tried to revive their version of the League after the Republicans returned to power in 1920. But at the time all of them were more uneasy about what one writer has termed Wilson's "moral imperialism."[23] They were not eager to identify themselves with the memories of that blatant imperialism of the years 1895 to 1905, but neither did they like Article X. That proviso caught them from both sides—it illegalized changes initiated by the United States and obligated America to restore a status quo to some aspects of which they were either indifferent or antagonistic. But least of all were they anxious to run the risk that the Wilsonian rhetoric of freedom and liberty might be taken seriously in an age of revolution. Either by choice or default they supported the idea of a community of interest among the industrialized powers of the world led by an American-British entente as against the colonial areas and the Soviet Union.

This postwar concept of the community of interest was the first generation intellectual off-spring of Herbert Croly's *Promise of American Life* and Herbert Hoover's *American Individualism*. Croly's opportunistic nationalism provided direction for Hoover's "greater mutuality of interest." The latter was to be expressed in an alliance between the government and the "great trade associations and the powerful corporations."[24] Pushed by the Croly-Hoover wing of the old Progressive Party, the idea enjoyed great prestige during the twenties. Among its most ardent exponents were Samuel Gompers and Matthew Woll of the labor movement, Owen D. Young of management, and Bernard Baruch of finance.

What emerged was an American corporatism. The avowed goals were order, stability, and social peace. The means to those objectives were labor-management co-operation, arbitration, and the elimination of waste and inefficiency by closing out unrestrained competition. State intervention was to be firm, but moderated through the cultivation and legalization of trade associations which would, in turn, advise the national government and supply leaders for the federal bureaucracy. The ideal was union in place of diversity and conflict.[25]

Other than Hoover, the chief spokesmen of this new community of interest as applied to foreign affairs were Secretaries of State Hughes and Stimson. In the late months of 1931 Stimson was to shift his ground, but until that time he supported the principle. All three men agreed that American economic power should be used to build, strengthen, and maintain the co-operation they sought. As a condition for his entry into the cabinet, Hoover demanded—and received—a major voice in "all important economic policies of the administration."[26] With the energetic assistance of Julius Klein, lauded by the National Foreign Trade Council as the "international business go-getter of Uncle Sam," Hoover changed the Department of Commerce from an agency primarily concerned with interstate commerce to one that concentrated on foreign markets and loans, and control of import sources.[27] Hughes and Stimson handled the political aspects of establishing a "community of ideals, interests and purposes."[28]

These men were not imperialists in the traditional sense of that much abused term. All agreed with Klein that the object was to eliminate "the old imperialistic trappings of politico-economic exploitation." They sought instead the "internationalization of business."[29] Through the use of economic power they wanted to establish a common bond, forged of similar assumptions and purposes, with both the industrialized nations and the native business community in the colonial areas of the world. Their deployment of America's material strength is unquestioned. President Calvin Coolidge reviewed their success, and indicated the political implications thereof, on Memorial Day, 1928. "Our investments and trade relations are such," he summarized, "that it is almost impossible to conceive of any conflict anywhere on earth which would not affect us injuriously."[30]

Internationalization through the avoidance of conflict was the key objective. This did not mean a negative foreign policy. Positive action was the basic theme. The transposition of corporatist principles to the area of foreign relations produced a parallel policy. American leadership and intervention would build a world community regulated by agreement among the industrialized nations. The prevention of revolution and the preservation of the sanctity of private property were vital objectives. Hughes was very clear when he formulated the idea for Latin America. "We are seeking to establish a *Pax Americana* maintained not by arms but by mutual respect and good will and the tranquillizing processes of reason." There would be, he admitted, "interpositions of a temporary character"—the Secretary did not like the connotations of the word intervention—but only to facilitate the establishment of the United States as the "exemplar of justice."[31]

Extension to the world of this pattern developed in Latin America was more involved. There were five main difficulties, four in the realm of foreign relations and one in domestic affairs. The internal problem was to establish and integrate a concert of decision between the government and private economic groups. Abroad the objectives were more sharply defined: circumscribe the impact of the Soviet Union, forestall and control potential resistance of colonial areas, pamper and cajole Germany and Japan into acceptance of the basic proposition, and secure from Great Britain practical recognition of the fact that Washington had become the center of Anglo-Saxon collaboration. Several examples will serve to illustrate the general outline of this diplomacy, and to indicate the friction between the office holders and the office dwellers.

Wilson's Administration left the incoming Republicans a plurality of tools designed for the purpose of extending American power. The Webb-Pomerene Law, the Edge Act, and the banking consortium were but three of the more obvious and important of these. Certain polishing and sharpening remained to be done, as exemplified by Hoover's generous interpretation of the Webb-Pomerene legislation, but this was a minor problem. Hoover and Hughes added to these implements with such laws as the one designed to give American customs officials diplomatic immunity so that they could do cost accounting surveys of foreign firms. This procedure was part of the plan to provide equal opportunity abroad, under which circumstances Secretary Hughes was confident that "American business men would take care of themselves."[32]

It was harder to deal with the British, who persisted in annoying indications that they considered themselves equal partners in the enterprise. Bainbridge Colby, Wilson's last Secretary of State, ran into the same trouble. Unless England came "to our way of thinking," Colby feared that "agreement [would] be impossible." A bit later Hughes told the British Ambassador that the time had come for London's expressions of cordial sentiment to be "translated into something definite." After many harangues about oil, access to mandated areas, and trade with Russia, it was with great relief that Stimson spoke of the United States and Great Britain "working together like two old shoes."[33]

Deep concern over revolutionary ferment produced great anxiety. Hughes quite agreed with Colby that the problem was to prevent revolutions without making martyrs of the leaders of colonial or other dissident movements. The despatches of the period are filled with such expressions as "very grave concern," "further depressed," and "deeply regret," in connection with revolutionary activity in China, Latin America, and Europe.[34] American foreign service personnel abroad were constantly reminded to report all indications of such unrest. This sensitivity reached a high point when one representative telegraphed as "an example of the failure to assure public safety . . . the throwing of a rock yesterday into the state hospital here." Quite in keeping with this pattern was Washington's conclusion that it would support "any provisional government which gave satisfactory evidence of an intention to re-establish constitutional order."[35]

Central to American diplomacy of the twenties was the issue of Germany and Japan. And it was in this area that the government ran into trouble with its partners, the large associations of capital. The snag was to convince the bankers of the validity of the long-range view. Hoover, Hughes, and Stimson all agreed that it was vital to integrate Germany and Japan into the American community. Thus Hughes opposed the French diplomacy of force on the Rhine, and for his own part initiated the Dawes Plan. But the delegation of so much authority to the financiers backfired in 1931. The depression scared the House of Morgan and it refused to extend further credits to Germany. Stimson "blew up." He angrily told the Morgan representative in Paris that this strengthened France and thereby undercut the American program. Interrupted in the midst of this argument by a trans-Atlantic phone call from Hoover, Stimson explained to the President that "if you want to help the cause you are speaking of you will not do it by calling me up, but by calling Tom Lamont." Stimson then turned back to Lamont's agent in Europe and, using "unregulated language," told the man to abandon his "narrow banking axioms."[36]

Similar difficulties faced the government in dealing with Japan and China. The main problem was to convince Japan, by persuasion, concession, and the delicate use of diplomatic force, to join the United States in an application of its Latin American policy to China. Washington argued that the era of the crude exploitation of, and the exercise of direct political sovereignty over, backward peoples was past. Instead, the interested powers should agree to develop and exercise a system of absentee authority while increasing the productive capacity and administrative efficiency of China. Japan seemed amenable to the proposal, and at the Washington Conference, Secretary Hughes went a great distance to convince Tokyo of American sincerity. Some writers, such as George Frost Kennan and Adolf A. Berle, claim that the United States did not go far enough.[37] This is something of a mystery. For in his efforts to establish "cooperation in the Far East," as Hughes termed it, the Secretary consciously gave Japan "an extraordinarily favorable position."[38]

Perhaps what Kennan and Berle have in mind is the attitude of Thomas Lamont. In contrast to their perspective on Europe, the bankers took an extremely long-range view of Asia. Accepting the implications of the Four and Nine Power Treaties, Lamont began to finance Japan's penetration of the mainland. Hughes and Stimson were trapped. They continued to think in terms of American business men taking care of themselves if given an opportunity, and thus strengthening Washington's position in the world community. Hughes wrote Morgan that he hoped the consortium would become an "important instrumentality of our 'open door' policy."[39] But the American members of the banking group refused to antagonize their Japanese and British colleagues, and so vetoed Washington's hope to finance the Chinese Eastern Railway and its efforts to support the Federal Telegraph Company in China.

In this context it is easy to sympathize with Stimson's discomfort when the Japanese Army roared across Manchuria. As he constantly reiterated to the Japanese Ambassador in Washington, Tokyo had come far along the road "of bringing itself into alignment with the methods and opinion of the Western World."[40] Stimson not only wanted to, but did in fact give Japan every chance to continue along that path. So too did President Hoover, whose concern with revolution was so great that he was inclined to view Japanese sovereignty in Manchuria as the best solution. Key men in the State Department shared the President's conclusion.[41]

Stimson's insight was not so limited. He realized that his predecessor, Secretary of State Frank B. Kellogg, had been right: the community of interest that America should seek was with the Chinese. The Secretary acknowledged his error to Senator Borah, who had argued just such a thesis since 1917. Stimson's letter to Borah of February 23, 1932, did not say that America should abandon her isolationism, but rather that she had gone too far with the wrong friends. The long and painful process of America's great awakening had begun. But in the meantime President Hoover's insistence that no move should be made toward the Soviet Union, and that the non-recognition of Manchuko should be considered as a formula looking toward conciliation, had opened the door to appeasement.

Notes

1. F. Bacon, *Novum Organum,* Headlam's translation as revised by C. P. Curtis and F. Greenslet, *The Practical Cogitator* (Boston: Houghton Mifflin Co., 1945), pp. 14–16.

2. A. M. Schlesinger, *Paths to the Present* (New York: The Macmillan Co., 1949), 69, 201; L. M. Hacker, "American International Relations," in *The United States and Its Place in World Affairs,* 1918–1943, ed. by A. Nevins and L. M. Hacker, (Boston: D. C. Heath and Co., 1943) p. 166; S. F. Bemis, "The Shifting Strategy of American Defense and Diplomacy," in *Essays in History and International Relations in Honor of George Hubbard Blakeslee,* ed. by D. E. Lee and G. E. McReynolds (Worcester: Clark University, 1949), p. 9.

3. In sequence, these quotations come from S. Adler, "The War-Guilt Question and American Disillusionment, 1919–1928," *The Journal of Modern History,* XXIII, No. 1 (March, 1951), p. 27; A. K. Weinberg, *Manifest Destiny. A Study of Nationalist Expansion in American History* (Baltimore: Johns Hopkins Press, 1935), p. 473; L. M. Hacker and H. S. Zahler, *The United States in the 20th Century* (New York: Appleton-Century-Crofts, Inc., 1952), pp. 278, 302; W. Wilson, quoted in Weinberg, *Manifest Destiny,* p. 473; F. D. Roosevelt, *Foreign Affairs,* vi, No. 4 (July, 1928), p. 577; W. Johnson, *The Battle Against Isolation* (Chicago: Chicago University Press, 1944), p. 132. For similar expressions see S. F. Bemis, *A Diplomatic History of the United States* (3rd ed., New York: Henry Holt and Co., 1950), p. 705; J. D. Hicks, *The American Nation* (Boston: Houghton Mifflin Co., 1949), p. 565; D. Perkins, *The Evolution of American Foreign Policy* (New York: Oxford University Press, 1949), p. 110; and A. Nevins, *America in World Affairs* (London: Oxford University Press, 1941), p. 80.

4. D. F. Fleming, *The United States and World Organization, 1920–1933* (New York: Columbia University Press, 1938), title of Chapter VI.

5. This literature is far too vast to cite, but even a perusal of *The Reader's Guide to Periodical Literature* will indicate the great volume of such material. It is vital to note, however, that the so-called disillusionment writers did not make this mistake—whatever their other errors. They criticized the policies of the time, but documented, in such journals as *The Nation,* the active character of the diplomacy.

6. Quotations, in order, from Weinberg, *Manifest Destiny,* pp. 473, 454; H. U. Faulkner, *American Political and Social History* (6th ed., New York: Appleton-Century-Crofts, Inc., 1952), pp. 700, 701; J. A. Garraty, *Henry Cabot Lodge. A Biography* (New York: Alfred A. Knopf, 1953), pp. 348, 364–65; F. L. Paxton, *American Democracy and the World War. Postwar Years. Normalcy, 1918–1923* (Berkeley: University of California Press, 1948), p. 367. For other examples of this ambiguity see D. Perkins, *The American Approach to Foreign Policy* (Cambridge: Harvard University Press, 1952), p. 26; T. A. Bailey, *A Diplomatic History of the American People* (4th ed., New York: Appleton-Century-Crofts, Inc., 1950), p. 682—where he says that the Harding Administration "retreated into what ex-President Wilson described as 'sullen and selfish isolation'"; H. J. Carman and H. C. Syrett, *A History of the American People* (New York: Alfred A. Knopf, 1952), pp. 264–65 and title of Chapter XII; S. E. Morrison and H. S. Commager, *The Growth of the American Republic* (4th ed., New York: Oxford University Press, 1950), Volume II, p. 497; and H. B. Parkes, *The United States of America* (New York: Alfred A. Knopf, 1953).

7. R. W. Van Alstyne, "The Significance of the Mississippi Valley in American Diplomatic History, 1686–1890," *Mississippi Valley Historical Review*, XXXVI, No. 2 (September, 1949), 238; L. L. Leonard, *Elements of American Foreign Policy* (New York: McGraw-Hill Book Co., Inc., 1953), p. 220; among the many others who characterize Lodge in this manner is S. Adler in his recent article on isolation, "Isolationism Since 1914," *The American Scholar*, XXI, No. 3 (Summer, 1952), p. 340; W. G. Carleton, "Isolationism and the Middle West," *Mississippi Valley Historical Review*, XXXIII, No. 3 (December, 1946), pp. 381–82; C. A. and M. R. Beard, *The Rise of American Civilization* (New Edition. Two Volumes in One. Revised and Enlarged. New York: The Macmillan Co., 1933), pp. 681–83; and compare D. Perkins, *The American Approach to Foreign Policy*, 26, with D. Perkins, "The Department of State and Public Opinion," Chapter IX in *The Diplomats 1919–1939*, ed. by G. A. Graig and F. Gilbert (Princeton: Princeton University Press, 1953), p. 308. Interestingly enough, both Carleton and Van Alstyne addressed their remarks to meetings of the Mississippi Valley Historical Association, and their articles later appeared as lead articles in the *Review*. On the same program with Van Alstyne, furthermore, was Professor Richard Leopold, whose comments were of a similar nature and whose paper was also printed. This professional audience seems to have ignored their keen suggestions. Professor Weinberg's article, "The Historical Meaning of the American Doctrine of Isolation," *The American Political Science Review*, XXXIV (1940), pp. 539–47, offers certain concepts that would go far to resolve the contradictions in his earlier *Manifest Destiny*, but he did not apply the ideas to any later period. H. Feis writes of America's active foreign economic policy in *The Diplomacy of the Dollar, First Era, 1919–1932* (Baltimore: Johns Hopkins Press, 1950), but fails to note that these facts contradict the idea of isolation. The same approach is taken by G. Soule, *Prosperity Decade. From War to Depression: 1917–1929* (New York: Rinehart and Co., Inc., 1947), pp. 252–74. Far more stimulating than either Feis or Soule is S. Kuznets, "Foreign Economic Relations of the United States and Their Impact Upon the Domestic Economy," Chapter 11 in his *Economic Change* (New York: W. W. Norton and Co., 1953), pp. 296–333. See also the neglected work of A. D. Gayer and C. T. Schmidt, *American Economic Foreign Policy. Postwar History, Analysis, and Interpretation* (New York: no publisher given, 1939), especially pp. 11–17.

8. R. E. Osgood, *Ideals and Self-Interest in America's Foreign Relations. The Great Transformation of the Twentieth Century* (Chicago: University of Chicago Press, 1953).

9. This is strange for a realist trained in the school of Professor Hans J. Morgenthau's *Realpolitik*. For the realists emphasize the fact that the relationship between power and ideals is reciprocal. Not only do ideas fail to have consequences without power, but the sources and the nature of the power have some correlation with the character of the ideals. Thus it would seem doubly unrealistic to slight the sources of power and at the same time discuss the ideas without reference to the private as well as the public record of the groups and individuals in question.

10. C. E. Hughes, "The Centenary of the Monroe Doctrine," *The Annals of the American Academy of Political and Social Science*, Supplement to Volume CXI (January, 1923), p. 7.

11. G. L. Grassmuck, *Sectional Biases in Congress on Foreign Policy* (Baltimore: Johns Hopkins Press, 1951), pp. 32, 93, 162, 49.

12. Hamilton to the British Minister, as quoted by S. F. Bemis, *Jay's Treaty. A Study in Commerce and Diplomacy* (New York: Macmillan and Co., 1924), p. 246.

13. R. W. Leopold, "The Mississippi Valley and American Foreign Policy, 1890–1941: an Assessment and an Appeal," *Mississippi Valley Historical Review*, XXXVII, No. 4 (March, 1951), p. 635; H. C. Lodge, "Foreign Relations of the United States, 1921–1924," *Foreign Affairs*, II, No. 4 (June, 1924), p. 526.

14. None of the authors cited above makes this association of events central to their discussion of the League issue. Few of them even connect the two. The integration has, of course, been made: most notably by E. H. Carr, *The Soviet Impact on the Western World* (New York: The Macmillan Co., 1947); M. Dobb, *Political Economy and Capitalism. Some Essays in Economic Tradition* (New York: International Publishers, 1945), Chapter VII, and *Studies in the Development of Capitalism* (New York:

International Publishers, 1947), Chapter VIII; H. J. Laski, *Reflections on the Revolution of Our Time* (New York, 1947); Sir L. Namier, *Conflicts. Studies in Contemporary History* (London: The Macmillan Co., 1942), Chapter I; and, of especial significance, H. Hoover, *American Individualism* (Garden City: Doubleday, Page and Co., 1923).

15. W. Wilson, remarks to the Council of Ten, January 16, 1919, *Papers Relating to the Foreign Relations of the United States. Paris Peace Conference* (13 vols., Washington, D. C.), III, p. 583.

16. See the excellent essay by J. H. Foote, "American Industrialists and Foreign Policy, 1919–1922. A Study in Attitudes," Master's Thesis, University of Wisconsin, Madison, 1947; for a typical expression see the remarks of Senator Walter E. Edge—"we wasted, practically wasted, two years of the opportunity presented to us at that time, unequaled, as I say, in the history of the world"—in National Foreign Trade Council, *Official Report of the Eighth National Foreign Trade Convention, 1921* (New York, 1921), p. 553.

17. W. Wilson, remarks to the Big Five, February 14, 1919, *Foreign Relations. Russia, 1919* (Washington, D. C., 1937), p. 59.

18. C. Vevier reviewed these early expansionist sympathies of the Progressives in "The Progressives and Dollar Diplomacy," Master's Thesis, University of Wisconsin, Madison, 1949. W. E. Leuchtenburg later published a summary of his own study of the same question as "Progressivism and Imperialism: The Progressive Movement and American Foreign Policy, 1898–1916," *Mississippi Valley Historical Review*, XXXIX, No. 3 (December, 1952), pp. 483–504. It would seem, however, that Leuchtenburg missed the split within the Progressives over Wilson's foreign policy. For in note 38, page 493, he considers it "remarkable" that the Progressives fought Wilson in view of the degree to which the President "was involved with American imperialist aspirations." This writer's information on the division comes from the manuscript papers of Calvin Coolidge, William E. Borah, William Judson, Samuel N. Harper, Theodore Roosevelt, Alexander Gumberg, Raymond Robins, and Woodrow Wilson; from the materials in the National Archives; and the *Congressional Record*.

19. See, for example, the debates on the Webb-Pomerene Act in *Congressional Record*, Volume 56, Part 1, pp. 69–71; and the votes on the same legislation, pp. 168, 186.

20. Especially pertinent are the remarks of Borah, *Congressional Record*, V54:1:636; V57:1:190; V58:3:3143–44; and his letter to F. Lynch, August 1, 1919, *Papers of William E. Borah*, Library of Congress, Manuscript Division, Washington, D. C. Also important are the comments of Senator Hiram Johnson, *Congressional Record*, V53:1:503, 505. Eric Goldman's penetrating study of the Progressives, *Rendezvous With Destiny. A History of Modern American Reform* (New York: Alfred A. Knopf, 1952), completely misses this development. On pp. 273–74, Goldman remarks that the "most striking deviation of American progressivism in foreign affairs from its attitudes in domestic affairs was the enthusiasm for international order in the form of the League of Nations." He proceeds, then, to argue that if the Progressives had applied the same criticism to the League as they had to its laissez faire counterpart in domestic affairs "they could hardly have emerged with a favorable attitude." But the key point is that the hard core of the Progressives did exactly this and came out in opposition to the League.

21. This paragraph is based on much the same material cited in note 18. But see, as representative, Cummins' remarks on the loans, *Congressional Record*, V55:11:757, 762; Borah on economic factors, V64:1:930–31; and the parliamentary maneuvers over the Liberian Loan, V63:1:287–88.

22. Stimson, Diary entry of December 3, 1919, quoted in H. L. Stimson and McGeorge Bundy, *On Active Service in Peace and War* (New York: Harper and Brothers, 1948), p. 104.

23. H. F. Cline, *The United States and Mexico* (Cambridge: Harvard University Press, 1953), p. 141.

24. H. Croly, *The Promise of American Life* (New York: The Macmillan Co., 1909); H. Hoover, *American Individualism*, p. 43; and Hoover, quoted in Goldman, *Rendezvous with Destiny*, p. 309. Goldman makes this identification between Croly and Hoover, but does not develop it, either as corporatism or in foreign affairs. Other Americans had spoken the language of the community of interest. J. P. Morgan

used it to describe his ideal in the economic realm. Brooks Adams warned Theodore Roosevelt that such coordination at the national level was necessary to insure American supremacy in the world. The Adams argument emphasized the need for an intellectual and political élite chosen from the upper classes to supervise the community of interest through control of the national government.

25. American corporatism is a neglected field. This writer is greatly indebted to Professor Paul Farmer, University of Wisconsin, for many long discussions of the question. Farmer brought to these conversations his intimate and extended knowledge of French corporative theory and practice as it developed to and culminated in the Vichy Government. His insights into the American scene were equally penetrating. At a later date M. H. Elbow, *French Corporative Theory, 1789–1948. A Chapter in the History of Ideas* (New York: Columbia University Press, 1953), was helpful in review. Of other published material, the following were most helpful: S. D. Alinsky, *Réveille For Radicals* (Chicago: University of Chicago Press, 1946); G. A. Almond, "The Political Attitudes of Wealth," *Journal of Politics*, VII, No. 3 (August, 1945); R. A. Brady, *Business as a System of Power* (New York: Columbia University Press, 1938); R. Bendix, "Bureaucracy and the Problem of Power," *Public Administration Review*, V, No. 3 (Summer, 1945); J. A. C. Grant, "The Guild Returns to America," *Journal of Politics*, IV, Nos. 3 and 4 (August, November, 1942); W. E. Henry, "The Business Executive: the Psycho-Dynamics of a Social Role," *American Journal of Sociology*, LIV, No. 1 (January, 1949); E. J. Howenstine, "Public Works Policy in the Twenties," *Social Research*, XII (December, 1946); F. Hunter, *Community Power Structure. A Study of Decision Makers* (Chapel Hill: University of North Carolina Press, 1953); R. S. Lynd, "Power Politics and the Post War World," in *The Postwar World. The Merrick Lectures for 1944* (New York: Abingdon-Cokesbury Press, 1945); and M. Weber, *The Theory of Social and Economic Organization*, trans. by A. M. Henderson and T. Parsons, ed. by T. Parsons (New York: Oxford University Press, 1947). For a revealing glimpse of the later bi-partisan movement toward corporatism, and the consequences thereof, see *The Welfare State and the National Welfare. A Symposium on Some of the Threatening Tendencies of Our Times*, ed. by S. Glueck (Cambridge: Addison-Wesley Press, Inc., 1952); and the last chapter in Goldman, *Rendezvous With Destiny*.

26. *The Memoirs of Herbert Hoover. The Cabinet and the Presidency, 1920–1933* (New York: The Macmillan Co., 1952), p. 36.

27. *Official Report of the 18th Foreign Trade Convention, 1931* (New York: 1931), p. 287.

28. C. E. Hughes, remarks concerning a substitute for Article X of the League Covenant, Union League Club Speech, New York, March 26, 1919.

29. J. Klein, *Frontiers of Trade* (New York: The Century Co., 1929), pp. 40, 46.

30. C. Coolidge, Address of May 30, 1928, *Congressional Record*, V69:10:10729.

31. C. E. Hughes, "Centenary of the Monroe Doctrine," *Annals*, p. 17; and Hughes, remarks to the Havana Conference, 1928.

32. The story of the fight over diplomatic immunity for consular officers can be followed in *Foreign Relations, 1925*, pp. 211–54; the quote from Hughes is by J. Butler Wright, in *Official Report of the 12th National Foreign Trade Convention, 1925* (New York, 1925), p. 165.

33. Colby to Wright, November 5, 1920, *National Archives of the United States* (hereafter cited as *NA*), 574.D 1/240b; Hughes, Memorandum of conversation with Geddes, September 20, 1921, *NA*, 500.A 4/190.5; Stimson, Memorandum of July 20, 1931, *NA*, 462.00 R 296/4594.5.

34. Colby to Russell, August 13, 1920, *NA*, 333.3921 L 96/3; Hughes to Cottrell, April 9, 1923, *NA*, 824.51/174; Hughes to Morales, June 30, 1923, *NA*, 815.00/2609; same to same, May 15, 1923, *NA*, 815.00/2574.

35. Kodding to Hughes, October 10, 1924, *NA*, 375.1123 Coleman and Delong/89; Hughes to Welles, April 10, 1924, *NA*, 815.00/3077a supplement.

36. Stimson, Memorandum of talks with representatives of J. P. Morgan and Co., Paris, July 17, 1931, *NA*, 462.00 R 296/4587.5.

37. G. F. Kennan, *American Diplomacy, 1900–1950* (Chicago, University of Chicago Press, 1951), p. 82; A. A. Berle, Jr., review of H. Feis, *The China Tangle*, in the *New York Times*, Book Review Section, October 4, 1953.

38. Hughes to Judge Hiscock, April 24, 1924, quoted in M. J. Pusey, *Charles Evans Hughes* (2 vols., New York, The Macmillan Co., 1951), II, p. 516; Hughes to Bell, October 22, 1924, *NA*, 893.51/4699; Hughes, Memorandum of conversations with Kato and Balfour, December 2, 1921, *NA*, 500. A4b/547.5.

39. Hughes to Morgan, August 8, 1921, *NA*, 861.77/2184.

40. Stimson, Memorandum of November 21, 1931, *NA*, 793.94/2865; and see Stimson, Memorandum of February 27, 1933, *NA*, 793.94/5953, for a clear review of his changing attitudes.

41. This writer is greatly indebted to Professor Richard N. Current, University of Illinois, for sharing his extended knowledge of the Manchurian Crisis. Professor Current's study will be published in the spring of 1954 by Rutgers University Press.

PART III
A Confused Culture

Divorce in the Progressive Era

WILLIAM L. O'NEILL

The decade of the twenties has always been most famous as a decade of "revolution" in social morality. The twenties has seemed to be a bizarre interlude during which Americans took something of a moral holiday from the more serious concerns of reform, World War I, and the depression. In formal histories, in fiction, in films, and in television programs, the twenties has been portrayed as an era when strains in the social fabric were widened into tears, and when some of the most neurotic features of American society became public habits.

In the following essay, Professor William L. O'Neill demonstrates that one of the most important measures of social tension and confusion came unhinged during the first two decades of this century. Divorce, as a fact and as a moral issue, was a prime national pastime before the twenties began, and most of the attitudes that still surround the issue today were exemplified on a broad scale before 1917. Like Professors Williams, May, and others, however, Professor O'Neill does not argue that *nothing* changed in the twenties. Indeed, he admits, the changes were "spectacular." He only claims that the divorce phenomenon, like other features commonly associated exclusively with the twenties, had its *origin* in the progressive period.

William L. O'Neill was trained at the University of California at Berkeley under Professor Henry F. May, as was Professor Samuel Haber. He is currently Associate Professor of History at the University of Wisconsin. The present essay formed part of his larger study entitled Divorce in the Progressive Era *(1967). He has also written on the related subject of feminism in an essay entitled* "Feminism as a Radical Ideology," *in* Dissent: Explorations in the History of Amercan Radicalism *(1968). In addition, he is the editor of* Echoes of Revolt: "The Masses," 1911–1917 *(1966).*

During the progressive years the divorce rate, which had been rising
steadily since the Civil War, attained critical dimensions. Consequently,
Americans of this period took a graver view of the problem than any
subsequent generation. Their varied responses proved to be decisive
as far as the future of divorce itself was concerned, and they illuminate
aspects of the Progressive Era which have received little attention from
historians.

The precipitate growth of the divorce rate can be easily demonstrated.
In 1880 there was one divorce for every twenty-one marriages; in 1900
there was one divorce for every twelve marriages; in 1909 the ratio
dropped to one in ten and by 1916 it stood at one in nine.[1] Naturally
this dramatic increase in the divorce rate stimulated public alarm.

In 1881 the New England Divorce Reform League was established
to conduct research on family problems, educate the public and lobby
for more effective legislative curbs on divorce.[2] Under the leadership
of Samuel Dike, a Congregational minister, the league enjoyed a long
and useful life, but Dike's reluctance to advance legislative solutions
to the divorce problem failed to deter others from resorting to politics.

Efforts to arrest the spread of divorce by legal means took two forms.
State campaigns were waged to amend local divorce laws, and repeated
attempts were made to achieve uniform marriage and divorce laws
either through a constitutional amendment or through the voluntary
enactment of uniform codes by the several states.[3] Typical of the many
local fights to alter state divorce laws was the successful battle in 1893
to end South Dakota's status as a divorce colony. After their admission
to the Union in 1889, North and South Dakota retained Dakota Territory's generous ninety-day residence requirement. Sioux City, largest

REPRINTED BY PERMISSION, FROM *American Quarterly*, 17 (SUMMER 1965),
203–217. COPYRIGHT, 1965, TRUSTEES OF THE UNIVERSITY OF PENNSYLVANIA.

and most accessible town in the two states, soon developed a substantial divorce trade and gained national fame as a divorce colony. The resulting notoriety provoked local resentment which was mobilized by the return from Japan of the popular Episcopal Bishop William Hobart Hare, who in 1893 led Protestants, Catholics and Populists in an attack on the ninety-day residence requirement. The state legislature was successfully petitioned to extend the residence requirement to six months and the migratory divorce trade was diverted to North Dakota.[4]

The South Dakota campaign conformed to what was already an established pattern. It was led by conservative clergymen, supported by women's groups, and met little apparent opposition. Although these local campaigns did not succeed anywhere in abolishing divorce, they were part of a widespread tendency toward stricter divorce legislation.[5] When such local crusades failed, it was usually because of public apathy, sometimes coupled with undercover resistance from commercial and legal interests which profited from the divorce trade.

Serious attempts to secure uniform marriage and divorce legislation through a constitutional amendment began in 1892 when James Kyle, the Populist Senator from South Dakota, introduced a joint resolution which read in full: "The Congress shall have the exclusive power to regulate marriage and divorce in the several states, Territories, and the District of Columbia."[6] Senator Kyle's resolution died in committee as did all later resolutions, presumably because of a disinclination on the part of Congress to increase the power of the Federal government at the expense of the states.[7]

More popular, if equally unsuccessful, was the movement to secure voluntary uniformity through the drafting of model statutes which were to be enacted by the states. The most persistent of the organizations dedicated to this goal was the National Conference of Commissioners on Uniform State Laws, which met annually in connection with the American Bar Association. It was established by the Bar Association in 1889 to frame model codes on a wide range of subjects. The Commissioners were usually appointed by their state governors, and over the years drafted seven model statutes concerning marriage and divorce.[8] However, few of the states demonstrated an interest in these models, and by 1916 the Commissioners were forced to admit that their approach had been a failure.

If the experience of the National Conference of Commissioners on Uniform State Laws to 1906 had not been conclusive, the fate of the National Divorce Congress in that year was. A national meeting to draft uniform legislation had been talked about for years on the grounds that it would attract sufficient attention to succeed where the more diffident Commissioners had failed. In 1906 President Roosevelt was persuaded to request a new census study of marriage and divorce, and the interest aroused by this led Governor Pennypacker of Pennsylvania to call a national conference to draft model uniform legislation on these subjects. The Congress met twice, once in Washington to appoint committees, and again in Philadelphia to ratify the proposed statutes. The first meeting was attended by delegates from 42 of the 45 states and consisted largely of clergymen and lawyers, many of the latter having also been members of the NCCUSL. Despite the widespread approval which met their efforts, few states adopted their model statutes.[9]

The antidivorce forces were also active within the established Protestant churches. During the Progressive Era repeated efforts were made in almost all the great Protestant denominations to stiffen their positions on divorce. The Episcopal Church, traditionally more hostile to divorce than most Protestant bodies, was in the van of this movement, thanks principally to William Croswell Doane, Bishop of Albany, New York. Doane was perhaps the most vocal and consistent enemy of divorce in the whole country. He favored prohibiting divorce altogether, and his activities within the Episcopal Church were directed at the canon which allowed the innocent party in an adultery suit to remarry. This canon was only slightly less severe than the refusal of the Roman Catholic Church to allow any divorced person to remarry, but it seemed dangerously lax to Doane and he regularly introduced an amendment which would have denied the sacraments to all divorced persons without exception.

In 1898 the House of Bishops, usually more conservative than the lower House, which included laymen, at the policy-making Triennial Convention, rejected Doane's amendment 31 to 24.[10] In 1901 his amendment was defeated by a narrower margin, but in 1904 it passed the House of Bishops only to fail in the House of Deputies, whose members felt that it was too far removed from the spirit of the country.[11] Thereafter enthusiasm within the Episcopal church for the Doane amendment declined, and while it was re-introduced at later conventions, it failed to pass even in the House of Bishops. Similar efforts were made in the other Protestant denominations with what proved to be an equal lack of success.[12]

American attitudes toward marriage and divorce during the Progressive years must be seen in terms of the widespread fear of divorce demonstrated by these examples. It is not too much to say that there was a national crisis generated by divorce. It was a crisis to begin with because people believed it was. As Daniel Bell has demonstrated in his *The End of Ideology*, it is not necessary for activities seen to be antisocial actually to increase in order to create a crisis atmosphere—it is enough if people simply believe that such activities are increasing.[13]

An even better example perhaps was the white slave panic of 1912–13. If anything, prostitution was declining, but irrespective of the facts, widespread public alarm over this presumed social evil was triggered by local investigations and newspaper publicity.[14]

However, divorce actually was increasing by leaps and bounds. When one marriage in twelve ended in divorce, there were legitimate grounds for concern. These were crucial years for divorce, finally, because the Progressive period was the last time when public opinion could reasonably have been expected to support genuinely repressive action. With the 1920s and the advent of the revolution in morals, the opportunity to abolish or seriously restrict divorce was lost forever. Some of the antidivorce leaders sensed that time was running out for them, and this awareness gave their strictures an urgent tone which became more shrill with the years.

Although divorce had political, psychological and other dimensions, the increase of divorce was usually seen as a moral and social problem.[15] It is difficult, if indeed not actually pointless, to try to determine which of these two aspects alarmed critics of divorce the most. The enemies of divorce invariably regarded it as both immoral and antisocial. Since most opponents of divorce were either clergymen or strongly religious people, it seems fair to assume that the moral side of the divorce question was what first engaged their attention, but having once declared divorce to be immoral, there is little more one can say in that direction, and most of the serious attacks on divorce emphasized its antisocial character.[16]

The attack on divorce hinged on the common belief that divorce destroyed the family, which was the foundation of society and civilization. Theodore Schmauk, editor of the *Lutheran Church Review*, President of the Lutheran General Council and a leading theologian, characterized the family as "the great and fundamental institution in social life."[17] *The Catholic World*, in an attack on H. G. Wells' view of divorce, felt that it had demolished his position when it observed that Wells failed to see that the family "was the cradle of civil society."[18] Lyman Abbott, an influential Progressive editor and associate of Theodore Roosevelt, once charged a prominent divorcee with being "the worst type of anarchist" because divorce, like anarchy, threatened to destroy society altogether.[19] President Roosevelt, in addressing Congress on the need for uniform legislation, described marriage as being "at the very foundation of our social organization. . . ."[20] Marriage and the family are, of course, quite different institutions, but the critics of divorce did not usually distinguish between them.

Felix Adler took this contention a step further when he insisted that divorce menaced "the physical and spiritual existence of the human race. . . ."[21] Adler was in some ways a surprising figure to find on this side of the divorce question. The founder of Ethical Culture and a leading advocate of liberal religion, he consistently attacked dogma and orthodoxy and supported a wide variety of social reforms.[22] He had earlier supported divorce, but by 1915 had changed his mind and accepted the point, usually advanced by the theologically orthodox, that divorce had to be suppressed as a matter of social survival. His conversion showed how this argument operated independently of its conservative religious base and helps to explain why some enemies of divorce attached such importance to their campaign. One could hardly play for higher stakes.

A related theme which engaged the attention of divorce critics was the role of woman. It was generally believed that the family was woman's special responsibility and its protection her primary concern. Moreover women were thought to be more active than men in securing divorces (and they probably were since about two-thirds of all divorces were awarded to women). The *North American Review* reflected this point of view when it entitled one of its divorce symposiums, "Are Women to Blame?"[23] The *Review's* female panelists charged women with responsibility for the divorce rate and accused them of being spoiled, romantic, impatient, jealous of men and usurpers of the male's time-honored functions. Many of these women were successful writers, as was Anna B. Rogers, a popular essayist, who repeated the same charges in her book, *Why American Marriages Fail,* nineteen years later.[24]

While the critics of divorce, especially the men, were inclined to argue that women were really happier when they stayed at home and held the family together, the more tough-minded accepted the fact that the woman's traditional role was often painful and difficult.[25] Few had a clearer picture of what was involved than the respected novelist Margaret Deland. Mrs. Deland was a warm supporter of many Progressive causes and a woman with courage enough to defend the rights of unwed mothers in Victorian Boston. But she believed that civilization "rests on the permanence of marriage."[26] For this reason women dared not turn to divorce, for it would mean the end of everything. "If we let the flame of idealism be quenched in the darkness of the senses," she cried, "our civilization must go upon the rocks."[27] Even adultery was no excuse for giving up the fight, she continued, because men were instinctively promiscuous and their lapses from grace had to be tolerated for the sake of the greater good.

Implicit in these arguments was the belief that the individual was less important than the group. Most opponents of divorce agreed that divorce was part of an unwholesome tendency toward a "dangerous individualism." Margaret Deland bewailed the absence of team-play among women and Professor Lawton called frankly for the "suppression of the individual in favor of the community."[28] Samuel Dike in his Cook Lecture attributed divorce to the rising tide of individualism menacing all progressive societies, while Felix Adler as early as 1890 was tracing the whole ugly business back to Rousseau's "false democratic ideals."[29] Although, as we shall see, most leading sociologists believed in divorce, Charles A. Ellwood did not. This future president of the American Sociological Society, despite his Progressive sympathies, also attributed divorce to excessive individualism.[30] Francis Peabody, an eminent theologian and student of the Higher Criticism, believed that the family's major enemies were scientific socialism and "the reactionary force of self-interested individualism. . . ."[31]

The opponents of divorce were more varied and had much more to say than I have been able to indicate, but the foregoing gives at least some idea of who they were and what they thought. The defenders of divorce, by way of contrast, were fewer in number and easier to locate. Opinion against divorce was so widespread and diffuse that it cannot be attributed to a handful of groups, but the sentiment favoring divorce was largely confined to sociologists, liberal clergymen and feminists. The defenders of divorce, like its enemies, viewed the problem primarily in moral and social terms. But unlike the critics of divorce, its supporters, who were with few exceptions liberals, were much more interested in the morality of divorce and more inclined to see its moral and social dimensions as too interrelated for separate discussion and analysis.

The case for divorce gained initial momentum in the 1880s and 1890s when a trickle of protest against Victorian marriage began to make itself heard. The plays of Henrik Ibsen, especially *A Doll's House* (1879) and *Ghosts* (1881), were affecting English audiences in the late 1880s and American opinion somewhat later. By the 1890s a number of Englishmen were attacking marriage, and the views of Mona Caird and Grant Allen became well known in the United States through their own writings and through the publicity given their ideas by the American press. Mona Caird was a feminist whose essays appeared for the most part in high-quality limited circulation periodicals. Her most controversial proposal was an attempt to substitute for divorce short-term marriage contracts whose expiration would leave both parties free to separate or to negotiate a new contract.[32]

Grant Allen's best-known statement on the question was a sensational novel boosting feminism and free love entitled *The Woman Who Did*.[33] Allen was really calling for an end to marriage altogether, but his polemics against the institution supported divorce as much as free love. Within a few years the radical attack on marriage enlisted such big guns as H. G. Wells, who, in a characteristically exuberant preview of the future in 1901, announced that monogamy was dissolving and sexual standards relaxing to the point where, in a hundred years, the present moral code "would remain nominally operative in sentiment and practice, while being practically disregarded. . . ."[34] Marriage was also under fire from the new moralists like the mystical Edward Carpenter, Havelock Ellis and his wife Edith, and the South African feminist Olive Schreiner, among others.[35]

The effect of this stream of marriage propaganda was to invigorate and inspire those Americans who believed in the right to divorce. Few respectable Americans were prepared to go as far as new moralists like Wells and Carpenter, but a substantial number of liberals were beginning to feel that traditional marriage was needlessly tyrannical and repressive, that it discriminated against women, and that divorce was not only an escape hatch for abused women, but offered real opportunities for a reform of the whole marriage system. At the bottom of most, if not all, of this sentiment was the feminist impulse, for most divorce liberals were acutely conscious of the usefulness of divorce as an instrument for the emancipation of women.

Unlike the new moralists whose feminism was concerned with freeing women for a fuller sex life, the American feminist was inclined to defend divorce because it freed women from sex. Benjamin O. Flower, who edited the populistic *Arena*, called for easier divorce laws as a way of protecting women from the excessive sexual appetites of their husbands. He argued that the common prostitute was "far freer than the wife who is nightly the victim of the unholy passion of her master. . . ."[36] By 1914 this argument had become so familiar that it was thought fit for the respectable readers of the cautious *Good Housekeeping* magazine. In that year Jesse Lynch Williams, feminist and playwright, asked rhetorically, "Is allowing herself to be owned body and soul by a man she loathes doing right?" before going on to delicately suggest, "that seems rather like a dishonorable institution more ancient than marriage."[37]

Many feminists contended that not only did traditional marriage make women the sexual victims of their husbands, but it also exaggerated the importance of sex by denying women the chance to develop their other traits of character though work and education, and by forcing them to compete in the marriage market largely on the basis of their sexual attractions. The most desirable women had the best marital opportunities and so, through a kind of natural selection, sexuality prospered at the expense of other attributes. Divorce, along with expanded opportunities for education and employment, was a way of combatting this pernicious tendency.[38]

If the impulse to defend divorce came first from feminists who agreed with Elizabeth Cady Stanton on the need for a "larger freedom in the marriage relation," social scientists performed a crucial service in coping with the public's fear of the social consequences of divorce.[39] The first man of stature to defend divorce was Carrol Wright, U.S. Commissioner of Labor Statistics and a self-trained social scientist, who, at the national Unitarian convention in 1891, boldly declared himself for liberal divorce laws. A few years later he wrote:

> The pressure for divorce finds its impetus outside of laws, outside of our institutions, outside of our theology; it springs from the rebellion of the human heart against that slavery which binds in the cruelest bonds human beings who have by their haste, their want of wisdom, or the intervention of friends, missed the divine purpose as well as the civil purpose of marriage.[40]

But it was not until 1904 that a leading professionally trained social scientist joined the fight. In his massive *A History of Matrimonial Institutions* and subsequent writings George E. Howard, an eminent historian and sociologist, tried to show how the divorce rate was the product of forces which were dramatically improving American society.[41] He argued that industrialization, urbanization and the other pressures which were breaking up the old patriarchal family produced not only more divorces, but a new kind of marriage marked by higher spiritual standards and greater freedom. Closing with the problem of individualism which so alarmed the enemies of divorce, he declared that the growing power of the state was tending to make the individual and not the family the functional unit of society and that this process not only freed the individual from familial authoritarianism but elevated the family by abolishing its coercive power and transforming it into a "spiritual and psychic association of parent and child based on persuasion."[42]

Within a few years Wright and Howard were joined by a host of social scientists including most of the leading men in the field.[43] The weight of sociological opinion was solidly on the side of divorce by 1908, when the American Sociological Society devoted its third annual meeting to the family.[44] President William G. Sumner, the crusty, aging president of the society who had done so much to establish sociology as an academic discipline, opened the proceedings by observing gloomily that "the family has to a great extent lost its position as a conservative institution and has become a field for social change."[45] The program of the convention confirmed Sumner's fears, for virtually every paper described the changes affecting the family, called for more changes, or did both. Charlotte P. Gilman read a paper summarizing her *Women and Economics*, and a group of papers dealt with the damage inflicted on the family by urban, industrial life.[46]

The high point of the meeting was George Howard's "Is the Freer Granting of Divorce an Evil?" Howard repeated his now familiar views and touched off a controversy which showed the drift of professional opinion.[47] He was attacked by Samuel Dike, who insisted that divorce was produced by a dangerous individualism and the decline of ideals, and by Walter George Smith. Smith was a prominent Catholic lawyer who had advocated stricter divorce laws for many years and was a leader in the campaign for uniform divorce legislation. His criticisms stressed divorce's incompatibility with orthodox religion and he accused Howard of condoning a social revolution that destroyed the divinely constituted order of things. Nothing, he declared, could alter the fact of feminine inferiority. Howard replied that marriage was a purely social institution "to be freely dealt with by men according to human needs."[48]

Despite this unusually spirited clash, Smith and his friends were making an illusory show of strength. The moralistic flavor of their language, so different in tone from Howard's, revealed their professional isolation. Theirs was the faintly anachronistic rhetoric of a discredited tradition of social criticism. The opponents of Howard's position were, moreover, all laymen with the exception of President Sumner and Albion Small, while on his side were ranged most of the speakers, including E. A. Ross, James Lichtenberger and other leading scientists. As a profession then, sociology was committed to a positive view of divorce at a time when virtually every other organized group in the country was opposed to it. But although heavily outnumbered, the sociologists were the only people who could claim to speak on the problem with expert authority, and in the Progressive Era expertise was coming to be highly valued. As experts, the social scientists conferred respectability on the cause of free divorce at the same time as they did much to allay public anxiety over its effects.

A final problem that remained for the divorce liberals was finding some way to weaken the general conviction that divorce was forbidden by the Bible and to diminish the impact of the clergy's opposition to divorce. It was here that the handful of liberal ministers who supported divorce performed a signal, and indeed indispensable, service. Simply by saying that divorce was a morally acceptable device, the liberal ministers endowed it with a certain degree of legitimacy. If supporting divorce with their moral prestige was the more important function performed by the liberal ministers, some went beyond this and effectively disputed the traditional charge that the Bible specifically prohibited divorce.

One of the most impressive statements of the liberal position was delivered by William G. Ballentine, classicist, Bible scholar, onetime president of Oberlin College and for twenty years editor of the *Bibliotheca Sacra*. Ballentine argued that "even if all thoughtful Christian men were today united in a resolute purpose of conformity to the letter of Scripture the path of duty would be far from plain."[49] He pointed out that a Biblical injunction against divorce cited by Bishop Doane in a recent magazine article appeared in the same passage as the admonition to resist evil. How, he asked, were Christians to know which commandment to obey and which to ignore? Ballentine described the life of Jesus as a struggle against Talmudic literalism:

> During His whole life, He fought against the tyranny of mere words, and for the lordship of the present living spiritual man. In His discourse He suggested great truths by parables, by questions, by metaphors, by paradoxes, by hyperboles, by every device that could elude the semblance of fixed judicial formulas. It is the irony of history that such language should be seized upon for statute law.[50]

Other scholars, theologians and Higher Critics attacked the presumed Biblical sanctions against divorce in different ways, but the effect of their work was to undercut the general belief that the Bible clearly forbade divorce.[51]

On a more popular level the Rev. Minot J. Savage declared that as love was the essence of marriage two people who no longer loved each other had every reason to get divorced.[52] This same conviction informed

the writings of John H. Holmes, a great civil libertarian and advocate
of liberal Christianity, who believed that the passing of love destroyed
marriage in fact if not in name.[53]

Gradually the climate of opinion began to change. As noted earlier
there was a substantial organized opposition to divorce during the Progressive period, but despite local victories, the movement to retard divorce
by legal and political means was resoundingly unsuccessful. There were
other signs which demonstrated that attitudes were being modified. Samuel Dike died in 1913 and his league expired shortly thereafter. It was
essentially a one-man operation, but it was supported by the enemies
of divorce, whose financial contributions had declined sharply even before his death, to the point where receipts after 1910 were about half of
what they had been in the 1890s.[54] The Committee on the Family, which
was routinely formed by the Federal Council of Churches in 1911, was
singularly inactive, and in 1919 it was dropped altogether.[55]

At the same time the solid wall of opposition to divorce maintained
by the nation's press was repeatedly breached. Before 1900 no important
American magazine defended the right to divorce except the radical
Arena. Articles favorable to divorce were very rare in the general press.
After about 1900, however, a few bold magazines like the *Independent*
endorsed the right of divorce editorially, and many more began to print
occasional articles defending divorce. The *North American Review*,
which was more interested in the problem than any other major periodical, began the new century with a rousing attack on the opponents of
divorce by the aging but still magnificent Elizabeth Cady Stanton.[56]
Other magazines, too numerous to mention, also began to print articles
favoring divorce. Even the uncompromisingly hostile *Outlook* unbent
to this extent, and in 1910 it conceded editorially that there were times
when divorce was permissible.[57] This shift influenced popular as well
as serious magazines. In 1910 the slick monthly *World's Work* announced
that "The True View of Increasing Divorce" was that the divorce rate
was not alarming, and that divorces should not be subject to excessive
restrictions.[58]

Obviously the changes in public opinion which these articles represented did not constitute a general recognition of the desirability of
divorce. Although a few journals accepted the liberal argument that
divorce was a therapeutic social mechanism, most did not. In many cases
nothing more was involved than the admission that there were probably
two sides to the question. This of itself, however, was a form of moral
relativism on the issue which would have been unthinkable in the 1890s.
This new tolerance of divorce coincided with the eruption of a number
of curious phenomena like the dance craze and the white slave panic
which marked the onset of the revolution in morals.[59]

Divorce was a part of the complex transformation of moral values and
sexual customs which was to help give the 1920s their bizarre flavor. It
was not only the most visible result of this vast social upheaval, but in

many ways it was the most compatible with traditional modes of thought. It was on the whole, an orderly, public and institutionalized process which took due account of the formal difference between right and wrong, guilt and innocence. It had the blessings of the highest socio-logical authorities, and it was recommended by many feminists as a cure for the brutalizing sexual indignities known to occur in some marriages. Conservatives could, therefore, more easily resign themselves to divorce than to other, more extravagant, demonstrations of the changing moral order.

Altough divorce has today assumed proportions undreamed of in the Progressive Era, the nature of the American response to mass divorce was determined at that time. Between 1905, when the magnitude of di-vorce as a social problem had become fully apparent, and 1917, when the movement to limit or direct the spread of divorce had clearly failed, something of importance for American social history had occurred. This was the recognition by moral conservatives that they could not prevent the revolution in morals represented by mass divorce. Their failure of morale in the immediate prewar period paved the way for the spectacular changes which took place after the war.

Notes

1. The definitive statistical study is Paul H. Jacobson, *American Marriage and Divorce* (New York, 1959). Two great government reports contain the raw materials —they are U. S. Bureau of Labor, *Marriage and Divorce 1867–1887* (1889), and the later, more comprehensive U. S. Bureau of the Census, *Marriage and Divorce 1867–1906* (1909). Interesting contemporary analyses are contained in E. A. Ross, *Changing America* (New York, 1912) and William B. Bailey, *Modern Social Conditions* (New York, 1906).

2. Its origins are described in an untitled autobiographical manuscript by Samuel Warren Dike in the Dike Papers, Library of Congress.

3. The legal and political history of divorce is described very fully in Nelson Manfred Blake, *The Road to Reno* (New York, 1962).

4. See M. A. DeWolfe Howe, *The Life and Labors of Bishop Hare* (New York, 1912), *passim;* Blake, "Divorce in South Dakota," *Nation,* IX (January 26, 1893), 61.

5. National League for the Preservation of the Family, *Some Fundamentals of the Divorce Question* (Boston, 1909). A pamphlet written by Samuel Dike and published by his organization, which had undergone two changes of name since its founding, deals with these changes at some length. They involved extending the time required to obtain divorces, and limiting the causes for which they could be granted.

6. U. S. Congressional Record, 52 Cong., 1st Sess. (February 3, 1892), p. 791.

7. See Senator Shortridge's candid remarks to this effect during hearings on a similar resolution years later. *Senate Judiciary Committee,* "Hearings on S. J. Res. 31" (November 1, 1921), *passim.*

8. "Secretary's Memorandum," *Proceedings of the 26th Annual Meeting of the NCCUSL* (1916).

9. See Blake, 140–45, and *Proceedings of the Adjourned Meeting of the National Congress on Uniform Divorce Laws* (Harrisburg, Pa., 1907).

10. "The Canon on Marriage and Divorce," *Public Opinion,* October 27, 1898.

11. "Remarriage After Divorce," *Outlook,* October 22, 1904.

12. The positions of the principal denominations on divorce and the efforts to change them are summarized in James P. Lichtenberger, *Divorce: A Study in Social Causation* (New York, 1909), chap. vii.

13. Daniel Bell, "The Myth of Crime Waves" (New York, 1961), pp. 151–74.

14. Roy Lubove, "The Progressives and the Prostitute," *The Historian*, XXIV (May 1962), 308–29.

15. Generalizations of this sort which depend upon a close acquaintance with the popular literature are notoriously hard to document. My own conclusions are derived from an examination of almost everything dealing with marriage and divorce published either in book form or in more than thirty leading periodicals from 1889 through 1919. For details see my unpublished, "The Divorce Crisis of the Progressive Era" (Doctor's dissertation, Berkeley, Calif., 1963).

16. By dismissing the moral side of the opposition to divorce so casually I do not mean to imply that it was not important, but only that it was unremarkable and required no detailed analysis. Divorce was considered immoral because it was forbidden by the New Testament, and because it encouraged lust. Naturally the clergymen who opposed divorce supported themselves with Scriptural citations. One of the most elaborate efforts to relate divorce to licentiousness was Samuel Dike's first major address on the subject, reprinted in *Christ and Modern Thought: The Boston Monday Lectures 1880–81*, ed. Joseph Cook (Boston, 1882).

17. "The Right to Be Divorced," *Lutheran Church Review*, XXVIII (October 1909), 661.

18. W. E. Campbell, "Wells, the Family, and the Church," *Catholic World*, XCI (July 1910), 483.

19. "The Worst Anarchism," *Outlook*, August 11, 1906, p. 826.

20. Bureau of the Census, *Marriage and Divorce 1867–1906*, p. 4.

21. *Marriage and Divorce* (New York, 1915), p. 15.

22. Henry Neumann, *Spokesmen for Ethical Religion* (Boston, 1951), deals with Adler's career at some length.

23. Rebecca Harding Davis, Rose Terry Cooke, Marion Harland, Catherine Owen, Amelia E. Barr, *North American Review*, CXLVIII (May 1889).

24. Boston, 1909.

25. Among the frequent male efforts to sentimentalize over the role and nature of woman were Lyman Abbott, *Christianity and Social Problems* (Boston, 1896), and Robert Lawton, *The Making of a Home* (Boston, 1914).

26. "The Change in the Feminine Ideal," *Atlantic Monthly*, CV (March 1910), 295; see also her interesting autobiography *Golden Yesterdays* (New York, 1940).

27. *Ibid.*, p. 297.

28. *The Making of a Home*, p. 594.

29. "The Ethics of Divorce," *Ethical Record*, II (April 1890), 207.

30. *Sociology and Modern Social Problems* (New York, 1913).

31. *Jesus Christ and the Social Question* (New York, 1903), p. 145.

32. *The Morality of Marriage and Other Essays on the Status and Destiny of Women* (London, 1897). A collection of articles which had previously appeared in the *North American Review*, the *Fortnightly Review*, the *Westminster Review* and the *Nineteenth Century*. Typical of the American press's treatment of her ideas are "The Millennium of Marriage—Mona Caird's Views," *Current Literature*, XVI (July 1894), reprinted from the *Boston Herald*. "The Practice of Marriage," *Current Literature*, XVIII (October 1895), reprinted from the *Saturday Review*.

33. Boston, 1895.

34. "Anticipations; An Experiment in Prophecy—II," *North American Review*, CLXXIII (July 1901), 73–74.

35. Carpenter, *Love's Coming of Age* (New York, 1911). *Little Essays of Love and Virtue* (New York, 1921), summarized the ideas Havelock Ellis had been advocating for years and the *New Horizon in Love and Life* (London, 1921), contains the thoughts of his wife, who died in 1916. Schreiner, *Woman and Labor* (New York, 1911).

36. "Prostitution Within the Marriage Bond," *Arena*, XIII (June 1895), 68.

37. "The New Marriage," *Good Housekeeping*, LII (February 1914), 184.

38. Charlotte Perkins Gilman, *Women and Economics* (Boston, 1898), was an especially influential exposition of this point of view. For other information on this remarkable woman's life and work see Carl N. Degler's appreciative article, "Charlotte Perkins Gilman on the Theory and Practice of Feminism," *American Quarterly*, VIII (Spring 1956). See also Rheta Childe Dorr, *What Eight Million Women Want* (Boston, 1910), and C. Gasquoine Hartley, *The Truth About Women* (London, 1914).

39. "Divorce vs. Domestic Warfare," *Arena*, I (April 1890), 568. Alone of the great feminist leaders, Mrs. Stanton was a lifelong supporter of divorce, and in her later years it became one of her major interests. In this respect she was hardly a typical feminist, for while most divorce liberals were also feminists, they remained very much a minority within the women's movement.

40. *Outline of Practical Sociology* (New York, 1900), p. 176.

41. Chicago, 1904.

42. "Social Control and the Function of the Family," Congress of Arts and Sciences, *Proceedings*, VII (St. Louis, 1904), 701. This abbreviated summary may not bring out the markedly utopian flavor which permeated discussions on the family by liberal sociologists and feminists during the Progressive period. Indeed, they entertained hopes for the future of the family which seem fantastically imaginative by the standards of our own more somberly clinical age. This visionary strain in Progressive social thought has been underestimated by historians in recent years, especially by Richard Hofstadter, whose influential *The Age of Reform* (New York, 1955), ignores the role played by feminism and the new morality in shaping the Progressive mood.

43. So many statements were made on marriage and divorce by sociologists during these years that I can list only a few of them here. Walter F. Willcox, *The Divorce Problem* (New York, 1891), was a seminal monograph that laid the statistical base for most later studies of divorce but which was not well known outside of the profession and did not have the impact of other works which were more widely publicized. Elsie Clews Parsons, *The Family* (New York, 1906), caused a minor sensation by calling for trial marriages. Mrs. Parsons was a student of Franz Boas and the most radical of the academicians who dealt with the problem. Arthur W. Calhoun, *A Social History of the American Family, From the Civil War* (Cleveland, 1919), Vol. III, was written from an avowedly socialist point of view and is still the only comprehensive work on the history of the American family.

44. *Papers and Proceedings of the American Sociological Society*, III (Chicago, 1909).

45. *Ibid.*, p. 15.

46. "How Home Conditions React Upon the Family," *Papers . . . of American Sociological Society*, pp. 16–29. Margaret F. Byington, "The Family in a Typical Mill Town," pp. 73–84. Edward T. Devine, "Results of the Pittsburgh Survey," pp. 85–92; Charles R. Henderson, "Are Modern Industry and City Life Unfavorable to the Family?" pp. 93–105, among others.

47. *Papers . . . of American Sociological Society*, pp. 150–60.

48. *Ibid.*, p. 180.

49. "The Hyperbolic Teachings of Jesus," *North American Review*, CLXXIX (September 1904), 403.

50. *Ibid.*, p. 447.

51. E.g., Ernest D. Burton, "The Biblical Teaching Concerning Divorce," *Biblical World*, XXIX (February and March 1907). Norman Jones, "Marriage and Divorce: The Letter of the Law," *North American Review*, CLXXXI (October 1905). Thomas S. Potwin, "Should Marriage Be Indissoluble?" *New Englander and Yale Review*, LVI (January 1892).

52. *Men and Women* (Boston, 1902).

53. *Marriage and Divorce* (New York, 1913).

54. *Annual Reports* of the National League for the Protection of the Family.

55. *Annual Reports* of the Executive Committee of the Federal Council of Churches of Christ in America.

56. "Are Homogenous Divorce Laws in all the States Desirable?" *North American Review*, CLXX (March 1900).

57. E. R. Stevens, "Divorce in America: The Problem," *Outlook*, June 1, 1907; "Just Grounds for Divorce," November 23, 1910.

58. *World's Work*, XIX (January 1910).

59. Henry F. May, *The End of American Innocence* (New York, 1959), II, Part IV, 333, 343–44.

Symbols of the Jazz Age: The New Negro and Harlem Discovered

GILBERT OSOFSKY

One of the most marked features of life among radical intellectuals in the progressive period was their tendency to identify psychologically with oppressed and outcast people. Immigrants, children, women, American Indians—all came in for a share of symbolic concern from young liberals and radicals. In the 1920s, as Professor Gilbert Osofsky shows in the following essay, the same phenomenon continued to play itself out and found an important new object, the Negro. The "Negro Renaissance" that centered in Harlem found an echoing response among fascinated white writers, poets, artists, and critics. These white intellectuals and some of their New York audience created for the decade an exciting mythic version of the "New Negro," projecting onto the Harlem community some of the most radical aspirations of white intellectual life during the period.

Gilbert Osofsky is Professor of History at the University of Illinois at Chicago, where he has taught since receiving his Ph.D. degree at Columbia University in 1963. The following essay has been incorporated into his book Harlem: The Making of a Ghetto *(1966). He has also published* The Burden of Race *(1967) and a related essay "The Enduring Ghetto" in the* Journal of American History *(1968). His work is part of the current and widespread surge of interest in both black and urban history.*

American society has anticipated the arrival of a "New Negro" for at least seventy-five years. In the white South of the 1890s, for example, it was common to contrast the former slaves with the first Negro generation born in freedom—to the detriment of the latter. "The good old Negroes," said a Southern farmer at the turn of the century, "are a first-rate class of labor. The younger ones [are] discontented and want to be roaming."[1] At about the same time Booker T. Washington surveyed America's racial scene and, contrary to the view of white Southerners, found it good. He related tales of Negro achievement and success since the Civil War that encouraged him to believe that the "Negro of to-day is in every phase of life far advanced over the Negro of thirty years ago." Washington hoped all Negroes would strive to achieve "the new life" and, accordingly, called his book *A New Negro for a New Century*.[2] The racial crises that followed the two world wars of the present century revived the concept. William Pickens, Negro educator and NAACP official, discovered a "New Negro" militancy and racial consciousness in 1916, and others have used the phrase to describe the Negro protest movements of the 1950s and 1960s.[3]

Amid the confusions that have hovered around the meaning of the term "New Negro" is one solid fact: the phrase entered the main stream of American thought in the 1920s, in the Jazz Age. A "New Negro," and his supposed place of residence, Harlem, were discovered by the white world then. Despite the romance and pride traditionally associated with the "Harlem Renaissance," the portrayal of the Negro that developed in the 1920s was *primarily* a product of broader changes in American society. It would be difficult to find a better example of the confusions, distortions, half-truths and quarter-truths that are the foundations of racial and

REPRINTED BY PERMISSION, FROM *American Quarterly*, 17 (SUMMER 1965), 229–238. COPYRIGHT, 1965, TRUSTEES OF THE UNIVERSITY OF PENNSYLVANIA.

ethnic stereotypes than the white world's image of the "New Negro" and Harlem in the 1920s.

The 1920s, as is well known, was a remarkable age in American intellectual history. A cultural rebellion of the first order erupted from beneath the complacency and conservatism that were dominant characteristics of American society and politics then. It was the time when writers, artists, scholars, aesthetes, and bohemians became aware of the standardization of life that resulted from mass production and large-scale, efficient industrialization—the "Machine Civilization," that "profound national impulse [that] drives the hundred millions steadily toward uniformity."[4] These intellectuals declared war on tenets of American thought and faith that had remained sacrosanct for three hundred years. As a by-product of their attack on traditional American middle-class values, which were constantly called "Puritanical," literary rebels and others discovered the Negro, America's "outcast," and created a semimythical dreamland which they came to idealize—"storied Harlem."[5]

In some part, this growing national awareness was caused by significant changes within Negro society. There seemed to be a new militancy in the Negro world after World War I—reflected in Harlem's well-known Silent Parade to protest the East St. Louis race riots, in the racial program and consciousness of Marcus Garvey, in A. Philip Randolph's struggling movement to found the Brotherhood of Sleeping Car Porters and Maids, in the numerous little leftist groups active in the Negro ghettos, in the national campaign to promote federal anti-lynching legislation. Yet American society never really took these movements seriously in the 1920s—Garvey was considered a comical figure; an anti-lynching law was never enacted; riots continued; Randolph's union made little headway until the Great Depression; the leftists were ignored or considered crackpots.

The 1920s also saw the rise of a noteworthy group of Negro writers and scholars, and America gave *them* considerable recognition. Some of the novels, plays, poems, books and articles of Countee Cullen, James Weldon Johnson, George S. Schuyler, Claude McKay, Wallace Thurman, Zora Neale Hurston, Jessie Fauset, Rudolph Fisher, Jean Toomer, Charles S. Johnson, E. Franklin Frazier, and others were good enough in their own right to justify public acclaim. The poetry of Langston Hughes continues to be widely read. Harlem was the center of this "New Negro Renaissance" and, like an "ebony flute," it lured Negro writers to it: "Harlem was like a great magnet for the Negro intellectual, pulling him from everywhere," wrote Langston Hughes.[6] Claude McKay came to Harlem from Jamaica, after two years at an agricultural college in Kansas; Jean Toomer was from an Alabama plantation; Langston Hughes arrived in 1921 after a sojourn in Mexico. "I can never put on paper the thrill of the underground ride to Harlem," Hughes recalled. "I went up the steps and out into the bright September sunlight. Harlem! I stood there, dropped my bags, took a deep breath and felt happy again."[7] Wherever they wandered in the 1920s, and many went to Paris or Africa for a time, the Negro literati always returned *Home to Harlem* (to use the title of a McKay novel). Little theater, art and political discussion groups flourished in the community. Negro literary and political magazines made their appearance: *Fire, The Messenger, Voice of the Negro, The Negro Champion, Harlem.* The 135th Street library became Harlem's cultural center. "The Schomburg Collection," remembered George S. Schuyler, "used to be a great gathering place for all the people of the Renaissance."[8] In the 1920s one could hear lectures there by such prominent people as Franz Boas, W. E. B. DuBois, Carl Van Doren, James Weldon Johnson, Carter G. Woodson, Kelly Miller, Melville J. Herskovits, R. R. Moton and Arthur A. Schomburg. Harlem became what contemporaries called the "Mecca of the New Negro."[9]

Some observers, Negro and white, looked to this outburst of literary and artistic expression as a significant step in the direction of a more general acceptance of Negroes by American society. Alain Locke, gifted writer and Howard University professor, argued that social equality would result from the recognition of the "New Negro" as an "artist class." ". . . it seems that the interest in the cultural expression of Negro life . . . heralds an almost revolutionary revaluation of the Negro," he wrote in 1927. It was "an augury of a new democracy in American culture."[10] Heywood Broun, well-known journalist and critic, addressed the New York Urban League at a Harlem church. He believed "a supremely great negro artist, [an artist] who could catch the imagination of the world, would do more than any other agency to remove the disabilities against which the negro race now labors. . . . This great artist may come at any time," Broun concluded, and he asked his audience to remain silent for ten seconds to imagine the coming of the savior-genius.[11] This same theme of a broad cultural acceptance evolving from the recognition of the "New Negro" as "a creator" dominates the writings of James Weldon Johnson in the 1920s. Johnson and others somehow believed that American racism was a process that could be reasoned with, a phenomenon that would crumble when whites recognized Negroes had extraordinary and unique artistic talents. "I am coming to believe," Johnson wrote his close friend Carl Van Vechten, "that nothing can go farther to destroy race prejudice than the recognition of the Negro as a creator and contributor to American civilization."[12] "Harlemites thought the millennium had come," remembered Langston Hughes. "They thought the race problem had at last been solved through Art. . . ."[13]

There was an element of realism in the romantic hopes of Johnson, Broun and Locke. For white Americans to grant that the Negro was capable of making *any* contribution to American culture was in itself a new idea—"that the Negro is a creator as well as creature . . . a giver as well as . . . receiver."[14] A new and more liberal vision of democracy developed among social scientists in the 1920s. Scholars like Robert E. Park, Herbert A. Miller, Franz Boas, Melville J. Herskovits, Charles S. Johnson, Bruno Lasker, E. Franklin Frazier and Horace M. Kallen attacked traditional American attitudes toward assimilation and "Americanization." A more vital and beautiful democracy would arise, they argued, by permitting ethnic groups to maintain their individuality, rather than conceiving them swallowed up (or melted down) in the one dominant American culture. Each group, given freedom of expression and development, would then make valuable contributions to American society. Diversity, cultural pluralism, should be fostered and encouraged, not stifled, they wrote.[15]

A spate of articles and books published in the 1920s seriously analyzed and attempted to understand the Negro's place in the nation. The dozens of volumes about Negroes written by pseudo-scientists and racists at the turn of the century were now replaced by works which attempted to cut through racial stereotypes ("generalized theories about racial qualities") and tried to find some viable program for "interracial cooperation." "The American Negro can no longer be dismissed as an unimportant element in the population of the United States," concluded one man. Bruno Lasker's *And Who Is My Neighbor?* and *All Colors* were among the earliest serious studies of American interracial attitudes.[16] *The Annals* of the American Academy of Political and Social Science printed a thick volume of studies on Negroes by the nation's leading social scientists.[17] *The World Tomorrow*, a fascinating Christian Pacifist journal, devoted two full issues to similar articles in the 1920s.[18] Most of the major periodicals of the decade contained large numbers of serious and important studies of Negro life. The artistic and human value of Negro spirituals, folk songs, folk legends and music was first recognized in the 1920s (many considered them America's most important contribution to world culture); Darius Milhaud, after listening to Negro music in Lenox Avenue cafes, composed pieces which made use of jazz rhythms and instruments; *In Abraham's Bosom*, one of Paul Green's many plays of Southern Negro life, won the Pulitzer Prize in 1926; Eugene O'Neill and Robert E. Sherwood constructed plays and novels around Negro characters and themes.[19] As important as this new recognition was, however, it was a minor trend in American thought. The generation that advocated cultural pluralism was also the generation that saw the revival of the Ku Klux Klan, and permanently restricted foreign immigration to the United States.

Had intellectuals like Johnson and Locke looked more critically at the stereotype of the "New Negro" that developed in the writings of most white commentators of the 1920s, they would have had further cause to question the extent of interracial understanding that existed then. White literary rebels created a "vogue in things Negro," "an enthusiasm for negro life and art" that bordered on being a cult.[20] They saw Negroes not as people but as symbols of everything America was not. The concept of the existence of a "New Negro" and the publicity given to it in the 1920s was primarily the result of this new awareness and interest in Negro society by what one writer called the "New White Man."[21] The generation that discovered "newness" all around itself—New Humanism, New Thought, New Woman, New Psychology, New Masses, New Poetry, New Criticism, and so on—also found a "New Negro"; and the concept became a cultural weapon: "Another Bombshell Fired into the Heart of Bourgeois Culture." "Negro stock is going up," wrote novelist Rudolph Fisher, "and everybody's buying."[22]

In the literature of the 1920s Negroes were conceived as "expressive" ("a singing race") in a society burdened with "unnatural inhibitions"; their lives were "primitive" and "exotic" (these two words appear repeatedly) in a "dull," "weary" and "monotonous" age; they could laugh and love freely in a "land flowing with Socony and Bryan and pristine Rotary purity." Negroes were presented as people who lived an "entire lifetime of laughs and thrills, [of] excitement and fun"—they had an "innate gayety of soul." "Ecstacy," wrote Joseph Wood Krutch in *The Nation*, "seems . . . to be his natural state."[23] The stereotype of the Negro that had existed in American society in the nineteenth century was largely untouched by the new interest in Negro life. It was continued, for example, in such "all-talking melodramas" as "Lucky Sambo," "Hearts in Dixie" and "Hallelujah," and in the new radio hit "Amos and Andy." In the 1920s, however, the ludicrous image of Negro as "darkey" became a subordinate theme, eclipsed by the conception of the Negro as sensuous and rhythmic African. Negroes were still thought to be alienated from traditional American virtues and values, as they had been since colonial times, but this was now considered a great asset. "To Americans," wrote a perceptive contemporary in 1929, "the Negro is not a human being but a concept."[24]

This was the background against which white America and the world came to know the "New Negro" and Harlem: "with our eyes focused on the Harlem scene we may dramatically glimpse the New Negro."[25] A large Negro community had gathered in Harlem prior to World War I but, aside from small numbers of dedicated social workers, American society seemed willing to overlook its existence. In the 1920s, however, Harlem was made a national symbol—a symbol of the Jazz Age. It was seen as the antithesis of Main Street, Zenith, and Gopher Prairie. Whatever seemed thrilling, bizarre or sensuous about Harlem life was made a part of the community's image; whatever was tragic about it, ignored.

Harlem of the Twenties was presented as a "great playground," America's answer to Paris.[26] The institution that best describes this aspect of Harlem's image was the white slumming party: "it became quite a rage . . . to go to night clubs in Harlem," recalled Carl Van Vechten.[27]

Cabarets were filled nightly with handsomely dressed white slummers who danced the Charleston, Turkey or Black Bottom, listened to jazz or watched risqué revues. Some night spots, like the Cotton Club (which had "the hottest show in town"), and Connie's Inn (which competed for the honor), catered exclusively to whites. They were, wrote a journalist, dives "where white people from downtown could be entertained by colored girls."[28] If one was looking "to go on a moral vacation," or wished to soften "the asperities of a Puritan conscience," Harlem's cabarets promised to do the job. The following is an advertisement, written especially for "white consumption" and distributed by a man who supplied "Slumming Hostesses" to "inquisitive Nordics" (each card was said to have a suggestive picture on it):[29]

> Here in the world's greatest city it would both amuse and also interest you to see the real inside of the New Negro Race of Harlem. You have heard it discussed, but there are very few who really know. . . . I am in a position to carry you through Harlem as you would go slumming through Chinatown. My guides are honest and have been instructed to give the best service. . . . Your season is not completed with thrills until you have visited Harlem.

"White people," editorialized a Negro journal, "are taking a morbid interest in the night life of [Harlem]."[30]

And the interest continued to grow throughout the decade. Carl Van Vechten's novel of Harlem life, *Nigger Heaven* (1925), sold 100,000 copies "almost immediately," and brought its author a substantial fortune. It was translated into French, Swedish, Russian and Japanese.[31] Van Vechten's book contained some interesting commentaries on the structure and problems of Negro society (the role of the middle class; "passing"; prejudice; color consciousness) but its plot was contrived, sensational and melodramatic; replete with orgies, drugs and seduction; a hodgepodge of *True Confessions* and the front pages of a tabloid. Its characters were unbelievable as people. "The squalor of Negro life, the vice of Negro life," wrote Van Vechten, "offer a wealth of novel, exotic, picturesque materials to the artist."[32] *Nigger Heaven* was "recognized in every quarter . . . as *the* portrayal of contemporary life in Harlem," said its publisher (and it undoubtedly was).[33] The white world looked curiously at the success of Marcus Garvey (whose movement basically reflected a profound Negro desire for racial pride and respect in a society that denied it), and concluded that Negroes "have parades almost every day."[34] White intellectuals and bohemians knew Harlem only through the cabarets, or the famous parties in the salon of the "joy-goddess of Harlem"—A'Lelia Walker's "Dark Tower": "dedicated to the aesthetes, young writers, sculptors, painters—a rendezvous where they may feel at home."[35] Bessie Smith, the great blues singer, toured America with her "Harlem Frolic" company. Josephine Baker ("Josephine of the Jazz Age") wowed them in Harlem as a young chorus girl, and went on to international acclaim in Europe. "From a world of stone with metal decoys/Drab stone streets and drab stone masses/New York's mold for the great middle-classes, Africa passes/With syncopated talking the Congo arouses."[36]

White audiences, like gluttons at a feast, vicariously tasted the "high yallers," "tantalizin' tans" and "hot chocolates" that strutted around in the Blackbird Revues, or in such plays as *Lulu Belle* (1926) and *Harlem* (1928)—and made them top box-office successes. (*Black Boy* and *Deep River*, dramas which emphasized a more serious side of Negro life, were failures.)[37] "Ten years ago," wrote one Negro reviewer of *Lulu Belle*, "this play would have been unprofitable. Twenty years ago it would have caused a riot."[38] The following is a handbill distributed to advertise the play *Harlem* ("A Thrilling Play of the Black Belt"):[39]

> Harlem! . . . The City that Never Sleeps! . . . A Strange, Exotic Island in the Heart of New York! . . . Rent Parties! . . . Number Runners! . . . Chippies! . . . Jazz Love! . . . Primitive Passion!

"How soon this common theme shall reach the nauseating state," remarked a caustic critic, "is not easy to tell."[40]

The Great Depression brought an abrupt end to the dream of a "New Negro" and the image of Harlem as erotic utopia. A nation sobered by bread lines no longer searched for a paradise inhabited by people who danced and loved and laughed for an "entire lifetime." Connie's Inn and other places of white entertainment closed down. Leading figures of the Renaissance: Wallace Thurman, Richard B. Harrison, A'Lelia Walker, Charles S. Gilpin, Florence Mills, Arthur A. Schomburg, died in the late 1920s or 1930s. Most of the Negro literati, though not all, stopped writing or, if they continued to do so, found a less responsive American audience for their works.[41] All the Negro literary magazines folded.

And, as the exotic vision of the 1920s passed, a new image of the Negro and Harlem emerged—a Harlem already known to stolid census-takers, city health officers and social workers. "The rosy enthusiasms and hopes of 1925," wrote Alain Locke ten years later, "were . . . cruelly deceptive mirage[s]." The ghetto was revealed in the 1930s as "a nasty, sordid corner into which black folk are herded"—"*a Harlem that the social worker knew all along but had not been able to dramatize. . . . There is no cure or saving magic in poetry and art for . . . precarious marginal employment, high mortality rates, civic neglect*," concluded Locke.[42] It was this Harlem, the neighborhood not visible "from the raucous interior of a smoke-filled, jazz-drunken cabaret," the Harlem hidden by the "bright surface . . . of . . . night clubs, cabaret tours and . . . arty magazines," that was devastated by the depression, and has remained a community with an inordinate share of sorrow and deprivation ever since. "The depression brought everybody down a peg or two," wrote Langston Hughes. "And the Negroes had but few pegs to fall." The myth-world of the 1920s had ended.[43]

Notes

1. *Report of the Industrial Commission on Agriculture and Agricultural Labor* (Washington, D. C., 1901), X, 50, 504, 770.

2. Booker T. Washington, *A New Negro for a New Century* (Chicago, 1900?), pp. 3 and *passim*.

3. William Pickens, *The New Negro* (New York, 1916); *The New Negro*, ed. Mathew H. Ahmann (Notre Dame, Ind., 1961); *The New Negro: Thirty Years Afterward*, ed. Charles S. Johnson (Washington, D. C., 1955).

4. Carl Van Doren, "The Negro Renaissance," *Century Magazine*, CXI (March 1926), 637.

5. Gilbert Seldes, "The Negro's Songs," *Dial*, LXXX (March 1926), 247–51.

6. Langston Hughes, *The Big Sea* (New York, 1940), p. 240.

7. *Ibid.*, p. 81.

8. "The Reminiscences of George S. Schuyler" (Oral History Research Office, Columbia University, 1962), p. 208.

9. Claude McKay, *A Long Way From Home* (New York, 1937), *passim*, and *Home to Harlem* (New York, 1927); "Harlem: Mecca of the New Negro," *Survey*, LIII (March 1, 1925), 629–724; Alain Locke, *The New Negro: An Interpretation* (New York, 1925).

10. Alain Locke and Lothrop Stoddard, "Should the Negro Be Encouraged to Cultural Equality?" *Forum*, LXXVIII (October 1927), 508; Locke, "Enter the New Negro," *Survey*, LIII (March 1, 1925), 631–34; Locke, "Negro Contributions to America," *World Tomorrow*, XII (June 1929), 255–57.

11. *New York Times*, January 26, 1925.

12. James Weldon Johnson to Carl Van Vechten, envelope dated March 6, 1927. James Weldon Johnson Collection of Negro Arts and Letters, Yale University.

13. *The Big Sea*, p. 288.

14. Johnson to Van Vechten, envelope dated March 6, 1927. Johnson Collection.

15. See, for example, Robert W. Bagnall, "The Divine Right of Race," *World Tomorrow*, VI (May 1923), 149; Herbert A. Miller, "Democracy and Diversity," *World Tomorrow*, VII (June 1924), 190–91; Robert E. Park, *The Immigrant Press and Its Control* (New York, 1922); Horace M. Kallen, *Culture and Democracy in the United States: Studies in the Group Psychology of the American Peoples* (New York, 1924).

16. "The Reminiscences of Bruno Lasker" (Oral History Research Office, Columbia University, 1957), p. 242 and chap. ix.

17. *The Annals of the American Academy of Political and Social Sciences*, CXL (November 1928).

18. *World Tomorrow*, VI (May 1923) and IX (April 1926).

19. Laurence Buermeyer, "The Negro Spirituals and American Art," *Opportunity*, IV (May 1926), 158–59, 167; Harry Alan Potamkin, "African Sculpture," *Opportunity*, VI (May 1929), 139–40, 147; James Weldon Johnson to Carl Van Vechten, envelope dated February 16, 1931, Johnson Collection; A. M. Chirgwin, "The Vogue of the Negro Spiritual," *Edinburgh Review*, CCXLVII (January 1928), 57–74; Darius Milhaud, "The Jazz Band and Negro Music," *Living Age*, CCCXXIII (October 18, 1924), 169–73.

20. Langston Hughes, "The Negro Artist and the Racial Mountain," *Nation*, CXXII (June 23, 1926), 693; Charles S. Johnson, "The Balance Sheet: Debits and Credits in Negro-White Relations," *World Tomorrow*, XI (January 1928), 13–16; Ernest Boyd, "Readers and Writers," *Independent*, CXVI (January 16, 1926), 77; George Jean Nathan, "The Wail of the Negro," *American Mercury*, XVIII (September 1929), 114–16; Claude McKay to James Weldon Johnson, April 30, 1928, Johnson Collection.

21. "The New White Man," *World Tomorrow*, X (March 1927), 124–25.

22. Rudolph Fisher, "The Caucasian Storms Harlem," *American Mercury*, XI (May 1927), 396.

23. Eugene Gordon, "The Negro's Inhibitions," *American Mercury*, XIII (February 1928), 159–65; Clement Wood, "Hosea Before the Rotary Club," *World Tomorrow*, VIII (July 1925), 209–10; Herman Keyserling, "What the Negro Means to America," *Atlantic Monthly*, CXLIV (October 1929), 444–47; Joseph Wood Krutch, "Black Ecstasy," *Nation*, CXXV (October 26, 1927), 456–58; George S. Schuyler, "Blessed

Are the Sons of Ham," *Nation*, CXXIV (March 23, 1927), 313–15; "Black Voices," *Nation*, CXIX (September 17, 1924), 278.

24. George Chester Morse, "The Fictitious Negro," *Outlook and Independent*, CLII (August 21, 1929), 648.

25. *A Long Way From Home*, p. 322.

26. Beverly Smith, "Harlem–Negro City," *New York Herald Tribune*, February 10, 1930.

27. "The Reminiscences of Carl Van Vechten" (Oral History Research Office, Columbia University, 1960), p. 196.

28. *Crisis*, XXXIX (September 1932), 293; *New York Age*, August 6, 1927. For a survey of Harlem cabarets see Archie Seale, "The Rise of Harlem As An Amusement Center," *Age*, November 2, 1935; and obituary of Moe Gale, owner of the Savoy Ballroom, *New York Times*, September 3, 1964.

29. "The Slumming Hostess," *New York Age*, November 6, 1926.

30. "Giving Harlem A Bad Name," "Is Harlem to be a Chinatown?" "In the Negro Cabarets," "Nordic Invasion of Harlem," *New York Age*, September 5, 1922; October 27, 1923; July 23, August 6, 1927; Committee of Fourteen, *Annual Report for 1928* (New York, 1929), pp. 31–34.

31. "The Reminiscences of Carl Van Vechten," p. 205.

32. Carl Van Vechten, *Nigger Heaven* (New York, 1925), *passim*.

33. "The Negro in Art—A Symposium," *Crisis*, XXXI (March 1926), 219–20; *Crisis*, XXXIV (September 1927), 248.

34. Chester T. Crowell, "The World's Largest Negro City," *Saturday Evening Post*, CXCVIII (August 8, 1925), 9. "The Caucasian Storms Harlem," *American Mercury*, XI (May 1927), 398.

35. "I am to be hostess at the Dark Tower Sunday Night April 21st, and I thought probably you and your friends would like to be present. . . ." A'Lelia Walker to Max Ewing, April 18, 1929. Ewing Collection, Yale University. A'Lelia Walker was the daughter and heir of the wealthy Madame C. J. Walker. Eric D. Walrond, "The Black City," *Messenger*, VI (January 1924), 14. *New York Age*, October 29, 1927.

36. Paul Oliver, *Bessie Smith* (New York, 1959), p. 45. Ermine Kahn, "Lenox Avenue —Saturday Night," *World Tomorrow*, VIII (November 1925), 337.

37. *New York Age*, November 27, 1926.

38. Hubert H. Harrison, "The Significance of Lulu Belle," *Opportunity*, IV (July 1926), 228–29; *Crisis*, XXXII (May 1926), 34; "Black Harlem Dramatized," *Literary Digest*, C (March 16, 1929), 21–24; James Weldon Johnson to Carl Van Vechten, envelope dated April 4, 1930, Johnson Collection.

39. Quoted in Diana N. Lockard, "The Negro on the Stage in the Nineteen Twenties" (Master's thesis, Columbia University, 1960), p. 38.

40. *Outlook and Independent*, CLII (August 21, 1929), 649; Charles S. Johnson, "Public Opinion and the Negro," *Proceedings of National Conference in Social Work, 1923* (Chicago, 1924), 497–502.

41. The most glaring exception to this generalization is Langston Hughes.

42. "Harlem had been too long the nighttime playground of New York. . . ." Alain Locke, "La Guardia and Harlem," manuscript in La Guardia Papers. Locke, "Harlem: Dark Weather-Vane," *Survey Graphic*, XXV (August 1936), 457–62, 493–95. Quotations in the above text are from the manuscript of this article in the La Guardia Papers. Italics mine.

43. Wallace Thurman, "Harlem Facets," *World Tomorrow*, X (November 1927), 466. E. Franklin Frazier, "Negro Harlem: An Ecological Study," *American Journal of Sociology*, XLIII (July 1937), 86. *The Big Sea*, p. 247; George W. Harris, "Harlem Gets a New Jail," *Nation*, CXXXIII (September 9, 1931), 258; "Negro Children in New York," *Nation*, CXXXIV (May 25, 1932), 588.

Sources and Nature of Intolerance in the 1920s

PAUL L. MURPHY

Modern American history is a complex affair, and every advance in the writing of twentieth-century history uncovers some new complexity. The decade of the twenties was extraordinarily confused, a patchwork of the most contradictory sorts of tendencies and events. One of the most confusing features of the period was the simultaneous development of "liberal" institutions like the American Civil Liberties Union, and the rise to prominence and power of other groups with contrary aims, such as the American Legion and the Ku Klux Klan.

In the following essay on the nature and causes of intolerance, Professor Paul L. Murphy attempts to spell out the underlying reasons for the apparent inflation of racist, nativist, and repressive behavior among Americans. What emerges from his essay is the possibility that the period of what he calls intolerance was not so much the twenties proper, but rather a decade running, roughly, from 1916 to 1926. He also makes it clear that the intolerance of the twenties was a response to difficult tensions in American life that were not sudden and temporary, but that had been deep-seated and enduring since the middle of the nineteenth century.

Paul L. Murphy holds a Ph.D. degree from the University of California at Berkeley. His principal field of work has been the history of civil liberties and civil rights in twentieth-century America. He is the author of The Meaning of Freedom of Speech *(1968) and coauthor of* Liberty and Justice *(2 vols., 1968). He is currently Associate Professor of both History and American Studies at the University of Minnesota.*

*In approaching that seamy side of the national character which periodi-*cally displays broad-scale intolerance, prejudice, nativism, and xeno-phobia, many American historians have sought in recent years to draw upon the findings of scholars in related disciplines in their attempts at meaningful analysis. Especially suggestive in this area has been recent work in sociology, social psychology, cultural anthropology, and Ameri-can studies.[1] Differences exist, however, as to how such findings can actually aid the historian and the degree of reliance he can confidently place upon them. Given the fact that the average historian must work in a past context in which precise empirical research is impossible, par-ticularly as it applies to a broad spectrum of public attitudes, and given the fact that modern social science studies draw the great body of their evidence from current materials, a question of relevance is raised. How safe is it for the historian to project such modern findings backwards in an attempt better to understand and grasp the tensions and pressures of a prior era? Are modern social science techniques reliable in the analysis of imprecise historical materials?

Some members of the historical guild feel that such borrowing of either materials or techniques is too dangerous to be acceptable. Others at times have relied too heavily upon such interdisciplinary aids in order to validate general presumptions otherwise difficult of documentation. Still others have used such materials cautiously and carefully, so cau-tiously and so carefully that they have come to differ among them-selves concerning their applicability. In the study of past intolerance, for example, there have been those who drew heavily upon a sociolog-ically oriented emphasis on status rivalries and who have emphasized ongoing tensions ever present in the slow process of ethnic integration

REPRINTED BY PERMISSION, FROM *Journal of American History*, 51 (JUNE 1964), 60–76.

in our dynamic society.[2] Yet such persons have subsequently been challenged to explain the plausibility of the cyclical nature of waves of intolerance and its frequently differing character as unique situations have produced unique expressions geared to immediate needs. Others who have made careful use of stereotyping or who have placed reliance upon ideological factors have been questioned. So too have those who have focused upon the concrete facts of the immediate situation, especially upon the influence of men of passion with ability to create or nurture moods of alarm by exploiting irrational myths. This has forced such persons to de-emphasize the constant factor of human irrationality in normal times even though it is always basic in assessing causation in all historical events.[3]

In many ways the study of intolerance in the 1920s raises in exaggerated form both a question of the applicability of related materials and of proper permissible use of such materials. That decade, despite its surface prosperity and supposed gaiety and exuberance, was characterized by waves of public intolerance seldom felt in the American experience. Much of this intolerance was merely an outbreak of familiar subsurface prejudices with antecedents in earlier expressed antipathies toward radicals, Catholics, Jews, Negroes, Orientals, and other minority groups. Yet such intolerance was not traditional. Fostered frequently, although seldom led directly by an apprehensive business community or aggravated by men seeking gratuities as brokers for that community or as brokers for men of property, it quickly gained its sanctions from that national consensus so clumsily branded "normalcy" and involved many Americans previously immune to its toxicity. As such it was an integral part of the 1920s, participated in consciously or unconsciously by the great majority of Americans. That it took on a changing character as the decade advanced is apt testimony to its virulence. That it either disappeared or took on different forms with the depression seems to reveal that it was specially suited to the peculiar culture and society of the jazz age.

The historian would be delighted if by merely adding the materials and utilizing the techniques of the social scientists he could say precise and scientific things both about the roots, nature, and manifestations of intolerance at this time. Yet, despite the siren's call of being able through empirical social research to reach quantitative answers, he is tempted to concentrate on the imprecise approaches of history, relying upon interdisciplinary tools as analytical devices only when they seem to have an obvious relation to known and documentable reality.

Clearly the sources of the intolerance of the 1920s can be traced to at least the late Progressive period, with obvious roots in the immediately preceding years. Clearly such intolerance had a relation to growing Progressive apprehensions over alarming developments which did not seem to be responding to normal controls. The IWW, the first effectively organized movement of militant workingmen to challenge the whole

American economic system, sent chills through the hearts and outrage through the souls of upper- and middle-class Americans. Here in the early years of the century was a group with the effrontery to make demands no decent citizen could honor and employ techniques no moral American could tolerate. But worse than this, these people and their Socialist "cousins" rejected the premises upon which the American system rested, namely that rights and privileges were open in a free society to anyone who was willing to work up patiently within the system. Or if the individual was incapable of utilizing this technique he would eventually be taken care of in a spirit of paternalism by the affluent class, as long as he stood with his hat in his hand and patiently waited. The alarming fact was that the IWWs and Socialists were no longer willing to wait. They were unwilling to accept the fact that only after one had gained a stake in society was he warranted in becoming a critic or a reformer. As one Progressive editor wrote during the Lawrence textile strike of 1912 (at the point which Paul Brissenden called "the high tide of the I.W.W. activity"):

> On all sides people are asking, Is this a new thing in the industrial world? . . . Are we to see another serious, perhaps successful, attempt to organize labor by whole industrial groups instead of by trades? Are we to expect that instead of playing the game respectably, or else frankly breaking out into lawless riot which we know well enough how to deal with, the laborers are to listen to a subtle anarchistic philosophy which challenges the fundamental ideas of law and order, inculcating such strange doctrines as those of "direct action," "sabotage," "syndicalism," "the general strike," and "violence"? . . . We think that our whole current morality as to the sacredness of property and even of life is involved in it.[4]

Also involved in it was the IWW practice of utilizing the rhetoric of American democracy as a device for obtaining their ends. The "free-speech fight" which assumed national proportions after 1910 was distressingly successful at times and was painfully difficult to counteract. For while many Americans could argue that utilizing free speech to gain personal economic ends was an abuse of American ideals, the alternative of arbitrary suppression hardly preserved them.

For those in this dilemma World War I afforded a satisfying rationalization for suppression. Woodrow Wilson's prediction, "once lead this people into war and they'll forget there ever was such a thing as tolerance,"[5] was clairvoyant, as the government quickly set out to turn the President's words into official policy that succeeded frighteningly well. Every element of American public opinion was mobilized behind "my country, right or wrong," dissent was virtually forbidden, democracy at home was drastically curtailed so that it could be made safe abroad, while impressionable children were either "educated" in Hun atrocities, or their time was employed in liberty loan, Red Cross, war saving stamp, or YMCA campaigns. It was not difficult then to channel an aroused nation's wrath against earlier boatrockers—a development made easier by the fact that many IWWs and Socialists stood out boldly against the war from the start. The Espionage Act of 1917, while ostensibly a measure to strike at illegal interference with the war effort, was so worded that it could be, and was, used to stamp out radical criticism of the war. Its subsequent 1918 amendment, the Sedition Act, was a less subtle device. Passed by the pressure of western senators and modeled after a Montana IWW statute, its purpose was to undercut both the performance and advocacy of undesirable activity. There was a clear implication that people who utilized speech as a means of gaining improper ends had to be restricted.[6] And with the subsequent federal prosecution of 184 members of the IWW in 1918 and 1919,[7] to say nothing of a crackdown on Socialists, German-Americans, conscientious objectors, and Non-Partisan Leaguers, the intent of the federal legislative and administrative program became crystal clear.

With peace and the end of conservative labor's wartime honeymoon, there was renewed fear on the part of the reinvigorated business community that an unholy union of dissident malcontents and elements of more orthodox labor, now feeling callously betrayed, was not only possible but probable. The strikes of the immediate postwar period could only be rationalized by business in these terms. And to create further alarm, not only was Bolshevism a reality in Russia, but American workers and even some influential leaders were studying its economic and political implications with interest if not with admiration. Catholics, when under fire in the past, had consistently denied their allegiance to the Vatican, but some of these Bolshevik admirers even proclaimed proudly and openly their allegiance to a new order functioning from the Kremlin.[8]

Fear led to irrationality and business found it impossible to analyze the meaning and implications of these developments or to understand what Gutzon Borglum called in 1919 the "real labor problem," which was labor's dependent condition. In response to a speech by Nicholas Murray Butler, rebuking labor for its lack of "reasonableness,"[9] Borglum wrote:

> Labor's recent political activity is due to a deep consciousness of the necessity of self-reliance to secure any and all improvement in its condition. And further, the political color that has recently appeared in its methods, is forced because of the utter faithlessness and failure of partisan government to give it relief.[10]

But to conservative leaders, protection was more important than understanding. With the wartime legislation now generally inapplicable, they sought to get onto the statute books peacetime sedition and criminal syndicalism laws to take its place. To accomplish this, business was frequently able to transfer its own fears of Bolshevism both to a broader public and to state legislators who served that public. The result was that such propagandizing, plus added apprehensions triggered by frequently specious bomb scares, produced wide demand for restriction. Thus, although much of the new legislation was enacted in a sincere desire to control agitators and dangerous seditionists, other more responsive legislators took care to be sure that resultant laws were carefully worded and did not appear to be class legislation. By 1920 thirty-five states had enacted some form of restrictive, precautionary legislation enabling the rapid crackdown on speech that might, by its expression, produce unlawful actions geared toward stimulating improper political or economic change. Such legislation was couched in terms which in Connecticut permitted punishment of "disloyal, scurrilous, or abusive language about the form of government of the United States," and in Colorado, "advocacy by word or in print of forcible resistance to constituted government either as a general principle, or in particular instances as a means of affecting governmental, industrial, social or economic conditions."[11]

That there was no legal need or justification for such legislation (the criminal codes of the states adequately covered conspiracy and libel)[12] further underlined the fact that its purpose was devious. It constituted intimidating legislation by which business subtly sought to institutionalize forms of prior curtailment and thereby free itself from the necessity of having personally to restrict those it considered a threat to the existing order. Henceforth such restriction and subtle regimentation could be left to the discretion of administrative officials who could develop standards to fit immediate and local needs,[13] and who, as the decade progressed, were to add the injunction as a further precautionary weapon.

Although this legislation was quickly implemented in 1919 in a number of states, it did not quiet all malcontents. Prompted by a multiplication of strikes and labor discontent, the more hysterical began to fear that local sanctions were not enough and proceeded to advocate a form of federal "direct action." Powerful federal activity such as the Palmer raids, the army-conducted deportation of 249 "dangerous Reds" aboard the "Soviet Ark" Buford, the contemporaneous effort of representatives and senators to rush through a federal peacetime sedition act, while a product of and response to excessive public hysteria, should also be understood as the partial culmination of an increasingly more pressing apprehensiveness which had obsessed conservatives for well over a decade. And the fact that many Americans were at the time able to rationalize and condone the most disgraceful, wholesale departure from fundamental guarantees of basic liberty and due process of law in American history further underscores the extent of their fears.[14]

Yet the Red scare of the 1920s introduced a new permanent dimension of intolerance. This was the aspiring, self-seeking individual or special interest group which sought to exploit the hysteria and intolerance of the moment for personal advantage. Such individuals and groups were not new in American history.[15] But the breadth of their operations was more sweeping in the 1920s, and the ambitiousness of their calculations was greater, as was the number of Americans they sought to affect. For aggressive politicians like A. Mitchell Palmer, Leonard Wood, or Albert S. Burleson, the ability to project themselves into the role of master defender of the endangered order could mean nomination to high office, hopefully the Presidency. To an Anthony Caminetti, the first person of Italian extraction to be elected to Congress and by then Commissioner of Immigration, this was an opportunity to demonstrate that he, as well as others of his national origin, were fully 100 percent American. To an aggressive bureaucrat like William J. Flynn, head of the Bureau of Investigation, or J. Edgar Hoover, head of the Bureau's newly created General Intelligence (antiradical) Division, here was a chance to enhance the power of the Bureau, and his own power and domain simultaneously.[16] To Flynn's successor, William J. Burns, the ability to guide public fears and even create fears where only apprehensions had existed was also an opportunity to stimulate a brisk private business for the Burns International Detective Agency until an increasingly more hostile public forced a curtailment and a housecleaning in the Department of Justice.[17]

At the group level motivations were equally divergent. The American Legion epitomized the service-oriented organizations, obligated to deliver a variety of specific benefits to its wide membership. To do this entailed sufficient flattering and assisting of those in power to convince them that the organization deserved favors. But to write the Legion off as "apple-polishing, flag-wavers of patriotism" is to miss the fact that most legionnaires received great satisfaction from ousting "Reds" and Americanizing everyone completely. Such patrioteering afforded an opportunity for members to demonstrate and articulate their faith and allegiance to basic ideals and institutions and thereby to gain acceptance and status with those who felt a similar need.[18] Thus in this and similar organizations there was a natural tie between aiding the "establishment" and crusading to save America. The professional patriots, on the other hand, had simpler and even less commendable motives. Primarily propaganda organizations, and the mouthpieces of single leaders or small cabals, their purpose was to ingratiate themselves with large private or corporate donors and thereby insure their continuation. This meant showing results, not only in broad distribution of literature but in providing speakers to help in mobilizing large elements of the general public against all manner of enemies of "the American way." Thus Harry A. Jung of the powerful National Clay Products Industries Association and later the American Vigilant Intelligence Federation could write to a potential subscriber:

> We cooperate with over 30 distinctly civic and patriotic organizations. . . . It would take me too long to relate how I "put over" this part of our activities, namely, "trailing the Reds." Should you ever be in Chicago, drop in and see me and I will explain. That it has been a paying proposition for our organization goes without saying. . . .[19]

And again, Fred R. Marvin, head of the Keymen of America, could for six dollars per annum supply potential private radical hunters with his *Daily Data Sheets* which conveyed the doings of the Bolsheviks and parlor pinks to nervous and apprehensive individuals.[20] It was Marvin's aim to inspire the leadership of such a group as the DAR to draw up and enforce a national "black-list" of undesirable speakers that included such public disturbers of the peace as Jane Addams, Sherwood Eddy, James Harvey Robinson, and William Allen White.[21] In all, over thirty such ultrapatriotic organizations came and went in the 1920s, all to a greater or lesser degree dependent upon the success with which they could mobilize and direct public intolerance and intemperance.[22]

In this context the Ku Klux Klan played a unique role. Although it was geared to financial gain, especially as the decade progressed and its leadership fell more and more into the hands of those who sought to utilize it solely for personal profit, it was content to draw its money and support largely from private citizens in small towns and rural communities, a fact which set it apart from most other intolerance purveyors in the 1920s. This also meant, however, that it operated upon poorly underpinned grounds, a fact graphically illustrated by its rapid collapse well before the onset of the economic crisis of the depression years.

The success which all these individuals and groups achieved would still not have been possible if great segments of the American public had not been highly susceptible to the various types of appeal which they made. The source of this susceptibility was neither simple, nor always rational. It stemmed from the turbulence of the decade as value patterns underwent modification from the impact both of external pressures and internal conflict. When the German sociologist Ferdinand Tönnies delineated in his 1926 volume[23] between what he called Gemeinschaft-Gesellschaft social structure, he inadvertently suggested the root of one of the sources of the chronic distress of the American middle-class mind. Tönnies' Gemeinschaft structure well described that segment of American society which was basically rural or rural oriented, homogeneous in its ethnic and religious structure and values, a society which functioned through traditional status arrangements and which was characterized by low mobility. The members of such a society had always in America fought off what they considered the deleterious effect of foreign values endemic in a Gesellschaft structure with its urban orientation, secular focus, heterogeneous ethnic makeup, its preference for ordering social and economic relations through contract, and its tradition of high mobility which too often seemed to operate on questionable standards. In fact, the decade had opened on the crest of a successful counterattack of superimposed Gemeinschaft values in the "noble experiment," prohibition. But such a victory was a nervous one as open defiance and hostility grew and as erosion seemed to be occurring elsewhere with the nation succumbing to the excitement and immediacy of a new, generally urban dispersed popular culture. Formerly insulated value orientations now were subjected to the lure of new behavioral patterns suggested by the radio, the movies, romance magazines, and national service clubs. Moreover, the automobile, and in time the airplane, were affording the physical mobility which inevitably speeded up actual social contact with those whose values may earlier have only been slightly known.[24] This does not suggest that either form of social organization was bound to prevail. What it does suggest is that with the pressures to standardize, elements of formerly isolated groups were being subjected to a new challenge to modify the intensity with which they held to their own unique ways as the only acceptable ones.

Those who were thus disturbed accepted dominant American values. However, they found that their interpretation of these values or the techniques that they found acceptable in attaining them frequently had to undergo more modification than they found comfortable. Yet "normalcy," incorporating as it did a multitude of simple virtues along with carefully contrived selfish ends, proved an acceptable home for most rural Victorians and Babbitts alike. Their concern, and often it was held with equal intensity by each, was not the system, but the deviator, who for one reason or another was unwilling to accept the system with its fairly rigid formulae as to how to succeed and who might succeed. Here two types of troublemakers invariably stood out. The one was made up of those who sought unjustifiably to reach the pinnacle of full attainment of the success symbols which the system held out. The other consisted of those whose hierarchy of values and, of necessity, methods for attaining them were totally at odds with the standards of the day. In the former group one inevitably found the targets of Klan antipathy, for example: the ambitious immigrant, non-Anglo-Saxon, non-Protestant, whose frequent tendency to "overachieve" led to actions to "keep him in his place." But the quiet "consensus" of the 1920s backed up the Klan's overt censuring with a type of silent coercion which was often far more effective, especially if a Jew wanted admission to the local country club, or a Catholic wanted the presidency of the nation. Although Americans may never be fully ready for "the functionally strategic convergence of the standards by which conduct is evaluated," to use Robin Williams' phrase,[25] they were not ready in the 1920s even to consider such a possibility as a desirable national objective. The deviators, although small in number, were even more of a threat. Radicals, militant labor leaders, other loud and unreasonable critics of the system, and the honest and misguided average citizens whom they seemed to be perverting, had to be clamped into place even more quickly and thoroughly and by virtually any means possible. In this many welcomed the aid of any and all self-proclaimed champions of 100 percent Americanism.[26]

This position constituted an interesting modification of an earlier confidence in progress through broad public participation and discussion, a process long boasted as inherent in American institutions. In 1931 Roger Baldwin attributed this to the manifestly declining postwar faith in democracy.[27] Others attributed it to the general insecurity of all Americans and especially the chronic dissatisfaction with what many had been led to believe would be the glorious life of a postwar world.[28] Regardless of the cause, the effect was to undercut one of the potentially important sources which might have brought significant relief. Having convinced themselves that deviators from the status quo were potential Bolsheviks, many Americans found it a simple step to renounce the mildest type of reformer or reform program, a view in which they had the most thorough encouragement from the self-seeking patriots of the decade. An organization like the American Civil Liberties Union, the Federal Council of Churches, various social justice elements within specific religious groups,[29] explicit social reform organizations like the American Birth Control League, the Consumer's League, the National Child Labor Committee, although in reality seeking to strengthen the system by eliminating its many defects, found basic communication difficult with a public conditioned to look askance at any but practitioners of normalcy.[30]

Despite the general similarity through the decade of the sources of broad scale intolerance, its public manifestations took a variety of changing forms. The early fears of Bolshevism could not be exploited indefinitely, especially when the sins committed in the name of its suppression were revealed and its purveyors were shown to be using it as a device for unscrupulous personal gain. Public indignation toward the excesses of the Palmer raids, for example, came quickly following the issuance by the National Popular Government League of the devastating report on the *Illegal Practices of the United States Department of Justice* in late May 1920.[31] Such indignation was sufficient to drive those who might have sought to extend similar techniques to adopt far more subtle and clandestine modes of approach, and also to turn hysteria-making over to the private professional patriot organizations. Thus, William J. Burns, for example, after carefully instituting the Bridgeman raids of August 1922 turned to Ralph Easley of the National Civic Federation, Richard M. Whitney of the American Defense Society, and Joseph T. Cashman of the National Security League to arouse the public to a fever pitch over their implications.[32]

Yet even Burns's string ran out in 1923–1924 as the misrule of the Department of Justice could no longer be ignored[33] and as antiradicalism (labor by this time having been quite thoroughly tamed) was becoming a tiresome broken record. This is not to say, as Sidney Howard wrote bitterly at the time, that certain business interests might not find it useful to tar their critics by turning to the "services of radicalism in almost any one of their patriotic clashes with social liberalism or rambunctious unions, or, even, child labor reformers."[34] But for the moment different targets were needed.

turn from anti-radicalism to idea of Catholic-Jewish anti-Prot conspiracy

For those distressed with the growing disruption of their Gemeinschaft society, the Ku Klux Klan offered avenues for assaulting those most surely responsible. And while all Americans might not have agreed with C. Lewis Fowler, editor of the *American Standard*, that a heinous conspiracy to destroy America was afoot between Roman Catholicism and anti-Christian Jewry,[35] the irrational myths and stereotyping surrounding these groups were sufficient to convince many they needed surveillance, if not repression. The Klan also impressed many with its pious objectives of uplifting the nation's morality through attacking its immoral desecrators. Atypical of the conservative, service-and-fellowship oriented organizations, or the professional patriot groups, stemming primarily from outside the urban business community, the Klan, nonetheless, for three or four years in the mid-1920s successfully attacked and insidiously exploited the shattering of old moral standards. Thereby the Klan could resort to direct action against progenitors of public immorality, as it did in the case of Judge Ben "Companionate Marriage" Lindsey in Denver.[36] Indirectly, it could also inspire others to heed the clarion call to expose the evil forces which had to be behind the callous disregard of traditional ways, a call answered by Calvin Coolidge, for example, in his public exposé of "Reds" in our women's colleges,[37] or by Texas representative Thomas L. Blanton's public assault on the ACLU which he branded the "UnAmerican Criminal License Union."[38]

For those patriots seeking essentially to play a broker's role for powerful interests, intriguing new opportunities were opening up in anti-pacifism and the baiting of antimilitarists. The official demise of Burns left the tradition of his office to the War Department. By that time the department was growing more apprehensive over the potential threat to its authority from antiwar sentiments that were increasingly prevalent as disillusion with the war experience intensified. As early as 1923, General Amos Fries, head of the Chemical Warfare Service, had publicly committed the government to support Preparedness Day, and by inference the continuation of an expanded military establishment. Fries had also encouraged Mrs. Lucia R. Maxwell, librarian of the Service, to prepare and circulate the famed "Spider Web Chart," which purported to study women's peace organizations in the United States and show, by ramification and association, that they were all Bolshevik inspired or at least deep pink.[39] Although the War Department eventually ordered retraction and directed Fries to inform persons to whom the chart had been circulated that its information was erroneous, the retraction fell on few careful ears. The chart was still being used by the Legion and the DAR in the early 1930s as an authentic exposé of the enemies of America. Such sentiments were also purveyed by such a professional militarist as General John J. Pershing, who, in a series of lectures for the American Defense Society, warned that "our situation is seriously complicated by the teachings of numerous pacifist organizations. . . ."[40]

The concern with pacifism does not imply, however, that earlier hostility toward radicals, social reformers, and other public disrupters had ended. On the contrary, the development of pacifism as a term of opprobrium was merely adding another liability to the large series of undesirable personality traits that these enemies of America were supposed to possess, one which could be stressed more strongly when public apprehensions of radicalism were relatively deflated. Certainly as explosive public episodes developed—the Passaic Textile Strike,[41] the furor over New York City's Stuyvesant High School, and by implication the use of any public building as a public forum even for liberals,[42] the Colorado Mine War of late 1927,[43] and above all the execution of Sacco and Vanzetti,[44]—the "Reds" and their dupes were held largely to blame, both for the episodes and for any number of people taking a remotely liberal view on the questions they raised. However, the dangers of such people could be brought home to a far more diversified audience if one talked of the "whole Pacifist-Radical-Communist movement in America [which] is foreign in its conception, if not actually under foreign influence, direction and control,"[45] or referred to such a leader as Roger Baldwin as a "slacker, radical, draft evader, and Leavenworth ex-convict."[46]

And the most effective agents of intolerance came more and more to have this focus. By 1925, the heyday of the Klan was over. The enactment of the National Origins Act in 1924, internal strife (endemic in the order from its beginnings), and burgeoning prosperity, all undercut prior strength. In its annual report for 1927, the American Civil Liberties Union announced that the principal purveyors of intolerance in the country were the War Department, the American Legion, and professional patriot societies. It declared that the American Legion had by then "replaced the Klan as the most active agency of intolerance and repression in the country."[47] The report was editorially criticized by Joseph Pulitzer's liberal New York *World* for such a value judgment, stating: "With scores of different organizations seeking to curtail liberty in scores of different ways, it is a wise man who can say that one is more active than any of the others."[48] To which Forrest Bailey, Director of the ACLU, responded by merely pointing out that this was the consensus of all the state units reporting to national headquarters for the year.[49]

It is not the purpose of this paper to attempt to explain the effect of the depression upon what had become fairly standard patterns of intolerance and intolerance-making. Nonetheless, certain clear developments can be recognized. On one hand, the professional patriots quickly found their traditional sources of income drying up. The National Civic Federation, for example, previously one of the bellwethers of such groups, was reduced to such belt-tightening by 1930 and the years following that its activities had to be cut to virtual ineffectiveness.[50] Other comparable groups collapsed completely. Faced with similar problems, the American Legion and the DAR found it expedient to do some of their cutting back in the area of antiradical activity. Pacifist-baiting no longer seemed a highly meaningful or relevant response to public problems.

On the other hand, vast evidence suggests that many businesses stepped up their antiradical activity. Deserting the intolerance purveyors who had formerly performed the function of subtly undermining and discrediting their critics, they now preferred to spend their money for direct action in the form of company guards, labor spies, strike breakers, and arms. Thus the American Civil Liberties Union could report a vast increase in the number of cases it received in the early depression years and generally the greatest suppression of individual liberties in the country since the days of the Red scare. Similarly, the number of instances of police brutality and flagrant abuse of local governmental power were well known.[51]

If one is to talk in terms of meaningful and internally consistent cycles of public intolerance, an era ends in 1929–1930. By this time, to defend the status quo as unassailable was to make oneself ludicrous, since a casual glance revealed the magnitude of its defects. Significantly, when Representative Hamilton Fish auspiciously launched a series of congressional investigations in 1930 in an attempt to throw the blame for the depression on domestic "Reds,"[52] the results of his crusade were to produce either large-scale public apathy or large-scale public antipathy.

The imperfect public record of the 1920s then would seem to reveal that many interwoven factors produced a concatenation of syndromes which made the country a peculiarly fertile seedbed both for intolerance and its shrewd manipulation. These undoubtedly included the tensions of economic dynamism, grossly unequal distribution of wealth, enhanced urbanization with the dislocation it produced both in the urban area and in its rural recruitment grounds, virulent disillusionment with democracy, and the confusing and contradictory assumptions concerning the increasingly unpopular war experience.

A moot question still exists as to whether more precise results could not have been reached by placing heavier reliance on social science. Undoubtedly if public opinion poll information were available or if scientific attempts had been made at the time to quantify a variety of public attitudes, the record would be more approachable. Certainly steeping ourselves in a more sophisticated analysis of present and future events enhances the understanding of social and human processes in general and affords a more precise appreciation of human behavior in a past context. Certainly the types of questions which the empirical social researcher is currently asking can be asked of that decade and the historian is derelict if he fails to ask them. Yet the basic problem is still how to gain essential information now lacking and difficult or impossible to obtain. The social science researcher is not much help here. In fact, he operates on the assumption that unless sufficient information is available to permit arrival at quantitative answers, little of value can be produced and one's energies are wasted in the effort.

The historian, proceeding on the assumption that almost all important questions are important precisely because of their subtle implications and overtones, their complexities, ambiguities, and ambivalences—because in other words, they are not susceptible to quantitative answers—then must plod on his dogged and imperfect way. He must approach incomplete materials not only semi-analytically, but impressionistically and eclectically, even at times attempting to devise his own ways to evaluate a great divergency of data which the social scientist scarcely feels worth considering due to its impreciseness and unsuitability to quantitative analysis. But the historian likes to feel that only if serious attempt is made to assess all the data, regardless of its nature or its incompleteness, can anything resembling past reality possibly be attained. And as a humanist viewing essentially human phenomena, even if in so imprecise a fashion, the historian also likes to feel that he may, as Arthur M. Schlesinger, Jr., has suggested, "yield truths about both individual and social experience which quantitative social research by itself could never reach."[53]

Notes

1. Particularly suggestive in this regard are the works of Gordon Allport, Bruno Bettelheim, Kenneth B. Clark, Allison Davis, E. Franklin Frazier, Marie Jahoda, Morris Janowitz, Clyde Kluckhohn, Kurt Lewin, Herbert Muller, Gunnar Myrdal, Arnold Rose, Gerhart Saenger, Edward A. Shils, James Vander Zanden, Robin Williams, and J. Milton Yinger.

2. For example, John Higham, "Another Look at Nativism," *Catholic Historical Review*, XLIV (July 1958), 150, in denigrating an ideological approach, argues: "Except on the subject of race (and in related forms anti-Semitism), the kind of accusations which nativists leveled against foreign elements remained relatively constant.... For the history of nativism, therefore, emotional intensity provided the significant measure of change."

3. David B. Davis confronts this dilemma with healthy open-mindedness in "Some Themes of Counter-Subversion: An Analysis of Anti-Masonic, Anti-Catholic, and Anti-Mormon Literature," *Mississippi Valley Historical Review*, XLVII (Sept. 1960), 205–24.

4. "After the Battle," *Survey*, XXVIII (April 6, 1912), 1–2. Such attitudes are explored in provocative detail in Reinhard Bendix, *Work and Authority in Industry: Ideologies of Management in the Course of Industrialization* (New York, 1956), 254–340.

5. Ray Stannard Baker, *Woodrow Wilson, Life and Letters* (8 vols., New York, 1927–1939), VI, 506–07. On the persecution of anti-war groups generally, see H. C. Peterson and Gilbert C. Fite, *Opponents of War: 1917–18* (Madison, 1957), and O. A. Hilton, "The Minnesota Commission of Public Safety in World War I, 1917–1919," *Bulletin of the Oklahoma Agricultural and Mechanical College*, LXVIII (May 15, 1951).

6. Zechariah Chafee, Jr., *Free Speech in the United States* (Cambridge, 1941), 39–41.

7. Philip Taft, "The Federal Trials of the IWW," *Labor History*, III (Winter 1962), 57–91.

8. Roger N. Baldwin, "The Myth of Law and Order," in Samuel D. Schmalhausen, ed., *Behold America!* (New York, 1931), 660–61. The appeal of the Soviet experiment in its early years stands out in various liberal organs. See, for example, *The Advance* (New York), 1919–1923. See also Matthew Josephson, *Sidney Hillman: Statesman of American Labor* (Garden City, 1952), 274 ff., and Christopher Lasch, *The American Liberals and the Russian Revolution* (New York, 1962).

9. Nicholas Murray Butler, *The Real Labor Problem* (n.p., [1919]), an address

delivered before the Institute of Arts and Sciences, Columbia University, October 13, 1919, and published as a pamphlet.

10. Gutzon Borglum, *The Real Labor Problem* (n.p., [1919]), a confidential pamphlet, privately printed.

11. See Fund for the Republic, *Digest of the Public Record of Communism in the United States* (New York, 1955), 266 ff. For a detailed history of this legislation and a careful state-by-state record of its framing see Eldridge F. Dowell, "A History of the Enactment of Criminal Syndicalism Legislation in the United States" (2 vols., doctoral dissertation, Johns Hopkins University, 1936).

12. "Criminal Syndicalism," *Columbia University Law Review*, XX (Feb. 1920), 232. The point was made regularly by liberals in the 1920s. See, for example, Brandeis' famous concurring opinion in the Whitney case (1927), 274 U.S. 357, 372 ff.

13. American Civil Liberties Union, *The Police and Radicals: What 88 Police Chiefs Think and Do About Radical Meetings* (New York, 1921). See also *Investigation of Communist Propaganda. Hearings before a Special Committee to Investigate Communist Activities in the United States.* House Exec. Docs., 71 Cong., 2 Sess., Pt. IV, Vol. I, 3; Vol. II, 574 ff. (1930).

14. National Popular Government League, *To the American People: Report upon the Illegal Practices of the United States Department of Justice* (Washington, 1920). On the impact of the report see Robert K. Murray, *Red Scare: A Study in National Hysteria* (Minneapolis, 1955), 255.

15. One is immediately reminded of the careful attempt of the Adams Federalists to exploit the half-war with France in 1798, Know-Nothingism in various periods of American history, bloody-shirt waving in the post-Civil War years, among other things. See James M. Smith, *Freedom's Fetters: The Alien and Sedition Laws and American Civil Liberties* (Ithaca, 1956).

16. Max Lowenthal, *The Federal Bureau of Investigation* (New York, 1950), 71–72, 90, 298 ff.

17. Don Whitehead, *The F.B.I. Story* (New York, 1956), 55–59; Alpheus T. Mason, *Harlan Fiske Stone: Pillar of the Law* (New York, 1956), 149–50; Methodist Federation for Social Service, *The Social Service Bulletin* (Feb. 1920), 1–4; *ibid.* (Sept. 1924), 1–4; Dowell, *Criminal Syndicalism Legislation*, 1026, 1129.

18. Rodney G. Minott, *Peerless Patriots: Organized Veterans and the Spirit of Americanism* (Washington, 1963), 112 ff.

19. Jung to Henry E. Niles, March 23, 1926, American Civil Liberties Union Collection, Microfilm Reel 333 (New York Public Library). The ACLU files are filled with material concerning the various professional patriot groups.

20. There is a complete run of the *Daily Data Sheets* in the ACLU Collection, Microfilm Reel 332.

21. On the blacklist see Martha Strayer, *The D.A.R., An Informal History* (Washington, 1958), 133 ff., and Walter Johnson, ed., *Selected Letters of William Allen White, 1889–1943* (New York, 1947), 278–83.

22. Norman Hapgood, ed., *Professional Patriots* (New York, 1927), concentrates on twenty-five or so of the major ones, although Fred R. Marvin, *Our Government and Its Enemies* (New York, 1932), by adding a variety of local auxiliaries, lists fifty-four organizations as making up the American Coalition of Patriotic Societies at the height of the movement.

23. Ferdinand Tönnies, *Gemeinschaft und Gesellchaft*, translated and edited by Charles P. Loomis (East Lansing, 1957). The danger for the historian in utilizing such a concept is well delineated by Robin M. Williams, Jr., *American Society* (2nd rev. ed., New York, 1960), 482–83. Highly provocative in this context is the assessment of value orientation within a culture in Florence R. Kluckhohn and Fred L. Strodtbeck, *Variations in Value Orientation* (Evanston, 1961), 24 ff., 340–44.

24. A perceptive contemporary understanding of this development was given by Judge Learned Hand in 1930; see Irving Dilliard, *The Spirit of Liberty: Papers and Addresses of Learned Hand* (New York, 1960), 66–83.

25. Williams, *American Society*, 557. In this regard see John P. Roche, *The Quest for the Dream* (New York, 1963), 261 ff.

26. Such champions sometimes used aggressive campaigns of "Americanization" geared especially toward education. See "Program for Promoting American Ideals," *American Bar Association Journal*, VIII (Sept. 1922), 587. See also Bessie L. Pierce,

Public Opinion and the Teaching of History in the United States (New York, 1926), and the same author's *Citizens' Organizations and the Civic Training of Youth* (New York, 1933).

27. Baldwin, "Myth of Law and Order," 658–59.

28. Walter Lippmann, whose own writings had reflected intense disillusionment with the "phantom public," attempted to analyze the general disillusionment of the decade in his volume, *A Preface to Morals* (New York, 1929). Revealing in this regard is the broad study of Joseph E. Clark, "The American Critique of the Democratic Idea, 1919–1929" (doctoral dissertation, Stanford University, 1958).

29. The Methodist Federation for Social Service, Unitarian Fellowship for Social Justice, Church League for Industrial Democracy (Episcopal), National Catholic Welfare Council, and Central Conference of American Rabbis are leading examples.

30. Clarke A. Chambers, "Creative Effort in an Age of Normalcy, 1913–1933," *The Social Welfare Forum* (1961), 252–71.

31. See National Popular Government League, *To the American People*.

32. Burns's dealings with Easley are revealed in some detail in the files of the National Civic Federation. See Easley to Howard E. Coffin, Oct. 9 and 19, 1922, National Civic Federation Collection (New York Public Library). See also Richard M. Whitney, *The Reds in America* (New York, 1923), and Joseph T. Cashman, *America Asleep: The Menace of Radicalism* (New York, 1923).

33. American Civil Liberties Union, *The Nation-Wide Spy System Centering in the Department of Justice* (New York, 1924); Mason, *Harlan Fiske Stone;* Whitehead, *F.B.I. Story*.

34. Sidney Howard, "Our Professional Patriots: V, The New Crusade," *New Republic*, XL (Sept. 24, 1924), 93.

35. A typical *American Standard* story caption read: "Ochs (Jew) wants Smith (R.C.): Owner of 'New York Times' Would Give Wet Papist Life Tenure of New York Governorship," Sept. 1, 1925. On the modern Klan and southern racism generally see James W. Vander Zanden, "The Southern White Resistance Movement to Integration" (doctoral dissertation, University of North Carolina, 1958).

36. Ben B. Lindsey and Rube Borough, *The Dangerous Life* (New York, 1931), 388 ff.

37. Calvin Coolidge, "Enemies of the Republic: Are the 'Reds' Stalking Our College Women?" *The Delineator*, XCVIII (June 1921), 4 ff.

38. *Cong. Record*, LXVII, Pt. 2, 1217 ff. (Dec. 19, 1925). The story of the assault was widely reprinted. Harry A. Jung wrote to 600 trade secretaries urging support for Blanton in his fight against the ACLU. ACLU Collection, Microfilm Reel 333.

39. Howard, "Our Professional Patriots," 94. Howard quotes Fries as referring to "the insidious pacifist, who is more to be feared than the man with the torch, gun or sword."

40. ACLU Collection, Microfilm Reel 331, contains pamphlet reprints of a number of Pershing's public addresses.

41. The material on Passaic is voluminous. See especially Albert Weisbord, *Passaic* (Chicago, 1926); Mary Heaton Vorse, *The Passaic Textile Strike* (New York, 1927); Joseph Freeman, *An American Testament* (New York, 1936), 392 ff.; *American Labor Year Book, 1927* (New York, 1927), 105 ff., 156.

42. The Annual Report of the American Civil Liberties Union for 1927, *Free Speech, 1926* (New York, 1927), referred to the ACLU's struggle with the New York City School Board in the Stuyvesant case as the "most important 'free speech fight' of the year." This struggle revealed the existence of a "blacklist" against individuals whose opinions did not conform to those of board members.

43. American Civil Liberties Union, *The War on Colorado Miners* (New York, 1928); Donald J. McClurg, "The Colorado Coal Strike of 1927: Tactical Leadership of the IWW," *Labor History*, IV (Winter 1963), 68–92; Dowell, "Criminal Syndicalism Legislation," 806 ff.; *The Advance* (New York), Dec. 2, 16, 27, 1929.

44. See especially G. Louis Joughin and Edmund M. Morgan, *The Legacy of Sacco and Vanzetti* (New York, 1948), and Francis Russell, *Tragedy in Dedham* (New York, 1962).

45. Fred R. Marvin, quoted in Marcus Duffield, *King Legion* (New York, 1931), 177–78.

46. This was the standard indictment of Baldwin by his enemies throughout the

decade. The quote here is by Col. Leroy F. Smith of the Better America Federation of Los Angeles in an "exposé" entitled: *The American Civil Liberties Union: Its Mental Processes, Its Chums, Its Program and Purpose* (Los Angeles, 1930), 1. On the early activities of the Federation see Edwin Layton, "The Better America Federation: A Case Study of Superpatriotism," *Pacific Historical Review,* XXX (May 1961), 137–47.

47. *Free Speech, 1926,* p. 2.

48. Editorial, "The American Civil Liberties Union," New York *World,* May 17, 1927, p. 12.

49. Letters column, *ibid.,* May 18, 1927, p. 12.

50. Prior to 1929 the organization's subversive activities program was lavishly supported. In that year the only contribution so earmarked was $1,000 from John Hays Hammond. In 1930 the only contribution was $5,000 from Samuel Insull. By 1931 the amount had been reduced to $138, and in 1932, 1933, and 1934 there were no entries of money received for that purpose. National Civic Federation Receipt Book, National Civic Federation Collection.

51. See the popular summarization of the findings of the Wickersham Commission, Ernest J. Hopkins, *Our Lawless Police: A Study of the Unlawful Enforcement of the Law* (New York, 1931).

52. See footnote 13. The *Hearings* of the so-called Fish Committee were published in nineteen volumes. The hearings were responsible for a large "Deport the Reds" rally in Carnegie Hall on Jan. 10, 1931. A good cross section of national newspaper opinion on the rally (which was primarily hostile) is in the ACLU Collection, Microfilm Reel 464.

53. Arthur M. Schlesinger, Jr., "The Humanist Looks at Empirical Social Research," *American Sociological Review,* XXVII (Dec. 1962), 771.

The Meaning of Lindbergh's Flight

JOHN W. WARD

In the following essay on a "minor" event of the 1920s, Professor John W. Ward manages to get at some of the basic cultural confusions that underlay so much of American history during the early twentieth century. Lindbergh's flight was important, according to him, because of the ways it allowed Americans to celebrate, simultaneously, the values of rugged individualism and machine technology. In many ways, the meaning of modern American life is to be found in this conflict between machinery and organization on the one side, and the ideal of the free individual on the other. According to Professor Murphy's interpretation, this kind of conflict caused much of the "intolerance" of the 1920s. It is also quite possible that white people celebrated the Harlem Negro precisely because he seemed to offer a symbolic escape from the mechanized demands of twentieth-century life. Working outward from a "superficial" event involving a "minor" figure, Professor Ward establishes a context that goes deep into our society and well back into our history.

John William Ward is Professor of History at Amherst College. With his colleagues at Amherst, he has been one of the leaders of the "American Studies" movement, which is an effort to integrate history, literature, and related fields of study. Professor Ward's first book was Andrew Jackson, Symbol for an Age *(1955).* *He is the editor of* Society, Manners and Politics in the United States *(1962) and of* The Nature and Tendency of Free Institutions *(1968). His essays on various subjects have been republished in a book entitled* Red, White and Blue: Men, Books and Ideas in American Culture *(1969), which is as good an introduction to "American Studies" as is available.*

On Friday, May 20, 1927, at 7:52 a.m., Charles A. Lindbergh took off in a silver-winged monoplane and flew from the United States to France. With this flight Lindbergh became the first man to fly alone across the Atlantic Ocean. The log of flight 33 of "The Spirit of St. Louis" reads: "Roosevelt Field, Long Island, New York, to Le Bourget Aerodrome, Paris, France. 33 hrs. 30 min." Thus was the fact of Lindbergh's achievement easily put down. But the meaning of Lindbergh's flight lay hidden in the next sentence of the log: "(Fuselage fabric badly torn by souvenir hunters.)"

When Lindbergh landed at Le Bourget he is supposed to have said, "Well, we've done it." A contemporary writer asked "Did what?" Lindbergh "had no idea of what he had done. He thought he had simply flown from New York to Paris. What he had really done was something far greater. He had fired the imagination of mankind." From the moment of Lindbergh's flight people recognized that something more was involved than the mere fact of the physical leap from New York to Paris. "Lindbergh," wrote John Erskine, "served as a metaphor." But what the metaphor stood for was not easy to say. The *New York Times* remarked then that "there has been no complete and satisfactory explanation of the enthusiasm and acclaim for Captain Lindbergh." Looking back on the celebration of Lindbergh, one can see now that the American people were trying to understand Lindbergh's flight, to grasp its meaning, and through it, perhaps, to grasp the meaning of their own experience. Was the flight the achievement of a heroic, solitary, unaided individual? Or did the flight represent the trumph of the machine, the success of an industrially organized society? These questions were central to the meaning

REPRINTED BY PERMISSION, FROM *American Quarterly*, 10 (SPRING 1958), 3–16.
COPYRIGHT, 1958, TRUSTEES OF THE UNIVERSITY OF PENNSYLVANIA.

of Lindbergh's flight. They were also central to the lives of the people who made Lindbergh their hero.

The flight demanded attention in its own right, of course, quite apart from whatever significance it might have. Lindbergh's story had all the makings of a great drama. Since 1919 there had been a standing prize of $25,000 to be awarded to the first aviator who could cross the Atlantic in either direction between the United States and France in a heavier-than-air craft. In the spring of 1927 there promised to be what the *New York Times* called "the most spectacular race ever held—3,600 miles over the open sea to Paris." The scene was dominated by veteran pilots. On the European side were the French aces, Nungesser and Coli; on the American side, Commander Richard E. Byrd, in a big tri-motored Fokker monoplane, led a group of contestants. Besides Byrd, who had already flown over the North Pole, there were Commander Davis, flying a ship named in honor of the American Legion which had put up $100,000 to finance his attempt, Clarence Chamberlin, who had already set a world's endurance record of more than fifty-one hours in the air in a Bellanca tri-motored plane, and Captain René Fonck, the French war ace, who had come to America to fly a Sikorsky aircraft. The hero was unheard of and unknown. He was on the West Coast supervising the construction of a single-engine plane to cost only ten thousand dollars.

Then fate played its part. It seemed impossible that Lindbergh could get his plane built and east to New York in time to challenge his better equipped and more famous rivals. But in quick succession a series of disasters cleared his path. On April 16, Commander Byrd's "America" crashed on its test flight, crushing the leg of Floyd Bennett who was one of the crew and injuring Byrd's hand and wrist. On April 24, Clarence Chamberlin cracked up in his Bellanca, not seriously, but enough to delay his plans. Then on April 26, Commander Davis and his co-pilot lost their lives as the "American Legion" crashed on its final test flight. In ten days, accidents had stopped all of Lindbergh's American rivals. Nungesser and Coli, however, took off in their romantically named ship, the "White Bird," from Le Bourget on May 8. The world waited and Lindbergh, still on the West Coast, decided to try to fly the Pacific. But Nungesser and Coli were never seen again. As rumors filled the newspapers, as reports came in that the "White Bird" was seen over Newfoundland, over Boston, over the Atlantic, it soon became apparent that Nungesser and Coli had failed, dropping to their death in some unknown grave. Disaster had touched every ship entered in the trans-Atlantic race.

Now, with the stage cleared, Lindbergh entered. He swooped across the continent in two great strides, landing only at St. Louis. The first leg of his flight established a new distance record but all eyes were on the Atlantic and the feat received little notice. Curiously, the first time Lindbergh appeared in the headlines of the New York papers was Friday, the thirteenth. By this time Byrd and Chamberlin were ready once again but the weather had closed in and kept all planes on the ground. Then, after a week of fretful waiting, on the night of May 19, on the way into New York to see "Rio Rita," Lindbergh received a report that the weather was breaking over the ocean. He hurried back to Roosevelt Field to haul his plane out onto a wet, dripping runway. After mechanics painfully loaded the plane's gas by hand, the wind shifted, as fate played its last trick. A muddy runway and an adverse wind. Whatever the elements, whatever the fates, the decisive act is the hero's, and Lindbergh made his choice. Providing a chorus to the action, the *Herald Tribune* reported that Lindbergh lifted the overloaded plane into the sky "by his indomitable will alone."

The parabola of the action was as clean as the arc of Lindbergh's flight. The drama should have ended with the landing of "The Spirit of St. Louis" at Le Bourget. That is where Lindbergh wanted it to end. In "*WE*," written immediately after the flight, and in *The Spirit of St. Louis*, written twenty-six years later, Lindbergh chose to end his accounts there. But the flight turned out to be only the first act in the part Lindbergh was to play.

Lindbergh was so innocent of his future that on his flight he carried letters of introduction. The hysterical response, first of the French and then of his own countrymen, had been no part of his careful plans. In "*WE*," after Lindbergh's narrative of the flight, the publisher wrote: "When Lindbergh came to tell the story of his welcome at Paris, London, Brussels, Washington, New York, and St. Louis he found himself up against a tougher problem than flying the Atlantic." So another writer completed the account in the third person. He suggested that "the reason Lindbergh's story is different is that when his plane came to a halt on Le Bourget field that black night in Paris, Lindbergh the man kept on going. The phenomenon of Lindbergh took its start with his flight across the ocean; but in its entirety it was almost as distinct from that flight as though he had never flown at all."

Lindbergh's private life ended with his flight to Paris. The drama was no longer his, it was the public's. "The outburst of unanimous acclaim was at once personal and symbolic," said the *American Review of Reviews*. From the moment of success there were two Lindberghs, the private Lindbergh and the public Lindbergh. The latter was the construction of the imagination of Lindbergh's time, fastened on to an unwilling person. The tragedy of Lindbergh's career is that he could never accept the role assigned him. He always believed he might keep his two lives separate. But from the moment he landed at Le Bourget, Lindbergh became, as the *New Republic* noted, "*ours*. . . . He is no longer permitted to be himself. He is US personified. He is the United States." Ambassador Herrick introduced Lindbergh to the French, saying, "This young man from out of the West brings you better than anything else the spirit of America," and wired to President Coolidge, "Had we searched all America we could not have found a better type than young Lindbergh to represent the spirit and high purpose of our people." This was Lindbergh's fate, to be a type. A writer in the *North American Review* felt that Lindbergh represented "the dominant American character," he "images the best" about the United States. And an ecstatic female in the *American Magazine,* who began by saying that Lindbergh "is a sort of symbol. . . . He is the dream that is in our hearts," concluded that the American public responded so wildly to Lindbergh because of "the thrill of possessing, in him, our dream of what *we* really and truly want to be." The act of possession was so complete that articles since have attempted to discover the "real" Lindbergh, that enigmatic and taciturn figure behind the public mask. But it is no less difficult to discern the features of the public Lindbergh, that symbolic figure who presented to the imagination of his time all the yearnings and buried desires of its dream for itself.

Lindbergh's flight came at the end of a decade marked by social and political corruption and by a sense of moral loss. The heady idealism of the First World War had been succeeded by a deep cynicism as to the war's real purpose. The naïve belief that virtue could be legislated was violated by the vast discrepancy between the law and the social habits of prohibition. A philosophy of relativism had become the uneasy rationale of a nation which had formerly believed in moral absolutes. The newspapers agreed that Lindbergh's chief worth was his spiritual and moral value. His story was held to be "in striking contrast with the sordid unhallowed themes that have for months steeped the imaginations and thinking of the people." Or, as another had it, "there is good reason why people should hail Lindbergh and give him honor. He stands out in a grubby world as an inspiration."

Lindbergh gave the American people a glimpse of what they liked to think themselves to be at a time when they feared they had deserted their own vision of themselves. The grubbiness of the twenties had a good deal to do with the shining quality of Lindbergh's success, especially when one remembers that Lindbergh's flight was not as unexampled as our national memory would have it. The Atlantic was not unconquered when Lindbergh flew. A British dirigible had twice crossed the Atlantic before 1919 and on May 8 of that year three naval seaplanes left Rockaway, New York, and one, the NC-4 manned by a crew of five, got through to Plymouth, England. A month later, Captain John Alcock, an Englishman, with Arthur W. Browne, an American, flew the first heavier-than-air land plane across the Atlantic nonstop, from Newfoundland to Ireland, to win twice the money Lindbergh did, a prize of $50,000 offered by the London *Daily Mail.* Alcock's and Browne's misfortune was to land in a soft and somnolent Irish peat bog instead of before the cheering thousands of London or Paris. Or perhaps they should have flown in 1927.

The wild medley of public acclaim and the homeric strivings of editors make one realize that the response to Lindbergh involved a mass ritual in which America celebrated itself more than it celebrated Lindbergh. Lindbergh's flight was the occasion of a public act of regeneration in which the nation momentarily rededicated itself to something, the loss of which was keenly felt. It was said again and again that "Lindy" taught America "to lift its eyes up to Heaven." Heywood Broun, in his column in the *New York World*, wrote that this "tall young man raised up and let us see the potentialities of the human spirit." Broun felt that the flight proved that, though "we are small and fragile," it "isn't true that there is no health in us." Lindbergh's flight provided the moment, but the meaning of the flight is to be found in the deep and pervasive need for renewal which the flight brought to the surface of public feeling. When Lindbergh appeared at the nation's capital, the *Washington Post* observed, "He was given that frenzied acclaim which comes from the depths of the people." In New York, where 4,000,000 people saw him, a reporter wrote that the dense and vociferous crowds were swept, as Lindbergh passed, "with an emotion tense and inflammable." The *Literary Digest* suggested that the answer to the hero-worship of Lindbergh would "throw an interesting light on the psychology of our times and of the American people."

The *Nation* noted about Lindbergh that "there was something lyric as well as heroic about the apparition of this young Lochinvar who suddenly came out of the West and who flew all unarmed and all alone. It is the kind of stuff which the ancient Greeks would have worked into a myth and the medieval Scots into a border ballad. . . . But what we have in the case of Lindbergh is an actual, an heroic and an exhaustively exposed experience which exists by suggestion in the form of poetry." The *Nation* quickly qualified its statement by observing that reporters were as far as possible from being poets and concluded that the discrepancy between the fact and the celebration of it was not poetry, perhaps, but "magic on a vast scale." Yet the *Nation* might have clung to its insight that the public meaning of Lindbergh's flight was somehow poetic. The vast publicity about Lindbergh corresponds in one vital particular with the poetic vision. Poetry, said William Butler Yeats, contains opposites; so did Lindbergh. Lindbergh did not mean one thing, he meant many things. The image of itself which America contemplated in the public person of Lindbergh was full of conflict; it was, in a word, dramatic.

To heighten the drama, Lindbergh did it alone. He was the "lone eagle" and a full exploration of that fact takes one deep into the emotional meaning of his success. Not only the *Nation* found Sir Walter Scott's lines on Lochinvar appropriate: "he rode all unarmed and he rode all alone." Newspapers and magazines were deluged with amateur poems that vindicated one rhymester's wry comment, "Go conquer the perils / That lurk in the skies— / And you'll get bum poems / Right up to your eyes." The *New York Times*, that alone received more than two hundred poems, observed in trying to summarize the poetic deluge that "the fact that he flew alone made the strongest impression." Another favorite tribute was Kipling's "The Winners," with its refrain, "He travels the fastest who travels alone." The others who had conquered the Atlantic and those like Byrd and Chamberlin who were trying at the same time were not traveling alone and they hardly rode unarmed. Other than Lindbergh, all the contestants in the trans-Atlantic race had unlimited backing, access to the best planes, and all were working in teams, carrying at least one co-pilot to share the long burden of flying the plane. So a writer in the New York *Sun*, in a poem called "The Flying Fool," a nickname that Lindbergh despised, celebrated Lindbergh's flight: ". . . no kingly plane for him; / No endless data, comrades, moneyed chums; / No boards, no councils, no directors grim— / He plans ALONE . . . and takes luck as it comes."

Upon second thought, it must seem strange that the long-distance flight of an airplane, the achievement of a highly advanced and organized technology, should be the occasion for hymns of praise to the solitary unaided man. Yet the National Geographic Society, when it presented a medal to Lindbergh, wrote on the presentation scroll, "Courage, when it goes alone, has ever caught men's imaginations," and compared Lindbergh to Robinson Crusoe and the trailmakers in our own West. But Lindbergh and Robinson Crusoe, the one in his helmet and fur-lined flying coat and the other in his wild goatskins, do not easily co-exist. Even if Robinson Crusoe did have a tidy capital investment in the form of a well-stocked shipwreck, he still did not have a ten thousand dollar machine under him.

Lindbergh, in nearly every remark about his flight and in his own writings about it, resisted the tendency to exploit the flight as the achievement of an individual. He never said "I," he always said "We." The plane was not to go unrecognized. Nevertheless, there persisted a tendency to seize upon the flight as a way of celebrating the self-sufficient individual, so that among many others an Ohio newspaper could describe Lindbergh as this "self-contained, self-reliant, courageous young man [who] ranks among the great pioneers of history." The strategy here was a common one, to make Lindbergh a "pioneer" and thus to link him with a long and vital tradition of individualism in the American experience. Colonel Theodore Roosevelt, himself the son of a famous exponent of self-reliance, said to reporters at his home in Oyster Bay that "Captain Lindbergh personifies the daring of youth. Daniel Boone, David Crocket [*sic*], and men of that type played a lone hand and made America. Lindbergh is their lineal descendant." In *Outlook* magazine, immediately below an enthusiastic endorsement of Lindbergh's own remarks on the importance of his machine and his scientific instruments, there was the statement, "Charles Lindbergh is the heir of all that we like to think is best in America. He is of the stuff out of which have been made the pioneers that opened up the wilderness, first on the Atlantic coast, and then in our great West. His are the qualities which we, as a people, must nourish." It is in this mood that one suspects it was important that Lindbergh came out of the West and rode all alone.

Another common metaphor in the attempt to place Lindbergh's exploit was to say that he had opened a new "frontier." To speak of the air as a "frontier" was to invoke an interpretation of the meaning of American history which had sources deep in American experience, but the frontier of the airplane is hardly the frontier of the trailmakers of the old West. Rather than an escape into the self-sufficient simplicity of the American past, the machine which made Lindbergh's flight possible represented an advance into a complex industrial present. The difficulty lay in using an instance of modern life to celebrate the virtues of the past, to use an extreme development of an urban industrial society to insist upon the significance of the frontier in American life.

A little more than a month after Lindbergh's flight, Joseph K. Hart in *Survey* magazine reached back to Walt Whitman's poem for the title of an article on Lindbergh: "O Pioneer." A school had made Lindbergh an honorary alumnus but Hart protested there was little available evidence "that he was educated in *schools*." "We must look elsewhere for our explanation," Hart wrote and he looked to the experience of Lindbergh's youth when "everything that he ever did . . . he did by himself. He lived more to himself than most boys." And, of course, Lindbergh lived to himself in the only place conceivably possible, in the world of nature, on a Minnesota farm. "There he developed in the companionship of woods and fields, animals and machines, his audaciously natural and simple personality." The word, "machines," jars as it intrudes into Hart's idyllic pastoral landscape and betrays Hart's difficulty in relating the setting of nature upon which he wishes to insist with the fact that its product spent his whole life tinkering with machines, from motorcycles to airplanes. But except for that one word, Hart proceeds in uncritical nostalgia to show that "a lone trip across the Atlantic was not impossible for a boy who had grown up in the solitude of the woods and waters." If Lindbergh was "clear-headed, naif, untrained in the ways of cities," it was because he had "that 'natural simplicity' which Fenimore Cooper used to attribute to the pioneer hero of his Leatherstocking Tales." Hart rejected the notion that any student "bent to all the conformities" of formal training could have done what Lindbergh did. "Must we not admit," he asked, "that this pioneering urge remained to this audacious youth because he had never submitted completely to the repressions of the world and its jealous institutions?"

Only those who insist on reason will find it strange that Hart should use the industrial achievement of the airplane to reject the urban, institutionalized world of industrialism. Hart was dealing with something other than reason; he was dealing with the emotion evoked by Lindbergh's solitude. He recognized that people wished to call Lindbergh a "genius" because that "would release him from the ordinary rules of existence." That way, "we could rejoice with him in his triumph, and then go back to the contracted routines of our institutional ways [because] ninety-nine percent of us must be content to be shaped and moulded by the routine ways and forms of the world to the routine tasks of life." It is in the word, "must," that the pathos of this interpretation of the phenomenon of Lindbergh lies. The world had changed from the open society of the pioneer to the close-knit, interdependent world of a modern machine-oriented civilization. The institutions of a highly corporate industrial society existed as a constant reproach to a people who liked to believe that the meaning of its experience was embodied in the formless, independent life of the frontier. Like Thomas Jefferson, who identified American virtue with nature and saw the city as a "great sore" on the public body, Hart concluded that "certainly, in the response that the world—especially the world of great cities—has made to the performance of this Midwestern boy, we can read of the homesickness of the human soul, immured in city canyons and routine tasks, for the freer world of youth, for the open spaces of the pioneer, for the joy of battling with nature and clean storms once more on the frontiers of the earth."

The social actuality which made the adulation of Lindbergh possible had its own irony for the notion that America's strength lay in its simple uncomplicated beginnings. For the public response to Lindbergh to have reached the proportions it did, the world had by necessity to be the intricately developed world of modern mass communications. But more than irony was involved. Ultimately, the emotion attached to Lindbergh's flight involved no less than a whole theory about American history. By singling out the fact that Lindbergh rode alone, and by naming him a pioneer of the frontier, the public projected its sense that the source of America's strength lay somewhere in the past and that Lindbergh somehow meant that America must look backward in time to rediscover some lost virtue. The mood was nostalgic and American history was read as a decline, a decline measured in terms of America's advance into an urban, institutionalized way of life which made solitary achievement increasingly beyond the reach of ninety-nine per cent of the people. Because Lindbergh's ancestors were Norse, it was easy to call him a "Viking" and extend the emotion far into the past when all frontiers were open. He became the "Columbus" of another new world to conquer as well as the "Lochinvar" who all rode alone. But there was always the brute, irreducible fact that Lindbergh's exploit was a victory of the machine over the barriers of nature. If the only response to Lindbergh had been a retreat to the past, we would be involved with a mass cultural neurosis, the inability of America to accept reality, the reality of the world in which it lived. But there was another aspect, one in which the public celebrated the machine and the highly organized society of which it was a product. The response to Lindbergh reveals that the American people were deeply torn between conflicting interpretations of their own experience. By calling Lindbergh a pioneer, the people could read into American history the necessity of turning back to the frontier past. Yet the people could also read American history in terms of progress into the industrial future. They could do this by emphasizing the machine which was involved in Lindbergh's flight.

Lindbergh came back from Europe in an American man-of-war, the cruiser *Memphis*. It seems he had contemplated flying on, around the whole world perhaps, but less adventurous heads prevailed and dictated a surer mode of travel for so valuable a piece of public property. The *New Republic* protested against bringing America's hero of romance home in a warship. If he had returned on a great liner, that would have been one thing. "One's first trip on an oceanliner is a great adventure— the novelty of it, the many people of all kinds and conditions, floating for a week in a tiny compact world of their own." But to return on the *Memphis*, "to be put on a gray battleship with a collection of people all of the same stripe, in a kind of ship that has as much relation to the life of the sea as a Ford factory has! We might as well have put him in a pneumatic tube and shot him across the Atlantic." The interesting thing about the *New Republic's* protest against the unromantic, regi- mented life of a battleship is that the image it found appropriate was the Ford assembly line. It was this reaction against the discipline of a mechanized society that probably led to the nostalgic image of Lind- bergh as a remnant of a past when romance was possible for the indi- vidual, when life held novelty and society was variegated rather than uniform. But what the Ford Assembly Line represents, a society com- mitted to the path of full mechanization, was what lay behind Lind- bergh's romantic success. A long piece in the Sunday *New York Times*, "Lindbergh Symbolizes the Genius of America," reminded its readers of the too obvious fact that "without an airplane he could not have flown at all." Lindbergh "is, indeed, the Icarus of the twentieth century; not himself an inventor of his own wings, but a son of that omnipotent Daedalus whose ingenuity has created the modern world." The point was that modern America was the creation of modern industry. Lind- bergh "reveres his 'ship' as a noble expression of mechanical wisdom. . . . Yet in this reverence . . . Lindbergh is not an exception. What he means by the Spirit of St. Louis is really the spirit of America. The mechanical genius, which is discerned in Henry Ford as well as in Charles A. Lindbergh, is in the very atmosphere of [the] country." In contrast to a sentiment that feared the enforced discipline of the machine there existed an attitude of reverence for its power.

Lindbergh led the way in the celebration of the machine, not only implicitly by including his plane when he said "we," but by direct statement. In Paris he told newspapermen, "You fellows have not said enough about that wonderful motor." Rarely have two more taciturn figures confronted one another than when Lindbergh returned to Wash- ington and Calvin Coolidge pinned the Distinguished Flying Cross on him, but in his brief remarks Coolidge found room to express his partic- ular delight that Lindbergh should have given equal credit to the air- plane. "For we are proud," said the President, "that in every particular this silent partner represented American genius and industry. I am told that more than 100 separate companies furnished materials, parts or service in its construction."

The flight was not the heroic lone success of a single daring individual, but the climax of the co-operative effort of an elaborately interlocked technology. The day after Coolidge's speech, Lindbergh said at another ceremony in Washington that the honor should "not go to the pilot alone but to American science and genius which had given years of study to the advancement of aeronautics." "Some things," he said, "should be taken into due consideration in connection with our flight that have not heretofore been given due weight. That is just what made this flight possible. It was not the act of a single pilot. It was the culmination of twenty years of aeronautical research and the assembling together of all that was practicable and best in American aviation." The flight, concluded Lindbergh, "represented American industry."

The worship of the machine which was embodied in the public's response to Lindbergh exalted those very aspects which were denigrated in the celebration of the flight as the work of a heroic individual. Organization and careful method were what lay behind the flight, not individual self-sufficiency and daring romance. One magazine hailed the flight as a "triumph of mechanical engineering." "It is not to be forgotten that this era is the work not so much of brave aviators as of engineers, who have through patient and protracted effort been steadily improving the construction of airplanes." The lesson to be learned from Lindbergh's flight, thought a writer in the *Independent*, "is that the splendid human and material aspects of America need to be organized for the ordinary, matter of fact service of society." The machine meant organization, the careful rationalization of activity of a Ford assembly line, it meant planning, and, if it meant the loss of spontaneous individual action, it meant the material betterment of society. Lindbergh meant not a retreat to the free life of the frontier past but an emergence into the time when "the machine began to take first place in the public mind— the machine and the organization that made its operation possible on a large scale." A poet on this side of the matter wrote, "All day I felt the pull / Of the steel miracle." The machine was not a devilish engine which would enthrall mankind, it was the instrument which would lead to a new paradise. But the direction of history implicit in the machine was toward the future, not the past; the meaning of history was progress, not decline, and America should not lose faith in the future betterment of society. An address by a Harvard professor, picked up by the *Magazine of Business*, made all this explicit. "We commonly take Social Progress for granted," said Edwin F. Gay, "but the doctrine of Social Progress is one of the great revolutionary ideas which have powerfully affected our modern world." There was a danger, however, that the idea "may be in danger of becoming a commonplace or a butt of criticism." The speaker recognized why this might be. America was "worn and disillusioned after the Great War." Logically, contentment should have gone with so optimistic a creed, yet the American people were losing faith. So Lindbergh filled an emotional need even where a need should have been lacking. "He has come like a shining vision to revive the hope of mankind." The high ideals of faith in progress "had almost come to seem like hollow words to us—but now here he is, emblematic of heroes yet to inhabit this world. Our belief in Social Progress is justified symbolically in him."

It is a long flight from New York to Paris; it is a still longer flight from the fact of Lindbergh's achievement to the burden imposed upon it by the imagination of his time. But it is in that further flight that lies the full meaning of Lindbergh. His role was finally a double one. His flight provided an opportunity for the people to project their own emotions into his act and their emotions involved finally two attitudes toward the meaning of their own experience. One view had it that America represented a brief escape from the course of history, an emergence into a new and open world with the self-sufficient individual at its center. The other said that America represented a stage in historical evolution and that its fulfillment lay in the development of society. For one, the meaning of America lay in the past; for the other in the future. For one, the American ideal was an escape from institutions, from the forms of society, and from limitations put upon the free individual; for the other, the American ideal was the elaboration of the complex institutions which made modern society possible, an acceptance of the discipline of the machine, and the achievement of the individual within a context of which he was only a part. The two views were contradictory but both were possible and both were present in the public's reaction to Lindbergh's flight.

The Sunday newspapers announced that Lindbergh had reached Paris, and in the very issue whose front pages were covered with Lindbergh's story the magazine section of the *New York Times* featured an article by the British philosopher, Bertrand Russell. The magazine had, of course, been made up too far in advance to take advantage of the news about Lindbergh. Yet, in a prophetic way, Russell's article was about Lindbergh. Russell hailed the rise to power of the United States because he felt that in the "new life that is America's" in the twentieth century "the new outlook appropriate to machinery [would] become more completely dominant than in the old world." Russell sensed that some might be unwilling to accept the machine, but "whether we like this new outlook or not," he wrote, "is of little importance." Why one might not was obvious. A society built on the machine, said Russell, meant "the diminution in the value and independence of the individual. Great enterprises tend more and more to be collective, and in an industrialized world the interference of the community with the individual must be more intense." Russell realized that while the co-operative effort involved in machine technology makes man collectively more lordly, it makes the individual more submissive. "I do not see how it is to be avoided," he concluded.

People are not philosophers. They did not see how the conflict between a machine society and the free individual was to be avoided either.

But neither were they ready to accept the philosopher's statement of the problem. In Lindbergh, the people celebrated both the self-sufficient individual and the machine. Americans still celebrate both. We cherish the individualism of the American creed at the same time that we worship the machine which increasingly enforces collectivized behavior. Whether we can have both, the freedom of the individual and the power of an organized society, is a question that still haunts our minds. To resolve the conflict that is present in America's celebration of Lindbergh in 1927 is still the task of America.